**CHAMPIONS OF NAUGHT SIX: THE STORY OF THE CLEBURNE RAILROADERS
THE 1906 TEXAS LEAGUE PENNANT RACE**

CHAMPIONS OF NAUGHT SIX
THE CLEBURNE RAILROADERS
THE STORY OF THE 1906 TEXAS LEAGUE PENNANT RACE

D. WILEY WHITTEN, JR.
MINOR LEAGUE PRESS

© 2010
FORT WORTH, TEXAS

First Edition

ISBN 978-0-557-46955-0

The Champions of Naught-Six
The Story of the Cleburne Railroaders

The Champions of Naught Six

is based upon newspapers, magazines, and articles contemporary to the men who made the Cleburne Railroaders of the Texas League a great team, men who went onto to greater glory both on and off the field. At the time it is unlikly that the citizens of Cleburne, and the other five cities that compiled the Texas League in 1906 knew and understood what they had the privilege to see. The Railroaders were just another team in a small town simply trying to stay financially afloat. However, as time passed the local newspapers carried the exploits of the players it became more and more apparent to those back in Johnson County, and Texas that their players were pacing themselves at an extraordinary rate.

My journey to gather the information that I cheerfully share within these pages began with a series of interviews with a wide range of individuals, including as many of the children and realatives of the men of this great team. These interviews were largely done from 1990-1995.

This story was done for my pleasure, but as the years passed it became apparent to me that these stories were too significant to the community of Cleburne, to those baseball fans in Texas in Fort Worth, Dallas, Waco, Temple, and Greenville to keep to myself. And so with this minor publication I lay out for all who wish to enjoy what brought pleasure.

And so to Cleburne, to Johnson County, and the rest of the cities in the old Texas League, here is the story of the Champions of Naught Six, The Cleburne Railroaders of The Texas League, 1906.

SCORE 1 TO 1

For the love of the Great Game

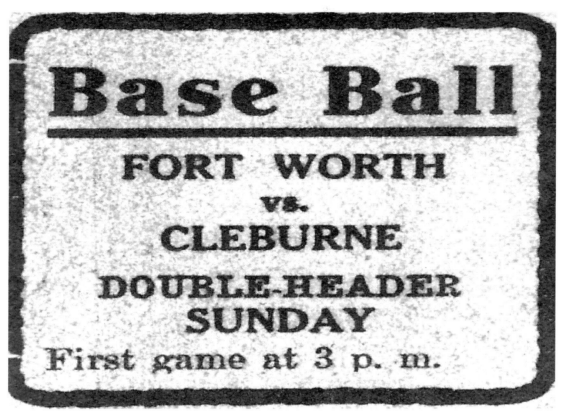

This book is dedicated to my mother, Helen Stafford Whitten, who taught me the love of the game, and to her father, Tobe Stafford, who shared his love for the game with his daughter, giving her a bond that she cheerfully shared with me. Years later, as she lay dying, for a brief moment she sat up to watch Mark McGwire hit his 70th home run. The two of us could forget her pain and for this one last time, share our common love for the great pastime, in the face of pain, we talked joyfully about baseball.

Major General Patrick Ronayne Cleburne

Born: March 17, 1828 Cork, Ireland
Died: November 30, 1864 at the Battle of Franklin

In Honor of this great Irishman, the men who served under his command gave his name to the city that would serve as the County Seat of Johnson County, Texas

CLEBURNE, TEXAS

For Those Who Love the Game Sharing is the Pleasure

The Very Latest Baseball News: Aug 10,1907

KINDRED SPIRITS: <u>*1907*</u> <u>*2010*</u>***:*** **what is compelling about writing of the exploits of 18 men gathered at some particular place at some particular time to play 9 innings of ball, and yet there are those of us who in fact find such activity mesmerizing and satisfying. On that August 10th Saturday in 1907 this unsigned post card was mailed to Mr. J. Winkler in Milwaukee, Wisconsin, written by an excited and detailed writer. We can only wonder why someone so far away would have been interested in the details of this Texas League game. Likely the excitement was more of the writer's doing than that of the recipient's.**

I understand the excitement: it is *he* in 1907, and *me* in 2010.

The Message as Written:
Saturday, August 10, (1907)
The very latest: Austin 2 Waco 0 at Waco. Austin made it three straight from Temple before leaving for Waco. They will be gone for 21 games and we hope they will keep up their good works. (Hugh B.) McCulley couldn't go on the trip as his wife is sick, so Alexander is playing short & Longley, who we got from Temple, is in right. Bailey, Sutor & McGill go to the National League next and Adams goes to the Southern League. Austin has a great "rep". We are at the head of the league and are several games to the good; Dallas is second, and S.A.(San Antonio) is in third. (The writer continues on the back of the card, but it is personal and no longer related to baseball).
* Austin was awarded the 1907 pennant, but not before San Antonio protested their late season acquisition of T.R. Vinson from Fort Worth past the season deadline for acquiring new players.

THE CHAMPIONS OF NAUGHT SIX

Contents

CLEBURNE, TEXAS...1906

Once from the banks of West Buffalo Creek the sounds of championship baseball echoed all over Texas. In the fall of 1906 the Texas League silver cup was awarded to the Cleburne Railroaders, the Champions of Naught Six. For a brief moment the city basked in the glory of greatness. Every so brief! Then it quickly ended. The team left town, left emptiness in the hearts of the fans, an emptiness in hastily built Gorman Park, its wood planks left to rot under the relentless hot Texas sun.

Those who were lucky enough to have witnessed that joyful season began to grow older, sadly one by one they left this earth. Without the collective memory of those old fans giving witnesses to the great team of 1906, the dark shroud that obscures history overtook the Champions of Naught Six and they exploits became largely forgotten.

Most minor league rosters at the turn of the century consisted of a collection of local boys, a few career minor league players, and perhaps a dash of an old veteran from the major leagues. Not so in Cleburne. The fans of the 1906 Railroaders watched, as the years passed, the group of men who were once the Railroaders developed into esteemed individuals: a future Hall-of-Famer, a man who for a short time shared playing time with Babe Ruth, a man who was one of the heroes of the 1918 World Series, a man who would be one of the greatest of Texas A&M football coaches, a man who would shock the world when he coached his team to upset Harvard, a man who would umpire in the National League for over 20 years, a man who was remembered by Ty Cobb as one of baseball's great hitters, a man who is considered the first regular pinch-hitter.

This book tells their individual story as well as their collective accomplishments of that season in 1906.

Doak Roberts, whose 27 year baseball career included ownership of several teams and 14 years as President of the Texas League, always considered his 1906 team his best, and remembered the players with great fondness. In short, the Cleburne Railroader club was an illustrious team made up of a remarkable collection of accomplished men.

The 1906 team is largely remembered as the team that gave Tris Speaker his start in baseball. It is also remembered for its owner and Texas League President, J. Doak Roberts, but the true hero, at least for the city of Cleburne, was a local, ambitious businessman whose contribution to the city has been totally forgotten. The only place his name appears in the city is on the tombstone he shares with his wife.

Charles H. Thacker came to Texas from Kentucky, first to Waco, then eventually settling in Cleburne in the 1890s. Along the way he became friends with Doak Roberts, a friendship that was fortuitous for the Johnson County city, when in 1905 the relationship that the two men had forged in Waco during the 1880s resulted in Cleburne being awarded a league franchise.

The Texas League proudly points back to its long history, going back to 1888. It would be nice to think of the circuit as having a one of the longest tenures for a minor association. The reality is that the modern league's foundation was built on shifting sands and more telling, shifting franchises. Teams came and went on a regular basis, franchises often failing during the season, disrupting schedules, creating uncertainty and insecurity for the league owners.

More than once, seasons were abandoned, or cut short when franchises failed. In 1899 the Texas League ceased operations, ostensibly due to the Spanish-American War which depleted the pool of professional baseball players. In 1902 baseball came back to Texas. The southern part of the state hosted the South Texas League, while in the north, there was the Texas League (erroneously referred to at times as the NORTH Texas League.) There was a North Texas League, but it was not associated with the modern Texas League of teams.

Doak Roberts was a successful Corsicana businessman, who was able to transfer his business acumen into the world of minor league baseball. Beginning ownership in 1902, Roberts' teams were highly successful on the field, but despite his ability to spot talent, his success was limited by the venue of his teams, first in Corsicana, then Temple, and finally Cleburne. With all the spirit these small towns could muster, they simply lacked the population to make their teams financially viable. In order to keep his teams on the field, Roberts had to reach into his own pockets to take money from his other business venture. After a while his wife grew weary of her husband throwing good money after bad, no matter how much he loved the game.

After transferring his operation to Temple for the 1905 season, Roberts continued to find himself in the red in his baseball ledger. He needed to find others willing to give him financial support if he were to remain in baseball.

Cleburne's Charles Thacker was privy to his old friend's problems, and so went to Roberts with a proposition which included the support of a dozen or so businessmen in Cleburne, provided the city would be included in the 1906 season. Thacker was the glue that held the two parties together, persuading the business leaders that they would benefit from the notoriety of a league team, while convincing Roberts that he was insulated from future monetary loss.

And so the 1906 Cleburne Railroaders franchise was brought to life.

Cleburne Railroaders: a team whose story needed telling.

On a cold rainy day several years ago I sought refuge in the library, leafing through sports books, when I came across a book detailing the history of minor league baseball. Having grown up in Fort Worth, a fan of the Fort Worth Cats, I knew a bit about the modern Texas League. For me, the circuit was made up of Fort Worth, Dallas, Houston, San Antonio, Austin and other large cities. Looking at the yearly standings I came across the 1906 season champions: Cleburne! When I read the name of Cleburne I was shocked that a town that small could ever have hosted a professional franchise, much less having won the title.

My curiosity piqued, I began looking for information about that championship team, only to discover that there was little printed material recalling the exploits of the Cleburne Railroaders. And so I began looking to see what I could discover. It was just a weekend hobby, and as it turned out, a delightful, but lengthy process. The men who played for the '06 club had long since died, but many had descendents who were kind enough to share their memories of their fathers and uncles with me.

Visits with the children, who were for the most part retired, were informal. I gathered information without thoughts of ever putting the details into book form, and so many of the details contained were not as well documented as would have been had I undertook the visits with the thought of publishing the details. Then again, this is about a baseball team, not a political history. There are events recounted that are no more than memories shared. Accuracy of memory eludes quantitative analysis. Again, does it really matter? It was the spirit of the team that intrigued me.

As far as I have been able to do, the details within these pages are as close to accurate as I was able to determine.

What we do know is that the Cleburne Railroaders consisted of some of the greatest men ever to play minor league baseball. For the folks of Cleburne, it was only the passage of time that brought into focus the true magic of that one hot, rainy summer in 1906, just a stone's throw from West Buffalo Creek.

If ever you have the chance, travel to modern day Hulen Park, at the southwest corner of the intersection of Westhill and Hillsboro. Reach down, pickup a handful of dirt. Hold it in your hands. Once long ago greatness walked on that very dirt. Perhaps you can still see the shadows of the illustrious men burned into the soil.

Herein is the story of those men. May their memories live long in the hearts of those who love the great game of baseball, the story of the Champions of Naught Six.

D. Wiley Whitten, Jr.
Wiley45@AOL.com
Fort Worth, Texas
2010

HULEN PARK: CLEBURNE, TEXAS

An Unmarked Tribute to the men of 1906

Hulen Park in Cleburne, Texas, sitting on the banks of West Buffalo Creek, was, until 1906, a vacant piece of land owned by the Trinity and Brazos Valley Railroad.

In 1905 Cleburne was awarded a baseball franchise for the upcoming 1906 season. Soon the search for *flat piece of land close to the square* was undertaken. Cleburne was a railroad town, so it was only fitting that TBVRR, affectionately known as *The Boll Weevil,* was approached about the possibility of obtaining land near West Buffalo Creek.

The Superintendent of the Boll Weevil agreed to lease the land, which was described by one man as *slicky, just smooth as a table top.* The agreement was for three years, and soon construction began on a new ball park. The field was ready for play in March, 1906, and for one summer there was a Texas League team in Cleburne. At the end of the season, the team left town, but the citizens of Cleburne had grown fond of the land on which the park sat, and over one hundred years later, the once leased property still brings pleasure to the citizens of Cleburne. The TBVRR is only a memory, but the place once owned by the old railroad continues to give to the community of Cleburne, Texas.

The original Gorman Park, made of wood, rotted, burned and was rebuilt several times. Eventually it physically disappeared, but remained in the collective memory of the people of Cleburne for many years. Today we can only estimate the exact spot where the ball park once sat. The site of Gorman Park faded into the twilight of time. There is no historical plaque to those men of 1906 who brought professional baseball to Cleburne, and for whom Hulen Park is a lasting monument to their accomplishments.

HULEN PARK
Modern Day Site of Historical Gorman Park
Cleburne, Texas

Approximate Site of Gorman Park: southwest corner, Westhill and Hillsboro Streets.

Google Earth

1

HULEN PARK

This aerial view of Hulen Park in Cleburne, Texas was taken in the late 1960's. A baseball field still occupied the land on which Gorman Park was first constructed in the winter of 1906. The baseball field in the lower left part of the picture is the approximate site of the original Gorman Park, which was named in honor Pat Gorman, the Superintendent of the Trinity and Brazos Railroad, who owned and later loaned the land to the city of Cleburne for a period of three years.

Hulen Park, which encompasses all of the land that surrounds the ball park, is named in honor of General John A. Hulen, who in 1932, acting for the Burlington and Rock Island Railroad, officially leased the 14 acres of land to the city of Cleburne for 99 years. Four additional acres were a gift from private citizens.

I.

CHAPTER ONE: A SUMMING UP

CHARLES H. THACKER
FAREWELL TO GORMAN PARK
LATE FALL 1906

THE SONG OF THE UNSUNG HERO
CHARLES H. THACKER
LATE FALL 1906

Charles Thacker shivered, awakening to an unexpected chill brought on by season's first *norther,* the heat of summer melting away with each gust of wind. He pulled himself up to side of the bed, aching, his joints rigid and reluctant. He was both surprised and offended that his body was losing its capacity to keep up with the demands he put on it.

As a young man he trained to become a bookkeeper, but he was never content to sit at a desk, living instead an active life, and now the prospect being physically limited irritated him. He was nearly 50, hardly old, but his strenuous life was taking its toll. He had always demanded of others, and now he would have to do the same in his own life. All he needed was to stretch, to start a fire, and boil some coffee. Heat and a hot drink: those things would put an end to his morning miseries.

He ambled slowly toward the kitchen, lighting the wood stove, then putting on a pot of water, ready to boil, ready for the coffee grinds. He washed the sleep from his eyes, put on his work clothes, the smell of the coffee soon filling the house. He poured a cup, still boiling, too hot to drink. He blew across the top of the cup, and slowly sipped the invigorating elixir.

He was right. The cure to his ills was simple: the stove warmed the room, and with a second cup of coffee in hand he was re-energized, stepping out of the house to fetch his mule and hitch her to his buggy. Yes, he felt fine. A blustery wind whipped through his hair, at which point he realized that he had not put on a hat, but he decided to brave the chill without head gear. The coffee helped, but he was still groggy. He had done this hundreds of times in his life, but this morning, in the stillness of the pre-dawn hours, the sound of hitching the mule to the wagon echoed, piercing his ears. Save for his activities, the neighborhood was very peaceful and incredibly quiet, his neighbors sleeping, taking advantage of Sunday's more leisurely pace.

The darkness of this pre-dawn hour provided Thacker a blanket of privacy as he prepared for his journey to Gorman Park. He finished his last cup of coffee, ate some peach preserves spread across a cold biscuit, put on his coat and hat and mounted the carriage. The mule waited for his command to move, then once given, began to trudge toward the park, a trip both man and beast knew well.

As the buggy lumbered onward, Charles slumped atop the bench of the buggy. He held the reigns lightly, ignoring, little noticing the familiar homes and businesses that lined one of Cleburne's busiest streets. Too much caught up in emotion of the moment, thinking back over the last 10 months, back to the beginning when he first made this very trip last January, when the flat piece of land on which the park would be built was still vacant.

On that cold day in January plans were in the work for Cleburne's baseball facility. As the plans began to fall into place during those early days of 1906, Thacker's excitement at seeing his baseball dream coming alive made him more boy than man, as excited as a child on Christmas morning. That was so many months ago, all in stark contrast to his somber mood this cold Sunday morning in November.

There was no need for him to rush to the park. No workers waited for his arrival. There were no fans at the gate. He was traveling alone and he would be alone when he arrived at the ball park, and that was the way he wanted it to be. He had no need for anyone to be aware of this, his last trip to Gorman Park.

Lost in thought as the wagon moved slowly along, Charles was startled to suddenly see the outline of the stadium, so lost in thought he had become oblivious to the trip. He brought his buggy to a halt, sat immobilized for a few moments, looking at the wooden structure, viewing it as a man might look at a dead loved one lying in a coffin. He coughed, cleared his throat. There may have been tears, but he would never have admitted such, even to himself. The cold wind was the cause of the mist in his eyes, of that he was certain.

He climbed down from the seat, tied up the mule to a post, looking at the forlorn bleachers, noticing that the leaves piled up against the fence were twisting in harmony with the harsh northerly gust. He unlocked the gate, and entered the grounds. The grass, once so carefully cropped, now brown, unkempt, in need of mowing, the park wrapped in silence, save for the occasional creaking sound of boards giving way to the cold prairie breeze, which in turn churned up the unattended infield dirt, producing a light dusty blanket covering both bleacher and grandstand seats.

As he walked about the depressing site, Thacker's shoulders bent downward, but with the cover of the darkness giving way to the sun's early morning rays, Charles becoming aware of his posture, stiffened and held himself erect, least he be seen in the unlikely event that someone might, at this early morning hour, pass by. He was a proud man who would not bear to be seen otherwise.

He was there on business. Checking out the stands and field, just as if there were a game scheduled later in the day. But in fact, there was no game. There was really no need for the trip this morning. Nothing left to do, except say goodbye to his ballpark.

The place would no longer need his services, but he was not about to abandon it without one last walk through. With the slightest of imagination, he could hear the players, yelling, playing pepper, jumping up and down in nervous and excited anticipation of a game, the crowd, mostly men and boys, yelling insults at the visitors.

There was the scorer's stand, specially built for him, a place where he could sit high above the stands, away from the irritating fans and their annoying questions. How could they expect him to maintain his official score card if they kept asking for information about the game? But those magical times were gone. The 1906 season had ended too soon, too suddenly. For a brief moment in the early days of November it appeared that Cleburne might be included in the 1907 schedule, but Thacker could not get any financial backing for the team, and so the league fathers withdrew their invitation. It was official. There would be no team to watch, no one to root for in '07.

Gorman Park, after only one season, was a relic, empty, destined to fall into disrepair. The ownership of the team had disintegrated. Thacker was a superintendent without a park, an official scorer without a team, an employee without an employer. He would have resigned as the superintendent, but there was no one left to accept his resignation.

Had it just been a year ago when so much excitement was generated with the announcement that professional baseball was coming to Cleburne, Texas? It was late summer of 1905 when the local papers gave hint of the city's elevated status in the world of baseball, then came all of the planning in the fall, becoming realty in 1906.

Cleburne's baseball stadium was designed, laid out, then constructed in the early days of the new year. By March games were being played at the new site. In April the mayor threw out the first pitch of the first game of Cleburne's first year in professional baseball. Up against teams from the big cities, Dallas, Fort Worth, and Waco, the little city's team prevailed. Was it ever a grand time, watching those boys of the summer of 1906, the Champions of the Texas League, the Cleburne Railroaders!

East Henderson Street, Cleburne, Tex.

Charles H. Thacker dreamed of a Cleburne beyond the dusty streets that surrounded the Johnson County Courthouse. He was a huge advocate of the newly opened Cleburne Country Club, and was hard at work in getting and keeping professional baseball in Cleburne, inspiring the local business community to put up the money to keep the team financially solvent.

Charles H. Thacker was a more illustrious man than the people of Cleburne ever realized. He had settled in their town in the early 1890's, building up his business on Chambers Street, accumulated a small amount of wealth, raised his daughter Lois, and then in February of 1906 said goodbye to his wife Kate, who faced death at the age of 37. He was one of the city's dynamic leaders, armed with a vision of a Cleburne beyond the dusty streets that encircled the courthouse. The Cleburne Country Club in part owed its existence to his ambition. It was his friendship with Doak Roberts that made it possible for Cleburne to soar to the lofty heights of professional baseball.

Before coming to Cleburne, Thacker had made a name for himself, once and long ago in another place, in another time, when he was an officer of the Texas League. That was way back in 1889 when he was living in Waco, and was appointed by the league leaders as the Secretary of the Texas League.

In 1888, the year before he became an official in the new league, he and his close friend Doak Roberts were a part of the group of men that enabled Waco to become a charter member of the first professional league in Texas. It was not easy, that first year of the Texas League. There was much to learn about running a professional circuit, handling the daily grind of travel, maintaining a regular schedule, paying salaries, hotel bills, train fares, along with all of the other financial obligations. Some teams folded, including, surprisingly, the Fort Worth team operated by Bill Ward.

Whatever discouragement the owners and players suffered in 1888 went away by the spring of the following year. The refreshment of hope comes with the arrival of each spring. The owners were convinced that they had learned invaluable lesson about operating professional ball from the previous year.

One of their mistakes in '88 was the lack of involvement of the local papers. They rectified that problem with the appointment of Charles Thacker as their secretary. With his training and talent as a bookkeeper, Thacker compiled detailed and accurate records and distributed them to the home town newspapers, who responded by giving the '89 season considerably more coverage. The result is that far more is known about the league's second season than their first. Thacker became one of the unsung heroes in Texas baseball history.

In 1951, Texas League historian Williams Ruggles published his monumental book on the history of the league and gave credit to Thacker's contribution to the league in 1889, but as it always seems to be with the unheralded hero, incorrectly identified him as *C.H. Thatcher*. The misspelling at that point probably didn't matter, for by that year in the early1950s, no one remembered Charles H. Thacker, not even those in Cleburne, who owed him a great debt.

Charles H. Thacker, Superintendent

When the Railroaders were scheduled to play in Gorman Park, Charles Thacker arrived early to get things ready for the afternoon crowd. He loved being there in Gorman Park, but it was a place of work for him, and he had no interest in being a *part* of the crowd. Even surrounded by hundreds of fans, he totally concentrated on the game at hand, keeping the fans at arm's length. He had an important job that required his entire attention, allowing the crowd to have the fun he denied of himself.

That was then, but now on this quiet Sunday morning there was no one about; he found himself in a solitary place, a place not supposed to be a place of solitude. Gorman Park came alive only when there were people in the stands, and players on the field. While Charles was seemingly indifferent to the fans during the season, he sorely missed them this morning.

When the season started, his scorer's table sat behind home plate, but it was too accessible to the prying eyes of the fans, which constantly disrupted his intense gaze at the game. They annoyed him in wanting to know details of the game. *How many hits...how many strikeouts....* He ordered his worker to build him a stand, 15 feet tall. He would be there, amongst the crowd, and yet high above them, unapproachable.

Now on this cold morning he stood at the base of the scorer's box, then for one last time, he climbed the ladder that lead to his chair and table. He loved it up here, with its unimpaired view of the park. As the cold winds washed his face, his eyes saw an empty, abandoned baseball diamond. There were no bags to mark the site of first, second or third base. The grass was dead, uneven. The lumber had turned an ugly grey, yielding to the unrelenting Texas sun and the hot summer showers. The chalk on the outfield scoreboard had mostly faded, nothing left to be read. No hint that once the proud Railroaders team rode to a championship level on this field. The cheers of the fans and the chatter of the teams had gone silent, broken only by sounds of the lapels of his suit jacket whipping in response to the wind against his chest.

For the moment he allowed himself a few pleasant memories of Gorman Park, of the Cleburne Railroaders, of the sound and smell of baseball. Then the reality of this Sunday morning plunged its blade into his heart. Doak Roberts had left town. The Cleburne Athletic Association no longer had a reason to exist.

November, 1906. Just days following the meeting in San Antonio, where he was promised that Cleburne would be included in the upcoming 1907 season, provided that he could obtain financial backing. It was not to be. The businessmen had no interest in investing in baseball. No one, save Charles Thacker, cared about defending the city's flag. He had given Cleburne a professional team, a club that made them champions of the league. They had challenged those big cities, Dallas and Fort Worth, and it was their little town that won the silver cup.

Thacker grieved. He was alone and abandoned. Only years later would the people of Cleburne, the businessmen of Cleburne, and the ball players themselves join him in their understanding of what they once had, but now had lost. By time of their realization, it was too late. The only thing left of the Champions of 1906 would be the legends, and soon even those would fade from memory, ending up as little more than an asterisk in the pages of Cleburne's history.

There was nothing left for him to do at Gorman Park. His services were no longer required or needed. He climbed down from the scorer's stand, walked past the grandstands, and then locked the gate behind him, returning to his buggy, where he untied his mule, climbed aboard the carriage, pointing the animal toward home.

The sun had risen, and the town was coming to life as its citizens made their way to the various churches that served the community. Thacker was not a church man, and so he headed back home. A few people waved as he journeyed back to his home on Main Street. His acknowledgement of their greeting was perfunctory, a mechanical wave in response. He arrived back at his empty home.

Katie, his wife of 15 years was no longer there, daughter Lois had returned to school. His house was as quiet now, as quiet as Gorman Park. He poured himself a glass of milk, walked to his desk. The ledger books for his sporting goods store were open. Thacker sat down, looked at the calendar hanging on the wall nearby. *1906.* What an incredible year. He would never forget. He missed his wife. He missed his daughter. He missed sitting at the scorer's table in Gorman Park. His life would never be the same. Charles sat at his desk, his head in his hands, looking at his ledger books. He needed to get them back in balance. Thacker picked up his pen, looked down at the numbers in the book, but they were blurry. He blinked tears, and wrote.

Charles Thacker's long friendship with Doak Roberts provided Cleburne with an opportunity to host a Texas League franchise in 1906.

Ironically, his wife, 37 year old Kate, died in February of 1906, just as the Railroaders were gathering for spring training.

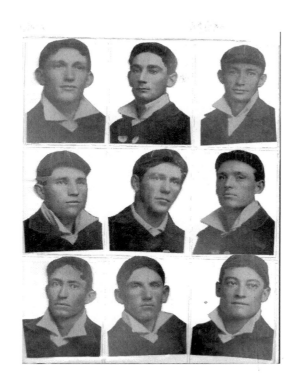

II.

THE FINEST MEN:

DOAK ROBERTS'
1906 CLEBURNE TEAM

...THE FINEST GROUP OF MEN I EVER KNEW..
The Cleburne Railroaders of 1906. . . the men of Gorman Park

National Pastime's Loss

J. DOAK ROBERTS.

J. DOAK ROBERTS DIED IN 1929

Doak Roberts never stopped adding players to this 1906 Cleburne squad until he had finally put together a championship caliber team, and indeed his team took the silver cup that year.

After a reported loss of about $1200, and the failure of the Cleburne Athletic Association to hold up their end of the bargain, Roberts decided to leave baseball, assigning most of his men to Claud Rielly's Houston team. However, by mid-season of 1907 Rielly begged him to join him, and for the next decade Roberts found a home in Houston. Eventually he returned to the Presidency of the Texas League. He was serving that capacity at the time of his death in 1929.

When he was nearing the end of his life J. Doak Roberts discussed his long association with organized ball that stretched back to the amateur days of Texas baseball. He was most proud of his 1906 Cleburne team: *as fine a group of players as I was ever associated with.* Despite all of the financial problems connected with that club, disputes with the business association that was supposed to provide monetary stability for the franchise, Roberts recalled that team with great fondness, and rightly so.

The Cleburne Railroaders existed but one short year, a class D franchise in a small league in an even smaller town. The citizens of Cleburne were afforded one of the greatest collections of players ever to grace a minor league diamond. The men who ran the club were themselves jewels of the game. Doak Roberts would spend that last decade of his life as the president of the Texas League during its golden era, the 1920's.

In his younger years, Roberts struggled to keep his franchises financially afloat, all the while he scouted Texas wide and far and signed player after player to play on his various teams. He signed hundred of young men, but his prize pupil was a star in the American League. By the time of Doak Roberts' death, Tris Speaker was out of baseball, one of the greatest centerfielders in the history of the game. Roberts back in Texas watched Tris' career with pride, keeping that first contract Speaker has signed in 1906. Sadly, Roberts did not live long enough to see him inducted into Baseball's Hall of Fame. Speaker was the star, however, there were others on his 1906 roster that, while they might not have reached the level of Tris, yet proved to be extraordinary in ability, and given the sheer numbers of excellent players in his fold, Roberts was shown to be one of the great scouts in the history of baseball.

TRIS SPEAKER

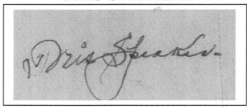

In May of 1906, Roberts spotted an 18 year old Hubbard boy playing for the Nicholson-Watson Store team in Corsicana. He offered the left hand pitcher a $50 a-month contract, sent him to on to Waco to join his Cleburne team. Tris Speaker was given a dollar for his rail fare, but pocketed the money and hopped a freight car. With that $50 contact, Speaker never looked back until 1937 when he was inducted into Baseball's Hall of Fame.

DODE CRISS

Tris Speaker's signing was enough to ensure Roberts' place in the history of the sport, but that same year he hired another left handed pitcher, who like Speaker, did not make his mark on the mound, but rather as a hitter. Dode Criss was a great Texas League pitcher, but was never able to translate that talent to the major leagues as a member of the St. Louis Browns. What he brought to his team was an extraordinary bat, a horrendous fielder, but a magnificent man at the plate. Had there been a designated hitter slot in this era, Criss would no doubt have become a superstar. As it were, he came off the bench so often for the Browns that he is considered almost to have invented the pinch hitter role.

The greatest tribute to Dode came from Ty Cobb, a man generally unwilling to give any man, except to himself, credit for hitting ability. In 1952 Life Magazine published an extensive assessment of the modern player as seen through the eyes of Ty Cobb, who had been out of baseball since 1928. Needless to say, Cobb did not like the players he watched in the '40's and early '50's. Who he did like was Dode Criss: below is Cobb's memory of Dode Criss:

"The St.Louis Browns used to have a fellow named Dode Criss, who I have often thought was one of the tragedies of baseball, a gold-plated case of a man who was born 20 years before his time. He seldom struck out, and nearly always hit a long ball. But with the old baseball, his drives didn't make enough difference, and since he wasn't a very good fielder, he spent most of his time on the bench. With the modern rabbit ball, Criss would have torn the league apart; he would have made today's so-called sluggers look sick. Could the Browns use him today!"

Ty Cobb, Life Magazine, 1952

GEORGE 'LUCKY' WHITEMAN

In 1906 the Fort Worth Panthers surprisingly cut George Whiteman from their roster. Roberts was quick to sign him. That year Whiteman would win the league batting title. He became one of the giants of the Texas League, playing in 1,432 league games, the most of any one man in the history of the league. In 1918 that he stepped into ball's greatest spotlight: the World Series. At age 35, as a member of the Boston Red Sox, he lead the Sox to the Championship over the Chicago Cubs. Earlier in 1918 he had lost his left field position to a left-handed pitcher, Babe Ruth. But the man who stole the spotlight in the World Series of 1918 was Whiteman, dubbed *Lucky*. He was involved in almost every rally, and in game six, he made a tremendous somersault catch that ensured the Red Sox 2-1 lead would hold up. It was his last game in the majors.

"UNCLE" CHARLEY MORAN

Even with Speaker, Criss, and Whiteman on the team, by far the most intriguing man ever to play in the Texas League, much less for Cleburne, was Kentucky's Charley Moran. He first played in the Texas League with Dallas. In 1906 Roberts was anxious to get him onto the Railroader's roster. For a while, due to his wife's illness, it appeared that Charley would not be playing that year, but at last he wired the worried Roberts and said he was on his way to Cleburne.

He had small stints in the major leagues, but he first established his credentials on the national stage as the football coach of Texas A&M, from 1909-1914. He left there to go to Carlisle, then at Centre College in Danville, Kentucky. At Centre College Moran became a true legend in the history of college football. The undisputed power house of football in 1921 was Harvard, national champions and undefeated in five years. On October 29, 1921 with 45,000 fans in the Harvard stadium, Moran's Prayer Colonels, David vs. Goliath, took to the field against the mighty Ivy League school.

At half-time, the score was a shocking 0-0 tie! The Harvard fans were not worried. It was only a matter of time before their club would take charge and put an end to Centre's impossible dream. Then in the third quarter Centre College quarterback Bo McMillin took off on a 32 yard run. He scored! 6-0! Harvard was not able to match Centre's score; the game ended. 6-0! The headlines were large. Moran's little club had clubbed the Mighty! The shock loomed long. Fifty years later, in 1972 the New York Times selected this as the greatest upset in the history of college football. At the midpoint of the 20th century, 1950, the Associated Press selected this game as the football upset of the first half of the century.

There is still more to the Charlie Moran story. For 22 years, 1916-1939, Charles Moran toiled in the National League as one of its outstanding umpires in the golden era of baseball. In 1940 his life in baseball was featured in the February edition of Baseball Magazine.

Charley Moran was the most interesting, most accomplished member of the 1906 Cleburne Railroaders. He left monuments at Texas A&M, Centre College, Bucknell, and in the National League. Uncle Charley Moran.

RICK ADAMS

Rick Adams was one of the outstanding pitchers in the Texas League. He too had his moments in the major leagues. In 1903 the New Orleans club sold him to the New York Americans (the Yankees). He was given a tryout with the big boys, but was cut before the season started. Finally in 1905 he got his moment in the sunshine as a member of the Washington Senators. He compiled a mediocre record with the American League team, 2-6, getting four hits in 23 at bats. He returned to Texas where he continued on with a long and outstanding minor league career.

WALTER "HICKORY" DICKSON

An extraordinary pitcher. In 1906 he was called upon several times to single handedly carry the Railroaders on his back when he pitched both ends of three double headers, including the decisive season ending double header in Fort Worth. Dickson played in five different seasons in the major leagues: 1910, 1912, 1913, 1914, and finally his last year, 1915.

WINGO CHARLIE ANDERSON

With his staff exhausted and with one week to go in the season, Doak Roberts reached out to Lillian, Texas to sign Wingo Charlie Anderson to a short contract. Two times within a space of three days Anderson pitched the Railroaders to crucial wins, setting the stage for the weekend series with Fort Worth that would determine the second half champion. Wingo Anderson was another of the many players that Roberts signed that eventually saw action in the major leagues. Wingo's shot came in 1910 with the Cincinnati Reds.

ROY MITCHELL

Roy Mitchell was one of Roberts' stars in Temple, but during spring training, he had to make financial and roster decisions. Having signed Dode Criss, who appeared not only to be an outstanding pitcher, but could handle the bat as well, and coupled with Mitchell's demands for more money, Roberts made a reluctant decision to remove him from the 1906 roster. Roy was another in the list of Roberts players who spent time in the big leagues, playing 8 seasons, five with the Browns, a couple with the White Sox, ending his career with Cincinnati Reds, where he got to witness firsthand the scandalous 1919 Black Sox World Series.

PARKER ARBOGAST

Cleburne struggled for a while to find a catcher to complement their excellent pitching staff. Arbogast finally brought stability to that position. He never made it to the major leagues, but he later proved himself as a steady, if not excellent catcher in the Pacific Coast League, which was considered by many at the time to be a west coast equivalence to the major leagues. Arbogast was described by the local papers as *fair and fuzzy haired.*

CHARLES H. THACKER

Not to be lost amongst the various famous players is a man who brought tremendous abilities to the operations side of the team. Charles Thacker's life and contributions to Cleburne have been largely lost, but without him, there would not have been Texas League baseball in Cleburne. He is briefly mentioned in William Ruggles' monumental work about the history of the Texas League.

J.DOAK ROBERTS

The story of Doak Roberts goes back to the fall of 1887 when the seeds were being planted for the creation of the Texas League. In 1902 he was amongst the men who revived the league after its two years hiatus. He was continually associated with the Texas League from 1902 until his death in 1929.

Few knew at the time that the Cleburne bunch would be the finest group of men most would ever know. Getting Doak Roberts to bring his franchise to Cleburne was a stroke of luck, in large part due to his lifelong friend, Charles Thacker, whose enthusiasm for baseball was unmatched in Cleburne. He was the catalyst who connected Roberts with the business community, convincing them that a baseball marriage was in the best interest of both.

It was not always a happy marriage and it ended in divorce at the end of the 1906 season. Only as the years passed did both sides grasp the magic and splendor of that one year in which the Railroaders played host in Gorman Park. As that generation grew older, a young set of men would visit the Cleburne fire department to look at the large framed picture of the old team and marvel that Tris Speaker actually played for Cleburne, Texas.

There was the team picture. Tris Speaker. But also Dode Criss, George Whiteman, the famous Texas A&M coach, Charley Moran, the President of the Texas League, Doak Roberts, Walter Dickson, pitcher. Did Chief Wilson actually play in Cleburne when the Fort Worth team came to town? Young boys could only wish that the team would come back. Then they became old men, and the story of the mighty Cleburne Railroaders was buried under dust, lost to clouded memories and became insignificant to the history of Cleburne.

THREE DOZEN FARMERS GATHER FOR A GAME OF COUNTRY BALL

III.

CLEBURNE, TEXAS
GETS A PROFESSIONAL TEAM

FROM COUNTRY BALL
TO THE TEXAS LEAGUE
SUMMER OF '05

CLEBURNE, TEXAS
COUNTY SEAT: JOHNSON COUNTY

SLEEPY DUSTY LITTLE TOWN……………

Fort Worth looks at its cousins from Cleburne….. *Fort Worth Telegram*

Those Hayseeds……

The newspapers in Fort Worth, and certainly in Dallas, looked askance at the citizens of Cleburne, located 30 miles south in Johnson County, a rural, sparsely populated area settled with little communities like Burleson, Joshua, Godley, Alvarado and Keene, mostly hidden away, mainly in existence to serve the surrounding farmers and ranchers. For those who lived in Johnson County it was easy to feel inferior, but their pride and individualism prevented them from buying into the gentle fun being poked their way.

If you picked up the Cleburne city directory for 1906, there would be a statement that the population was 14,000. Perhaps, but the official federal census in 1900 was 7,493, and had only increased to 10,364 in 1910. As far out as 1920 the census figure was still only 12,820, with the population not surpassing 14,000 until 1960 when the feds stated Cleburne's census as 15,381.

So what was the population in 1906? If the growth between 1900 and 1910 were steady, then the 1906 census was about 9,200. Not a good drawing base for professional baseball, but Thacker was certain that the people would turn out to support the endeavor.

Hogs, Hot Weather, Baseball, and City Life
1905

Visitors not accustomed to Texas weather soon wilted in the relentless summer heat that held sway over Cleburne from May until September. A Cleburne reporter spotted a traveling businessman debarking from the southbound Santa Fe, vigorously fanning himself with a rolled up newspaper. The stranger's quote made the next day's paper:...*I had expected it to be hot, but I was unprepared for this.* His words fell on deaf ears to the long suffering Texans, who took any complaint about their weather as an affront to God. However, if you were a Texan, it was okay to ask (and how often they asked!) *Hot enough for you?*

Twentieth century technology was finding its place in Cleburne, perhaps a bit slower than in some parts of the country, but a visitor from this era would find many items familiar to our daily life a hundred years later. The city was well wired for electricity, and at least in town, the Edison light bulb was a common feature in most homes. The telephone had by this time become an essential part of the business community, and many families were sharing a party line.

The modern day air conditioner was the work of Willis H. Carrier, who patented his device in 1902. There is no indication that anyone in Cleburne as of yet had a cooling unit, but certainly the ceiling fan was ubiquitous, at least in the businesses around the square.

There were now cars in Johnson County, estimated to be about 75 in number. The young men and the rich loved the automobile, but the transaction from farm animal to the gas engine was a bumpy ride, with the local papers filled with wild accounts of the meeting of man, beast and auto. There were attempts to keep the drivers at bay, but progress likes to progress. The mules, horses, and other varmints would just have to get used to the sputtering and spewing of the horseless carriage. Besides there were exciting stories about cars that could do a *mile a minute*. It was the stuff of Jules Verne's science fiction.

Cleburne was well served by two newspapers, mostly providing daily coverage of local events, but at times national stories made it into insular life of this small community.

THACKER AND THE COUNTRY CLUB
1905/1906

In the summer of '05 plans for the Cleburne Country Club was finalized and put on display, revealing a fine drawing of a two story building estimated to cost $5,000 with the starting date of construction hoped to be near. The opening of the club in May of 1906 was a huge move forward for Johnson County and Cleburne in particular, giving the city a place where visiting business executives and politicians could conduct business in a style suited for a growing community. Thacker's interest in sports played no small part in the planning and developing the club.

Charles Thacker put his final touch to the Cleburne Country Club when he took charge to see that the Blue Hole Road was paved. If the road went unimproved then the least rainfall would create a quagmire which would be nearly impassable by an automobile. How embarrassing that would be to the community to have a VIP to arrive only to not be able to make a planned meeting because of a muddy thoroughfare. Thacker personally oversaw the improvement of the access road soon to be known as Country Club Road. Thacker was into the exacting details, the finishing touch: pave the road before the rains come!

Cleburne Country Club House, Cleburne, Tex.

The Cleburne Country Club opened its doors in 1906, giving the city a place for business leaders to meet with visiting dignitaries.

The Cleburne Country Club was a signal that the county seat of Johnson County was determined to become an urban 20th century place, changing its focus from the farmer to the businessman. The farmers were welcomed to town, but they were not welcomed to live in town, not unless they were willing to become city-folk. Unfortunately for the city leaders, there were too many farmers in town who refused to recognize the fundamental traits of a modern city, and so a new ordinance was to soon take effect. And it was not a popular proposal.

AN ORDINANCE MIGHTIER THAN THE PEN..
……..well at least a hog pen

Hogs! The city had so many hog pens that the smell was becoming a distraction, and needless to say, unpleasant, except, of course, to those who stood to gain from the sale of their pigs. It was the custom of the time to dress out the hogs following the first cold snap. While some depended upon the fall ritual for food, for most it was a matter of finances. The hog was a cash crop, providing the few extra dollars it took to buy shoes, coats, and school books for the kids.

A proposed city ordinance by the city council would remove the hog from the city, and if it became law, the effect would be devastating for many families. They pleaded their case *how can we make up that lost money.* They were hard working people trying to make a good life for their families and to keep the children in school. They needed every cent just to make it.

The city council listened. A few years earlier they might have given in to those who begged for its defeat, but this was the progressive year of 1906. Cities of importance all across the state had passed similar laws against raising livestock within the city boundaries. If Cleburne were not to forever fall into the image of being just a bunch of country hicks, they too would have to pass similar ordinances.

Progress dictated the passage. If Cleburne were to ever be considered to be more than a dusty, backwoods place, it would have to look like a modern, clean city. The country club was one step, getting rid of hog pens was next. The city had other items on the agenda. Certainly paving the streets, bringing a street car line to the city was a couple of other issues facing the business community. But the easiest and quickest way to improve this city was the hog ordinance, a step in the right direction.

South Anglin Street

Cleburne had to battle its proximity to Dallas and Fort Worth. Perhaps had the city been 100 miles from their larger neighbors, their thrust to became a larger city, with increased business opportunities might have been easier, but the fact was that Fort Worth was only 30 miles away, Dallas about 50. At one time those were considerable distances for most travelers, but now with the convenience of the railroad and interurban, those mileages were less of a barrier. It was now too easy for the people of Cleburne to compare the lack of development in their city to its progressive neighbors, especially Fort Worth.

In 1905 the prospect of bringing professional baseball to Cleburne was looked at more in terms of the *image* of the city than for the mere presence of a team. As Thacker vigorous worked to find a group of men willing to put up their money to back the team, his primary selling point was for the publicity that being in the Texas League would bring to the little Johnson County community. And it was an excellent sell. The Cleburne Athletic Association was comprised of businessmen who could be swayed by the free publicity a league team would bring to their town and by association, to their business.

CLEBURNE, TEXAS
The Circus Comes To Town

Soon baseball as well would be coming to entertain the city!

PROVIDED SUITABLE GROUNDS CAN BE SECURED
Roberts and Thacker Discuss Baseball coming to Cleburne

On Wednesday, August 23, 1905 W.Y. Wilson was the first farmer in Johnson County to bring a bale of cotton to market. His load was described as *middling* and weighing 462 pounds. Being the first to bring cotton to the gin was a great personal honor for Mr. Wilson, earning him an extra $20 in celebration for his accomplishment.

While Mr. Wilson rejoiced at his good fortune, there were serious matters at hand. The citizens of Cleburne were up in arms. Recent rains had resulted in swarms of mosquitoes, and the people expected the government to take immediate actions. The city council members listened to the anguish cries for help, agreeing to fight the pesky critters with fire and crude oil. No puddle would be safe from the long arm of city workers, a few drops of oil, and a match.

There was news about the community amateur baseball team to report. A good number of men had gone to Godley to support their local Cleburne team. They returned to the city pointing with pride. Their boys had defeated Godley by a score of 3-2, thanks in large part to the battery tandem of Henry and Davis, and the paper gleefully noted that *not a single error was made by the Cleburne team.* Godley wanted a rematch, which would be played in Cleburne the following Saturday *provided suitable ground can be secured by that time.*

These were some of the important stories of the day in the town, but the most significant event that August 23rd of '05 went unnoticed and unreported.

Quiet Goings-on….

While the city of Cleburne went about it business that summer day, Doak Roberts quietly boarded the north bound train out of Temple. He was on his way back to Corsicana, returning from one of his frequent trips to check on the Boll Weevils. His team was doing fine, winning and leading the league. The 1905 flag seemed well within the reach of his Temple team. On the field, things were great. At the gate, attendance lagged, finances suffered. His wife Lola complained.

Perhaps his wife had a legitimate concern. She little cared that Doak loved his team, and that they were doing well. All she could see was what owning a team did do their banking account. The money always seemed to be going the wrong way.

Roberts conceded to her concerns. His love for the game could go only so far. *One more move, one more promise, one more chance.* Roberts desperately looked for ways of keeping his hand in the game, with his pocketbook protected. And so it was to that end that his old friend Charlie Thacker made a pitch. *Come to Cleburne and our men will set up an association with guaranteed funding in the unlikely event that the team was a fiscal failure.* Thacker was a man of honor and an acquaintance for many years.

On this trip home from Temple, Doak would stop in Cleburne and call on his old friend. He needed a miracle. Perhaps Thacker might be a financial angel, or at least a man with an angle.

Boarding the train, Doak removed his suit coat, lowered all the windows in the Pullman car for a cooling breeze, and hoped that a piece of soot did not end up in his eyes. He secured a seat, put his suitcase in the overhead, lit a Cremo cigar, reread his letter from Charles Thacker.

His old friend sounded optimistic about a future possibility for his Texas League club. Thacker promised to secure a collection of local business men with sufficient funds to underwrite a Cleburne baseball venture. *Bring your team here!* This was the message he wanted to here.

**CLEBURNE'S PASSENGER DEPOT:
THE CLEBURNE GULF, COLORADO, AND SANTA FE DEPOT**

Thacker did his best to hide his gleeful anticipation of the meeting with Roberts, to be conducted without coverage by the local papers. It was likely that few in the city had any idea who the President of the Texas League might be, and fewer would recognize Doak Roberts, thus it was not really difficult to keep such a meeting unknown to the city.

He journeyed to the depot to greet the north bound train carrying the man he had known since the days when both lived in Waco. Both men were genuinely glad to meet. From the train station it was a short jaunt to his sporting goods store. They talked about that day in Waco when they first saw a professional baseball club, when they were teammates on the local semi-professional team that took on John McCloskey's traveling Joplin, Missouri club. It was in November of 1887. The professional team had first stopped in Fort Worth, and was on its way to Austin to play a team composed of members of the New York Giants. Waco was a convenient stop, and another place to pick up some cash during the off-season for the Joplin boys.

A large crowd showed up for the game in Waco, giving the Joplin players a nice payday. McCloskey was impressed by the fan turnout in both cities, and by the time he reached Austin, he saw the potential of league ball in the Lone Star state.

Things went well for the traveling team, and by December, McCloskey, the father of professional baseball in Texas, was holding meetings with prospective owners. Incredibly, in the short span of a few months, the new league began play on April 8, 1888. The Texas League began play in Fort Worth, Dallas, Houston, Galveston, San Antonio, Austin, along with New Orleans. There were rough spots that first year, but the Texas League continued play until September.

Waco was not a part of the inaugural season, but when the second season began in 1889, the Navigators were included in the Texas League schedule. Charles H. Thacker was appointed as the league's Secretary and official scorer. His training as a bookkeeper served him well. Considerably more is known about the 1889 season than 1888, thanks to Thacker's accumulated statistics.

Then in 1890, when he and his new wife decided to make their home in Cleburne, Thacker left his post in the league, not to return to professional baseball until 1906.

John J. McCloskey may have been the *Father of Texas Baseball*, but he was one of the worst managers in the early history of the major leagues. He managed Louisville of the National League for 2 seasons, with records of 35-96, and 2-17. From 1906 until 1908 he managed the St. Louis Cardinals, compiling records of 52-98, 52-101, and 49-105. He managed in the majors five years, and only once had a team out of the cellar. The 1906 Cards finished 7th. McCloskey's major league lifetime record was 190-417 (.313)

Thacker had been out of professional baseball since 1889. As far as Roberts there is little known of any connection he had with the Texas League until 1902, when he helped revive the league following its two years hiatus (1900-1901).

Doak Roberts was doing quite well at the time with his coal and lumber businesses, providing him with the wherewithal to invest in the new 1902 Corsicana ball club, which is considered even today as one of the top 100 minor league teams, thanks to their 88-23 record, including the famous 51-3 win over Texarkana.

Thacker and Roberts had moved apart, but they continued to occasionally exchange correspondences. In '02 Roberts shared his excitement about becoming a team owner with his old Cleburne friend. Those letters would prove to be the basis for Cleburne eventually getting a pro team. Doak often shared both his accomplishments as well as his frustrations with his Cleburne friend. By 1905 his letters increasingly reflected a sense of desperation. Things were not going well financially with Roberts' team in Temple. Thacker was hungry to get back into the Texas League, and now he perceived a golden opportunity.

Charles Thacker composed a letter of invitation. The Temple team owner was lured into Cleburne, a city that would guarantee the monetary solvency of a Cleburne league team. And so Roberts boarded the train that morning out of Temple, mulling over Thacker's proposition.

As they settled in on this hot afternoon, the two men revived old memories, of times stretching back 20 years, but Roberts had a limited amount of time to speed, needing to catch the afternoon train. It was time to get down to business. Thacker presented a simple plan: Roberts would bring his team to Cleburne, continue to operate the organization; Thacker would help create an association of businessmen that would guarantee the financial stability of the team. In addition, the local men would secure a suitable ground for the team as well as to construct a suitable stadium.

Doak Roberts most likely looked around the town square, dirt streets, bucolic settings, a limited business community and wondered if indeed Cleburne was ready for league ball.

Thacker had an answer to all of his concerns. The city had proven that it was ready to expand its horizons and business opportunities. The Cleburne Country Club was up and running. The city had the Santa Fe yards, and the Trinity and Brazos Valley Railroad yards in town. A Texas League franchise would provide the business community with invaluable publicity throughout the state, and that is the very thing that company men wanted and needed. The small cost of operating a team would be far outweighed by the benefit of having their name constantly in the papers. There were only eleven league cities in the entire state.

Thacker could deliver the businessmen's money. His services to the club would be included for free. He had been there once, the Secretary of the Texas League, and he was ready to once again take his talents to the baseball league.

Roberts and Thacker were much alike and appreciated the similar qualities they saw in each other. While the Corsicana gentleman could not have been particularly impressed with the city, he had no alternative plan in hand. He liked and trusted his old friend from Waco. They shook hands, ate lunch, and then Roberts headed back to the Santa Fe station to return to Corsicana to mull over the offer. Roberts wrestled with serious doubts, but his obsession with baseball allowed him to look at the positives in Thacker's plan. In the end, he had few options if he were to remain associated with the league. The Cleburne proposition just might work.

Thacker was a man who had *presence*. He was trusted, he had a proven record of getting things done, a man with a singular mind, who once took on a task, would not let go until he not only had his way, but that it was completed, without those loose ends that often lead a project to failure.

When he made is presentation to the local business organization, those men knew he could attend to the details. Better still, Charles Thacker did not seek out recognition for himself. He was content with seeing things done right. Others could claim the notoriety. The reality was in such a small town, everyone truly knew the pecking order, and knew those who were blustery and those who were reliable.

Charles Thacker was both a business man as well as a sporting man. He knew both ends of the business of sports, and so he was quick to present a business plan for a minor league baseball team that emphasized the business needs. Sport was recreational. Most of the local leaders were pragmatic, and while they saw a sport as something entertaining, they had to understand how it would play into their financial realm.

The man, who initiated what would eventually become the Cleburne Athletic Association, did not discuss the glory of baseball. Instead he was careful to point out that in the entire state of Texas, there were less than a dozen cities with professional baseball. Thacker brought papers from Fort Worth and Dallas, as well as from a few other lesser cities, pointing to their sports section. The Texas and South Texas Leagues got prominent coverage throughout the entire state.

For a small guarantee from a local business association, Cleburne could be one of those dozen cities! All across the state, there would be the name of the city, alongside Dallas, Fort Worth, Waco, San Antonio, Houston, and Galveston. The leaders of Cleburne could not afford to buy that much publicity. Each would be able to attach their name to the Texas League, with the fame of the league enhancing their business.

There was much to be done, and only a short period of time to get the agreement in place. Charles was pleased to be able to share the initial agreement with his friend in Corsicana.

Doak Roberts wrestled with the idea. Corsicana was bigger, but the city had failed to support the team during its first three years, and the current team under different ownership was not in good shape. Temple suffered from the lack of newspaper exposure, and attendance was not supporting his move to that city.

While his businesses continued to support his lifestyle and helped to underwrite the business side of baseball, Roberts, no doubt under pressure from his wife, as well as the reality of seeing money spent without the hope of recoupment, Roberts had to make a serious decision. Underlying all of the business end of baseball was his great love for the sport. He could not imagine leaving the great game.

It was about the money. Cleburne would guarantee him against losses, and he would still be directing the team. J. Doak Roberts held out hopes that for one more season, he could be a baseball man.

The following letter, written on September 23, 1905, is one of the most important ever written in the history of Cleburne and Johnson County:

Corsicana, Texas
Sept. 23, 1905
Dear Sir and Friend:

At a recent meeting of the Texas Baseball League the plan of extending our circuit was discussed, and the idea was looked on favorably by all the directory, and I as President of the league was appointed as a committee to visit your city and go over the ground with those who might become interested in Cleburne being represented in the Texas League circuit in 1906.

If you think that your people will be interested in this proposed enterprise, advise me at your earliest convenience, and I will visit Cleburne in the near future and will go over the ground with them. I feel sure that we can show them the benefits derived by being represented in a good league in such a way that it will be very little trouble to make a success of the undertaking.

Yours truly,

J. D. Roberts

It is hard to imagine the excitement Charles Thacker was feeling as he raced to the two newspapers with the letter in hand. The papers took the good news to heart, and spun it to their satisfaction. The Morning News editor, in an attempt to look like a universal man, instead looked very provincial that day. The editor obviously had no idea of what it meant to become a league city, seeing the Texas League as he saw Cleburne.

As for players, there are a number of young men who reside here that can put up excellent games; in fact, several have gone from here to the larger places and signed with professional teams. Sam Byrd was manager and during that season defeated everything they went up against with the exception of the last game that year. They were defeated on the home grounds by Paris, but the game was given to the visitors mostly because of sympathy. (Obviously a pesky umpire...)

Cleburne Morning Review Sept 25, 1905

CLEBURNE HAD TWO DAILY NEWSPAPERS IN 1906

THE PRESIDENT COMES TO TOWN
October 26, 1905

On October 26, 1905 J. Doak Roberts made his first *official* appearance in Cleburne, and he brought good news. While the configuration of the league for the 1906 season was still uncertain, with Greenville, Sherman, and Cleburne in competition for Roberts' franchise, he reported that the Johnson County city had several advantages over the two other cities, not the least of which was the friendship between himself and Charles H. Thacker.

Roberts addressed the city leaders, flattering Cleburne in other ways. With the Santa Fe Rail Yards pumping a huge amount of dollars into their local economy, the people like to think of themselves as a "train-town" and Doak confirmed that when he talked about her railway and transportation facilities. Cleburne was centrally located to the other Texas League cities, no small consideration, since much of the cost of operating a team was related to travel. Thus the city had a great advantage over its two rivals. He continued with his praise of the city, of its size and growth, and the general feeling that the city would support league ball.

With all of his kind words, the Corsicana gentleman withheld a direct commitment to the city until he could meet in private with the business leaders who, in order to attract the team, would have to initiate a stock company capitalized at a sum of $2,000. Roberts himself, or someone he would appoint, would take one-half of the money:

> *A ballpark would be built by popular subscription to be property of the stock*
> *company, yet revert to the citizens of the company to the exclusion of the*
> *outside stockholders at the season's end. The team being secured will revert in*
> *this manner to the outside stockholders, himself or to the one he appointed and*
> *takes the one-half interest.*

This was the way in which the franchise operated in Temple, and Roberts claimed that stockholders had profited a little at the conclusion of the season.

Following his meeting with the press, Roberts, Thacker and the businessmen retreated to the law offices of Mr. Brown and Mr. Bledsoe for sustentative talks. Roberts planned on returning to his home that evening, and if Cleburne were to be seriously considered for the league, he would need to *carry back a tangible plan which will develop into a membership in the league and secure for her citizens great sport and a winning ball team for the next season.*

NEVER ON A SUNDAY
NOVEMBER 2, 1905

On November 2, 1905 County Attorney Mason Cleveland dropped a bombshell that threatened Cleburne's chances of hosting a professional franchise. A week earlier, Doak Roberts had inquired about the possibility of scheduling Sunday games in the Johnson County city. The answer Roberts hoped to get was not the decision that Cleveland delivered to the team and to the press. Cleveland's decision was based on a law that was over two decades old.

In April of 1883 the Texas Legislature imposed the religious concept of Sunday into the law, greatly restricting any commercial activity from occurring on Sunday. Four years later the law was amended, furthering the number of prohibitions while more clearly defining the types of activities which were not permitted on this particular day of the week. The law was expanded to include a definition for the term *places of public amusement:*

The term *public amusement* was defined within the pages of the new law:
..construed to mean circuses, theaters, variety theaters, and such other amusement as are exhibited and for which an admission fee is charged; and shall also include dances at disorderly houses, low dives, and places of like character, with or without fees for admission.....Chap 116, 20th , Texas Legislature Approved April 2, 1887

Excluded from the Sunday Law was the sale of burial or shrouding materials, ice, ice-cream, milk, the sending of telegraphs or telephone messages, as well as the keepers of drug stores, hotels, boarding houses, restaurants, livery stables, barber shops, or bath houses. It was okay to die, eat ice cream, or take a bath, but not much else was legal, if it involved the transfer of money between parties.

The Seventh Day Adventist Church, which opposed the law, feared that farmers, who attended their church services on Saturday, could be arrested for working their fields and farms on Sunday. Their pleas were ignored, and the law went into effect in its modified version.

Carefully note that the law was amended on April 2, *1887.* The date of the law would play an important role in the determination of whether or not professional baseball would fall under the category of *public amusement.* The decision would be based in part on the fact that *professional baseball* came to Texas in April of *1888,* a year after the passage of the Sunday law.

Texas was not the only state in which prohibition of entertainment requiring an admission fee was in effect. Major league teams faced the same difficulty in scheduling games on Sunday as in Texas.

The issue of playing games on that one day of the week was for the owners not a religious issue. It was about the money, and survival. According to the standards of the day, that being from the mid-1880's until World War I, about 1/3 of a season's total attendance was recorded on Sundays for teams that could schedule games on that day. Remember that during this time there was no *weekend* as we know it.

Most Americans worked six days a week, at least 10 hours a day, including, of course, Saturday. That left only Sunday as a day away from work, the only day of idleness, and the one day in which the average baseball fan could gather at the park for a game scheduled at 4 pm, normal working hours for most men.

Fearing that given the choice between amusements and church, the citizenry would choose to purchase diversions, law makers chose to enforce religious observance by taking away choice. Having no other options, the people would attend worship services.

As is so common, laws can often be breached *legally*. When it came to baseball, the law had a couple of loopholes, the primary being the applicable date of the statute, which took effect *one year before the Texas League began charging for admissions*. The gap between the two dates gave some credence to the argument that the law could not have been intended to include professional baseball since the law was in effect prior to the establishment of the Texas League.

The fight by the league to gain the right to play ball on Sundays took a dramatic turn in 1905, in of all places the Baptist stronghold of Waco. Henry Fabian was arrested for scheduling a game on that day. He was tried for the offense, and the issue was brought to the Court of Criminal Appeals, which ruled:

> *Since the law had been passed before baseball had become a professional*
> *sport, it did not apply to the entertainment of this character…* Judge Sam R. Scott

However, the judge left the door partly opened for those who opposed Sunday ball, leaving the right of communities to interpret the local in accordance to their local customs and traditions. Cities so choosing could schedule baseball games on Sunday afternoons, otherwise they could prohibit games along with other amusements.

Cleburne was a small, blue collar town. Attending games at four in the afternoon during weekdays was difficult for men who worked on an hourly basis. For many of the fans the only time they would have spare time were holidays and Sundays. Cities with *Sunday Ball* often found that 1/3 of their season attendance come through the gates on Sundays. It was essential that if Cleburne were to survive financially, the team would need to have Sunday games on its schedule.

The answer…

Then came the first week in November, 1905. Thursday, November 2nd. County Attorney Mason Cleveland announced that any effort to schedule baseball games in Cleburne would violate Article 199 of the Texas Penal Code. Mr. Cleveland challenged the ruling of Judge Scott:

…with all due respect for Judge Scott, and for his judicial opinion, I have only
this to say. He and I take virtually the same oath of office, he acts under
his oath and I undermine…Judge Scott's opinion cannot control when other
officials construe the meaning of the law differently. A great many just such
laws could be made much plainer, in fact, so plain as to need no construction
but that is the business of the legislature.

Mason Cleveland's ruling appeared to be devastating to Cleburne's chances of landing a team for the '06 season. Already at a disadvantage because of its size, the team would now lose the most important day of the week for scheduling. Clearly, the franchise was in jeopardy. As results of Cleveland's ruling, the Cleburne Athletic Association had to assume greater financial liability. Already somewhat reluctant to take on the guarantee, Thacker was forced to approach each member with the assurance that the gate would be sufficient to exclude any significant loses.

Roberts challenged the ruling, asking Cleveland: *Are you not in favor of Cleburne being in the state league?*

Mason Cleveland shot back: *Unanimously and by acclamation!* Despite several other objections and the potential negative effect of his ruling, Cleveland stood firm by his decision to oppose Sunday ball. To him it was a simple matter of rescheduling the games to another day.

Doak Roberts had operated his teams in both Corsicana and Temple without the benefit of a Sunday schedule, and so was less disturbed by Cleveland's ruling than Thacker. Of course, Roberts had incurred losses in each of his previous years in the league, and surely must have wanted the opportunity of having additional gate receipts, but with the association promising to cover him in 1906, Roberts accepted the ruling, and the process of setting up the club continued forward.

Until his death in 1929, no one individual played a greater part in the success of the Texas League than J. Doak Roberts. This picture taken in 1906 was during one of his most difficult periods. He had helped to revise the league in 1902, providing the league with some of its greatest teams and players, but against the backdrop of financial struggles. By the end of 1906, he had concluded that his time in the Texas League was over. Fortunately, he was able to team up with Claud Reilly in Houston, where his teams resumed their domination, and where eventually he would resume his role as President of the Texas League.

J. DOAK ROBERTS, 1906

The Texas League's 1923 Record
(Class A)
President, DOAK ROBERTS
Houston, Texas

SUNDAY BLUE LAWS IN THE MAJOR LEAGUES
TROUBLE IN GOTHAM
Sunday Ball: New York City
Sunday Laws Affected Both Minor and Major Leagues

While tiny Cleburne sought to challenge the Sunday "Blue Laws" in Texas, a similar challenge was taking place in New York City.

Back in 1880 Cincinnati, Ohio was stripped of its National League franchise for not only allowing liquor to be sold in its stands, but worse for having games scheduled on Sunday. Cincinnati's expulsion by President William Hulbert directly led to the formation of the rival American Association, which was not opposed to liquor, gambling, or Sunday ball.

Eventually the major leagues gave into the desire of teams to play on the one day in the week that most Americans did not work. In both Cincinnati and in St. Louis, large crowds attended Sunday games.

The leagues might have chosen to play on Sundays, but this was not their decision. They were at the mercy of state law and city ordinances. Churches were still a powerful force in many communities.

In 1906 Brooklyn and Cincinnati scheduled a game on Sunday, well realizing that this would lead to an arrest. The game was played under the Contribution box system. Fans were not charged for the game, but were expected to voluntarily give the team money when they attended the game. Everyone knew this was a ruse, including local law enforcement.

The Brooklyn game was intended as a direct confrontation of local blue law. Someone would be going to jail.

Each team designated an arrest victim. Cincinnati manager Ned Hanlon designated Charlie Chech to be the victim of the ordinance. Chech begged off, and so Hanlon offered $25 to any man who would volunteer. Chick Fraser took the bait. He would be the lead-off batter. Brooklyn selected Mal Eason as his sacrificial goat. He would be sent to the pitcher's box, notwithstanding the fact that the actual scheduled pitcher was to be Doc Scanlon. Scanlon would remain in the bull pen until the arrest of Eason before taking to the mound.

After the umpire cried Play Ball! Plain clothed officers stepped onto the field and took custody of Fraser and Eason. The 10,000 fans in the stands found the process amusing, hooting at the officers accordingly. The players grinned and waved at the crowd. The officers tried to look severe, but they could not help smiling at the whole process. For a few moments they were in the spotlight.

With their two conspirators in hand, the police left the park and the game continued without further disruption. When the two players arrived at the police station, they were accompanied by Brooklyn President Charles Ebbets, Manager Pat Donavon, and Manager Hanlon of Cincinnati. Their lawyer was ex-Police Commissioner Bernard York. The two men had to show bail, and were scheduled to appear before Magistrate Naumer in the Vanderbilt Avenue Court.

President Ebbets returned to Washington Park before the game had been concluded and did not appear to be in the least disconcerted by the arrest, claiming this playing on Sunday by the contribution box scheme is not an evasion of the law, and we propose to have the matter decided as quickly as possible. In the meantime we shall continue to play games on Sunday in Washington Park.

FALL, 1905

PROGRESS IN CLEBURNE: *..... it will not do to have a piking team...*

Tuesday, November 14, 1905:

That Tuesday ominous headlines in the Cleburne paper read PANICKY MONEY MARKET! This was no idle story for the farmers around Cleburne: cotton had dropped 30 to 40 points, resulting in a dollar-a-bale loss in New Orleans.

While the cotton growers worried about their crop, Charles Thacker met with the local papers to report that the league leaders were scheduled to meet in Dallas on December 10th. The importance of the meeting was not lost on the citizens and business leaders in Cleburne. During the meeting, the league fathers were to be prepared to make a *formal* invitation for Cleburne to join the Texas League.

The story continued with the news that Cleburne would not only be getting a Texas League franchise, Doak Roberts would continue his association with the franchise, meaning that he would bring most of the players from the '05 Temple club, the team that barely lost the league pennant. A large number of the players were contracted to him personally, meaning, in Thacker's words:

the city to be able to draw around him some first class players and this is the kind of team Cleburne will want when she gets into the league. **It will not do to have a piking team**. *Fast men will win a record for the town*

His remarks continued: still of concern was *locating close-in grounds to ensure that the team gets a full attendance.* Fans would not have the convenience of a trolley-line to bring them to the game. Many would have to walk to the new park, while others would arrive by buggy, and horseback.

Charles Thacker proudly reported that along with Doak Roberts, he would be in attendance at the December meeting.

Wednesday, November 29, 1905..more good news…

From reports coming out of Temple, it has been definitely ascertained that J.D. Roberts, who owned the Temple franchise in the Texas Baseball League last season, and who also managed the club, will be connected with the new Cleburne team next season. Inasmuch as all of the old Temple players are under contract to Mr. Roberts, it means the Cleburne will secure the reserved players on last season's local team and that Temple will have to hustle an entirely new team. **The Cleburne Morning-Review, Nov.30, 1905**

MANAGER *OR* CAPTAIN…….

For the fan of 1906 and the current baseball fan, the term *manager* has different meanings. Roberts' position as manager referred to the overall operation of the team, much like the term General-manager of today's sport. The on-field decisions were made by the Captain of the team, who in most instances was a playing member of the team. Ben Shelton was the captain and first baseman of Roberts' franchise.

AT THE ORIENTAL HOTEL
DECEMBER 10, 1905

On December 10, 1905 the executives of the Texas League met in Dallas at the Oriental Hotel in what at first appeared to be little more than a routine gathering. The group included J.E. Edens, Temple, W.D. Simmons and Lee Dawkins, Waco, William "Bill" Ward, Fort Worth, H. H. Mock, and Horace Kelton, Greenville, Charles H. Thacker and J.Doak Roberts, Cleburne, and J. W. Gardner, Dallas.

Cleburne and Greenville were formally inducted into the league schedule; with each franchise limited to a payroll of $1,000 a month, exclusive of the captain, the roster limited to 12 players, with the 13th player being the team's captain.

The Texas League officials also announced that they were seeking an upgrade from Class D ball to Class C. The higher classification would bring more prestige to the league, but the true benefit was financially. One of the primary sources of income for the owners was the sale of players under contract. The higher classification translated into the potential value of the player when his contract was sold.

One of the requirements for "C-ball" was a combined population of the league of at least 200,000 for those cities represented. The mayors of the six cities scheduled for the 1906 season were requested to submit the official census of their community.

The league compiled the figures and released the following totals:

In an attempt to reach the 200,000 combined population figure for all teams in the league, the league fathers submitted this list to baseball's minor league association: Figures are based upon data submitted by the cities:

Dallas	90,000
Fort Worth	57,000
Waco	30,000
Cleburne	14,000
Temple	12,000
Greenville	12,000

Oriental Hotel, Dallas,

With the routine business completed, the agenda took a dramatic turn. Dallas owner and general manager J. W. Gardner asked that the representatives of the new cities to come forward to present details of their ownership. There were in fact three towns with new owners. The three cities included Temple, Cleburne, and Greenville. Temple had been in the league in 1905, but with Doak Roberts taking his franchise to Cleburne, Temple had new ownership, headed up by Roberts' acquaintance and friend, J. E. Edens, also of Corsicana.

Doak Roberts was the first to speak, taking the opportunity to present information about the two companies that had been formed in Cleburne and in Temple to protect the two teams from bankruptcy. Over its entire history, the league had been plagued by teams dropping from the schedule for financial reasons, creating havoc, and often resulting in the cancellation of the season. Other times, franchises were shifted around in hopes of finding a city that would support the club at the gate.

Gardner was intent on avoiding similar problems in the 1906 season. Roberts understood the Dallas owner's concerns, and concluded with the information that he would maintain control of the Cleburne team, with the financial backing of the Cleburne Athletic Association, while Edens would control the Temple club with a similar arrangement with their local businessmen. Hence, both clubs were guaranteed to complete the entire season, even if attendance lagged.

The next speaker was H. H. Mock who declared that he represented a stock company from Greenville, promising that Greenville would support the Texas League team, noting in the previous year fans continue to attend games in spite of its losing record in the old North Texas League. Mock stated that he would turn the club over to men who knew how to operate a baseball club, and completed his remarks with a promise of providing a new park for the Texas League club in Greenville.

FURY AND FRACTIOUS

It was at the point that the meeting took on a fractious tone. While most of the other members were satisfied by the Greenville proposal, Joe Gardner of Dallas stated that the new Greenville franchise should be awarded to him. Doak Roberts was caught off guard and angered that the Dallas man would even consider such an arrangement. W.D. Simmons of Waco joined Roberts in condemnation of Gardner, stating he strongly opposed such a proposition, since it would look like "syndicated" ball, with Greenville becoming little more than a training team for Dallas. Simmons stated *I don't believe that things can be square if one man owns two teams.*

An arrogant and belligerent Gardner addressed the meeting from the strength of owning a club in the largest city in the league:

> *It has always been necessary for Dallas and Fort Worth to help out*
> *the smaller teams before the season was over. Last year they had*
> *wanted Waco in, but no one was willing to go down and shoulder*
> *responsibility. It is a natural advantage of the larger towns that they*
> *had a paying position and that they had always come to the help of*
> *the little towns with players and money.*

There was unanimous opposition to the Gardner plan, including J. E. Edens, supporting Roberts' concerns, strongly stating his opposition to Gardner's arguments. The heated debated went on for over an hour, with Gardner becoming more upset. A vote was finally taken amongst the franchise representatives. Dallas ownership of the Greenville club was denied.

An irritated Joe Gardner then proposed an amendment to the league's rules, a proposal that was personal in nature, targeting Doak Roberts. Gardner demanded that anyone holding an elective office not be permitted to own a franchise, citing the possibility of a conflict in interest. His amendment was discussed, but the Dallas owner had not made any friends at the meeting, and for a second time his proposition was defeated. J. Doak Roberts would both operate the Cleburne franchise as well as serve as the president of the Texas League.

The final business of the meeting was concluded, with T.J. Darling appointed as the Secretary of the Texas League. At that point the members were exhausted and voted to postpone the selection of umpires as well as selecting the official league ball until the next meeting, to be held in Waco on January 7, 1906.

AT LAST, "PIE" IN THE SKY

"Pie" Bailey, having witnessed the cantankerous exchanges amongst the executives, sought to bring a more civilized ending to the meeting. Bailey's name had been mentioned as a possible president of the league in lieu of the official winner, Roberts. Seeking reconciliation and ever gracious in his loss to Roberts, Bailey addressed the meeting on a positive note: *The fact that Texas is to have a six team league is evidence of the popularity of the game, and in fact the more the merrier will stimulate fan interest.* The meeting was adjourned.

Cleburne Fans delighted to learn that the city was now a part of the famed Texas League

Dapper Pie Bailey ended the contentious meeting on a positive note.

CHRISTMAS IN THE TEXAS LEAGUE.

CHRISTMAS 1905:
Cleburne and Greenville:
Celebrating their Christmas franchise gift from the Texas League

PROFESSIONAL BASEBALL COMES TO TEXAS

CLEBURNE JOINED THE LEAGUE THAT FIRST PLAYED IN 1888:

In 1869 the Cincinnati Red Stockings became the first professional club in the United States. Nineteen years later Dallas, San Antonio, Houston, Galveston, Austin, and Fort Worth joined together to form the Texas League, bringing organized baseball to the state.

The inaugural season in Texas was not without problems. The San Antonio team won only 6 of its 33 games, resulting in miserable attendance, causing the owners to withdraw from the league, leaving the circuit with only five teams. Shortly afterward Bill Ward found himself in financial difficulties, and so after only 44 games, and a record of 19-25 the 1888 season was over for the Panthers. Troubles continued. McCloskey's Austin franchise was near throwing in the towel, until new ownership in San Antonio revitalized the team, resulting in the shifting of the Austin team to San Antonio. With Austin and Fort Worth gone, the league was reduced to four teams. However when the Southern League folded, New Orleans sought entry into the Texas League, once again creating a five team schedule. It was an awkward set up, but the Texas League managed to complete the season, with Dallas crowned as the league's first champion with a record of 55-27.

THE 1888 FORT WORTH PANTHERS NEWSPAPER PICTURE:

Fort Worth Panthers Roster
April 5, 1888 vs. Houston

William Geiss – Second Base
William L. Works – Left Field
Charles A. Sunday – Center Field
John Rodemaker – Shortstop
Mike O'Connor – Right Field
William Joyce – Third Base
Emmett Rodgers – Catcher
Mike Firle- First Base, Captain
George B. Kittle – Catcher
F. S. Fudger – Pitcher
Dan O'Leary – Pitcher
William Goodenough - Pitcher

Captain Mike Firle,

Pitcher Dan O'Leary,

IV

THE 1906 TEXAS LEAGUE: SIX CITIES
Fort Worth-Temple- Waco
Dallas – Cleburne - Greenville

TEXAS LEAGUE PARKS: 1906

As the opening date of the 1906 season loomed ever closer, both Cleburne newspapers boastfully proclaimed their team to be the best bunch in the league. It was spring and spring time in baseball is always a time of absolute optimism, and it has always been that way, even long before the Railroaders came to Cleburne. Six cities in north Texas readied for the new season, each confident about the rapidly approaching season, certain of success on the field, and equally convinced that their city's fans would be there in good numbers to support their ream. Given the history of the Texas League, the owner's confidence perhaps should have been tempered by reality.

Of the six cities that would make up the league in 1906, two would be hosting professional baseball for the first time, Cleburne and Greenville, and since Doak Roberts had abandoned Temple following the '05 campaign, that city was in many ways new to the league. Clearly half of the league in 1906 was novice, and that factor alone hung ominously over the financial well being and stability of baseball in north Texas. But it was spring and no one was willing to concede to the negative. The emphasis was on the positive and upon signing players capable of bringing the championship to their city. The right to brag was an integral part of life in Texas at the turn of the century.

Two cities were still without ball parks, more than a slight problem that had to be addressed before opening day, but there was little urgency about the lack of a playing facility. A few hundred dollars, maybe a thousand, about 4 weeks, and a level piece of land was all that was needed for the construction of a local diamond.

A SELLOUT CROWD WATCHING THE CORSICANA OILERS

Texas League ball parks were similar to the other parks that hosted minor league teams around the United States. The parks were made of wood. A steel and concrete structure would not come to the Texas League until 1911, when Fort Worth constructed Morris Park, later called Panther Park. In Texas as well as in most parks around the country, the grandstands, as well as the barrier surrounding the playing field, were made of lumber, and gave rise to one of the early sports of young boys: watching a professional league game through a knothole, one of the enduring images from the early days of baseball. A hundred years later, long after wood ceased being used, *Knothole Gangs* are still a part of many baseball organizations.

The prized seating area, the section that garnered the highest price ticket were those under the grandstand, whose protective roof provided a haven from both rain, and, since all games were day games, from the harsh sun. Most teams rented seat cushions, not only to relieve the patron from the uncomfortable hardness of the bench, but as much from the dangers of splinters. Of rain and sun, it was the sun that was the greater threat and hindrance to attendance.

Another characteristic of the ballparks of the early years of the twentieth century was the crowd, its makeup, and attire. Owners, tired of battling rude behavior, open gambling, and in hopes of increasing crowd size, began encouraging the attendance of ladies at the game. In 1906 women at the game was still fodder for editorial comment from the sports writers, and generally appreciated by all except the most traditional of fans. One thing did not change. Most generally, as is evident in photos of the era, for both men and women, baseball games were attended by fans that were well dressed. Men wore their hats, as well as white shirts and a suit.

Bowie Blue Caps, Bowie, Texas

> *There were only eleven professional teams in Texas, which meant that most other cities were dependent upon amateur and semi-pro teams for baseball. Semi-Pro teams were organized by a business willing to buy uniforms and to pay the players for publicity. Amateur clubs were made up of local boys playing nearby communities for the honor of their city.*

Ladies at the games were becoming more common, and the gentleman came to the games in their business clothes, including hats. Gambling and rough language was still a problem, but the owners were reluctant to offend their ticket buying fans.

The dimensions of the old ball parks were generally not mentioned, and only occasion can we guess at the distances from home plate to left, right and center fields. The dead ball era included the minor leagues, which used basically the same ball as found in the major leagues, generally the *Official Reach Baseball.* Home runs were still a rarity, and distinguished by "over the fence home run" when that was the case. Inside the park home runs were more common, given the huge distances and dimension of the stadium.

Many games, including the major leagues, were played with only one ball for the entirety of the contest. Foul balls were returned to play. Young boys outside of the park were traded a ticket for recovery of a ball, a ticket more prized than the ball itself. Texas League umpires were given three balls before the start of the game. The ball had to be gratuitously damaged before the umpire dismissed it from play. After inning after inning of pounding, the ball by the end of the game had softened considerably.

The games were expected to be over within two hours, preferably sooner. One Dallas writer admonished the Giants when they played a slow game lasting two hours and fifteen minutes.

The umpire made announcements through a megaphone.

The official scorekeeper had to fight off fans who wanted to know details of the game as it continued on. Charles Thacker of the Cleburne Railroaders became enraged by the constant interruption by the fans and had a booth constructed towering over the field and away from the fans.

Although few scorecards from the era have survived, they were available for those wishing to keep notes of the game. Programs sold for a nickel. The scorecards were generally published with the lineup already typed in place. The players could only be identified by sight. There was no numbering system, nor names on the uniforms. The Cleburne players had a block maroon "C" on the front of their uniform.

Souvenirs were almost non-existent, except perhaps a pennant. Baseballs were not kept as keepsakes. They were utilitarian, and put into play by the boys and men who had few other toys. Baseball cards given away free in cigarette packages were one of the few items that young boys managed to save from their youthful love of the game. Tobacco cards are still a prized find by baseball collectors today.

In 1906 the camera was still a bulky, nearly unmanageable piece of equipment, making anything less than posed or staged photo shots almost impossible. There were few photographed images of players in action carried in any of the local Texas papers during the season. The only images showing movement was in the form of cartoons. The newspapers in Dallas and Fort Worth printed pictures of baseball teams frequently, but they were generally studio or studio type photos, with the player's static, posed.

WOODBURY, TEXAS
Recess: Time for Baseball

THE INTERURBAN PROVIDED TRANSPORTATION FOR THE SIX TEAMS AND THEIR FANS

The cost of rail tickets and hotel rooms was one of the major expenses incurred by the teams, and so distances from one park to the next was carefully measured and considered when the makeup of the league changed. One of the advantages of having Cleburne in the league was its central position on the rail lines. In fact, once the 1906 league configuration was finalized, Cleburne was nearly equal with both Dallas and Fort Worth for composite distances in the league. Temple and Greenville's distances were the greatest in the league, and later would play a devastating role in their fate.

TEXAS LEAGUE MILEAGE CHART

TRAVEL DISTANCES of SIX CITIES IN THE TEXAS LEAGUE IN 1906						
TEAM	**Dallas**	Greenville	Cleburne	Ft Worth	Waco	Temple
Dallas	----------	56	49	31	92	127
Greenville	56	--------------	103	87	147	182
Cleburne	49	103	-------------	31	72	108
Ft Worth	31	87	31	---------	88	123
Waco	92	147	72	88	---------	38
Temple	127	182	108	123	38	----------
Composite	**355**	**575**	**363**	**360**	**437**	**578**

Being a baseball fan in Texas was not an easy proposition, with hard timbers full of splinters for seats, generally without a back, and with all games scheduled in the heat of the day, it took hardy individuals to endure the elements in order to watch a game.

In Fort Worth fans commonly moved away from their seats to sit in foul territory where the shade of the stadium provided some relief from the relentless heat of the sun. During one game the proximity of the fans to fair territory would play a deciding factor in the outcome.

```
┌─────────────────────────────────────────────────────────────┐
│            TEXAS LEAGUE CITIES AND PARKS IN 1906:             │
│                                                               │
│   CLEBURNE RAILROADERS:        GORMAN PARK                    │
│   FORT WORTH PANTHERS:         HAINES PARK                    │
│   DALLAS GIANTS:               GASTON PARK                    │
│   WACO NAVIGATORS:             KATY PARK                      │
│   TEMPLE BOLL WEEVILS:         FREEMAN HEIGHTS PARK           │
│   GREENVILLE HUNTERS:          COTTON BELT PARK               │
└─────────────────────────────────────────────────────────────┘
```

THE PARKS:

CLEBURNE: *Gorman Park*

The Texas League awarded Cleburne a franchise in the fall of 1905, yet in January of 1906 there still was no stadium suitable for professional baseball in the city. With the preseason less than two months away, the Cleburne Athletic Association was quickly running out of time to get construction under way. Their primary problem was locating a flat piece of land within a convenient distance from the town square. There was such property located along the banks of West Buffalo Creek, but it was owned by the Trinity and Brazos Valley Railroad.

The land was vacant and the railroad had no immediate plans to use the site for any business purposes, and so when the company was approached by the business association, they agreed to let the city build the baseball diamond on their property. Pat A. Gorman, General Superintendent of the TBVRR and the Cleburne Athletic Association worked out details for the lease of the land in early 1906.

The association had allocated about $500 (there are varying published figures) for the cost of lumber and construction, and in the cold of winter, the project took life. The barren land was soon a hub of activity, as the raw wood began to take the shape of a minor stadium, simila in design to the other league parks around the nation.

The seating was made of simple planks of wood, which meant not long afterwards, splinters would be a major hazard to the fans, making seat cushions a necessity, and indeed, in many parks, cushion rental was common. After the carpenters completed the grandstand, the next step was to add the roof. In Texas this was not so much to protect fans from rain as it was from the sun. Of course, in 1906 there were no night games, and with most games starting at 4pm, shade was of the premium for fans, and generally seating under the roof required an extra charge, usually a dime in addition to the quarter admission charge.

Cleburne's park was laid out over a huge area, and as the fence line was marked, it became apparent that the association park would have the longest distances to the outfield walls in the Texas League. Centerfield was estimated at 550 feet. The distances later proved daunting, with only one "over-the-fence" homer hit in Cleburne for the entire 1906 season.

Dugouts were not yet common. Instead players from both teams would be sitting on benches level with the playing field. The benches were covered for shade and some privacy from the fans.

As the stands were being built, other workers began to prepare the field. Sand was brought in and poured onto the surface, and then a heavy roller was used to pack the soil, and to assure that the players would have a reasonable flat surface to play on. The construction crew did not add seed or new plantings to the field. What grass that was there was native to the field, and consisted as much of weeds as grass, and was cut by a hand mower. There was little done to otherwise enhance the appearance of the field. There would be no water sprinklers. If it rained, the grass and weeds were watered. Otherwise, the players played on a dry, parched field. The infield was all dirt.

In the larger communities, advertising billboards were attached to the outfield walls, but in Cleburne only a few businesses opted to pay the cost of having the sign painted, then the cost to the ball club for displaying it. The sound system consisted of a megaphone used by the umpire to announce the starting lineup, as well as any changes during the game. The players did not wear numbers on their uniforms, so it was difficult for the fans to know who the players were, especially visiting teams.

At the completion of construction, Cleburne's baseball stadium was given the official title *Cleburne Athletic Association Park*. However, that name was short-lived. On the eve of the first official pitch of the 1906 season, the association decided to give the ball park a more proper name. Charles Thacker, secretary of the Cleburne association advised Mr. M. Sweeney, the current General Manager of the Trinity and Brazos Valley Railroad that the park would be named in his honor. Mr. Sweeney listened attentively, but declined the offer, indicating that he was honored to have been chosen, but suggesting that the park might more properly be named after Pat A. Gorman, the ex-General Superintendent, under whose leadership the deal to lease the land was made.

The Association accepted the suggestion, and on April 24, 1906 the stadium was officially christened *Gorman Park,* and so in this railroad town, the field would honor the name of *"one of the best and well known railroad man in Texas."*

THE LOCATION OF GORMAN PARK

According to the 1907 city directory, Cleburne Ball Park was *located at the intersection of Bishop and Hillsboro, the southwest corner*. Today those streets do not intersect, so using the description of the city directories of that era is confusing for anyone attempting to relocate the park. Bishop Street was later changed to Buffalo Street, which was described in the city directory of 1907 as being *the seventh street south from Chambers, running west from Main Street to the limits*. With the name of Bishop having been changed to Buffalo Street, travelers were often confused, since there was already a North and South Buffalo Street. Eventually the city fathers recognized the problem, rectifying the situation by again renaming the street, this time to Westhill. Thus today, the address of Gorman Park would be at the southwest corner of the intersection of Westhill and Hillsboro, today the site of Hulen Park, Cleburne, Texas.

GORMAN PARK FROM BLURRY NEWSPAPER PHOTO

Cleburne leased land from the Trinity and Brazos Valley Railroad to build Gorman Park, named in honor of the railroad company's superintendent, Pat A. Gorman.

Cleburne's Park Superintendent and Official Scorer for the 1906 season, Charles Thacker, was the most experienced baseball man in Cleburne. Thacker had been an official scorer in the Texas League back in 1889.

Charles H. Thacker: Secretary of the Texas League, 1889

Nothing daunted by the failure of the 1888 league, the Texas League was reorganized for the succeeding year. Over winter, there was talk of a Texas-Southern circuit. Dallas actually accepted a franchise in the Southern. The organization meeting was held on January 4th in Fort Worth at which Louis Newburg of Waco was elected president and A.D. Triplett of Fort Worth temporary secretary, with Houston (McCloskey), Galveston (Jeff Turin), Waco (Newburg) and Jack Pettiford, manager, and Fort Worth (John Cella) present. $800 was fixed as the salary limit. Apparently efforts to arrange a larger meeting for January in Austin failed, but on February 13th the circuit elected Newburg its president with C.H. Thatcher, of Waco, as secretary, although it had not been able to interest two more clubs definitely. A fortnight before the season opened, Dallas and Austin arranged to come in. …The History of the Texas League of Professional Baseball Clubs 1888-1951, by William B. Ruggles, p.62.

In 1905 the local papers noted that Charles H. Thacker had once been the Secretary of the Texas League, but no date was mentioned. William Ruggles' book confirms Thacker's claim, although when his name was included in the 1951 publication, it was as *Thatcher,* not Thacker.

Charles trained as a bookkeeper in Christian County, Kentucky, and when he became the league's secretary in 1889, he brought his eye for detail to the league, compiling the league's stats, but more importantly distributing his compilations to the local papers, which resulted in much greater press coverage in '89 than the 1888 season received. Publicity was essential to the continued health of the Texas League.

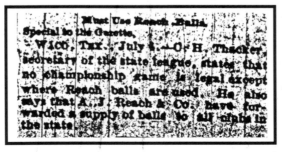

Must Use Reach Balls
Special to the Gazette,
Waco, Tex. July 4th,--C.H. Thacker secretary of the state league states that no championship game is legal except where Reach balls are used. He also says that A.J. Reach and Co have forwarded a supply of balls to all the clubs in the state
The Fort Worth Gazette, July 4th, 1889

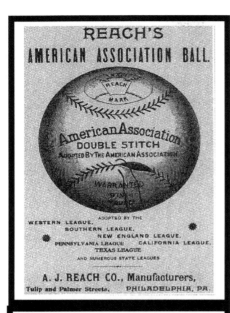

THE REACH BALL:
The "Official Ball" for the 1889 Texas League Season..
..Charles Thacker, League Secretary 7/4/1889

CLEBURNE ATHLETIC ASSOCIATION MEMBERSHIP:

Phil Allin, President –Mayor of Cleburne
C.H. Thacker, Secretary, Treasurer, General Manager
G. W. Anderson – VP of Bradford Brothers
Jacob D. Oliger – President of Farmer's Oil Company
R. J. Corson – Agent Buick Auto 213 E. James
Alta Souther –Livery and Boarding Stable   No. Anglin
Arthur Chase – City Engineer 216 W. Henderson
W.W.Murphy –Manager Cleburne Cotton Co Compress
Frank N. Graves – Printer: 105 N. Field
Tom B. Harris

The Cleburne Athletic Association:
comprised of Cleburne businessmen urged to join forces in order to bring professional baseball to Cleburne.   Charles Thacker had convinced the city leaders that having a team in the Texas League would bring a great deal of publicity to the city and with it increased business opportunities.   The Association lasted one year, reneged on their financial agreement with Doak Roberts, then abandoned the team, killing any chances for the city to return to league play in 1907.

Cleburne Hotel

1900-1910 RAPID POPULATION GROWTH IN TEXAS
Federal Census Records

	1900	1910
Cleburne	7,493	10,364
Dallas	42,638	92,104
Ft.Worth	26,288	73,320
Greenville	6,860	8,850
Temple	7,065	10,993
Waco	20,676	26,425

FORT WORTH

THE PANTHERS' (CATS) FIVE LOCATIONS SINCE 1887:

The Fort Worth Panthers (shortened to Cats) have played in only five locations since 1887. Bill Ward built *a park south of town* for the 1887 season. When the Texas League made Fort Worth a charter member in 1888, the team played in the same stadium until the opening of the new park, at first called the **Spring Palace Grounds** (due to its proximity to the Spring Palace), then later after it burned, the park was referred to as the T&P Grounds (Texas & Pacific). The third location was **Haines Park** on property owned by the Northern Traction Company just south of modern day Lancaster at its intersection with Pine St. In 1911 the team moved to the north side, near 6th Street, west of North Main, **Morris Park**, changed to Panther Park, then in 1925 moved to the present site of modern day **La Grave Field.**

Fort Worth's First Park: October 1887...just south of town

In 1888 Fort Worth joined the Texas League with the team slated to play in an unnamed ball park, referred to in the press simply as **"the park just south of town...."** Under the ownership of Bill Ward, Fort Worth's first baseball stadium was constructed in the fall of 1887, with seating for 1,000 fans. The exact location of the park has never been defined to an exact degree. The park was built to accommodate Fort Worth's first look at professional baseball when John J. McCloskey brought his Joplin, Missouri team to town for a three game series with Bill Ward's team. The series drew large crowds, at least for the first two games. By the third game there was no doubt as to the superiority of the visitors, and attendance dropped. The Fort Worth series was the first of three cities on Joplin's barnstorming trek to Texas. After leaving Fort Worth, Joplin traveled to Waco, then on to Austin. John McCloskey was impressed with the crowds and the enthusiasm for baseball shown by the state, and within months, under his urging, the Texas League was born, kicking off the first season of professional league baseball in the spring of 1888.

Joplin, Missouri was the first professional league team to play in Fort Worth when they played October 30, 31st and November 1st, 1887 against Bill Ward's semi-pro Fort Worth Panthers in the new park "just south of town".. Probably Near the T&P tracks.

BILL WARD, OWNER OF PANTHERS   OCT.17, 1887 NEW PARK

Monday Oct. 17, 1887

Yesterday the Dallas base ball team played a match with the Fort Worth club at the new ball park, which resulted in an overwhelming defeat of the Dallas players. This was rather a surprise to those who were posted as to the merits of the two organizations. Both clubs had made great preparation for this game, particularly that of Dallas, but the visitors were not able to make anything more than a practice game for the doughty Ft.Worth boys. Neither club played a remarkably good game...Dallas because she could not; Ft.Worth because she need not to. The new player with the home team, O'Connor, did excellent work and has already established himself as a favorite in the grandstands. Jeff Davis also did first class work, making the only three base hit of the day and beautiful running catch of a fly to left field that brought great applause from the spectators. A double play by Buckley and Firl for the home club, and one by the visitors were good plays. The score stood 21 to 8 in favor of the home team. Only seven innings were taken by Ft.Worth and 8 by Dallas. Mr. Ball of Dallas undertook to umpire the game, but at the end of the third he was superseded by Mr. Louis, who gave very good satisfaction.

It has not been decided yet what team will be brought here next Sunday, but it will be either from Galveston, New Orleans, or Joplin, Missouri. It is now become so that no club in the state, unless it be Galveston, can furnish a game with Ft.Worth. There will be no trouble in get-ting outsiders to come here, as Ft.Worth has the reputation of drawing the largest crowds to the game of any town in the state.
The Fort Worth Gazette.....Oct.17, 1887

Apparently as late as October 17th Bill Ward was still in negotiation with John McCloskey about bringing his Joplin team to Texas. McCloskey was likely looking for the best spots for a big draw. Ward was in a jubilant mood, with his excellent ball club headed up by Mike O'Connor. He had built a nice ball park that could seat around a thousand fans, and was anxious to get his team some serious competition. The amateur Galveston team was also a well-organized club, and they might have been invited to Fort Worth, but when the chance came to play a professional league team, Ward was there with open arms.

COLORED BALL PLAYERS TOURNAMENT:
Prof. W.A. Driffle, umpire and manager of the colored baseball tournament, to take place during the Colored State Fair, arrived at the city yesterday morning from Dallas. He speaks very favorably of the grand time anticipated during the fair. He is accompanied by several of the sporting fraternity from Dallas and other cities. The Cuban Giants of New York, and the Union Base Ball club of New Orleans will cross bats here on Friday, the 28th of October, 1887. *The Fort Worth Gazette, Monday, October 24, 1887*

"MISSOURI SPHERE MANIPULATORS"...Fort Worth Gazette
October 30 - October 31-November 1, 1887
FIRST PROFESSIONAL GAMES IN FORT WORTH
PANTHERS vs. JOPLIN, MISSOURI "Independents"

Those two days leading up to the first day of November of 1887 are without a doubt three of the most important days in the history of Fort Worth baseball, and indeed, for the state of Texas.

William H. Ward, owner of the White Elephant Restaurant, had taken pains to hire some of the most expensive talent available in Texas, including the legendary Mike O'Connor. The Panthers, as they were called, had held up their bargain, defeating teams for the surrounding towns, including, and most importantly, Dallas. The famous Dallas insult had given Fort Worth its nickname, the Panthers..something a Dallas writer said about the city being so sleepy that a Panther was seen resting on Main Street, like the city, sleeping.

There was baseball, the only wagering sport besides horse racing. Unlike the equine sport, the ball team carried both the name of the city and its nickname. Going into battle, the team carried the hopes of their city, a chance to excel over a rival.

Bill Ward had done it. Put together a strong team that could, and in fact, did humiliate the boys from Dallas. And now there were new worlds to conquer. The details of the origin of the match are not clear, but from most accounts, John J. McCloskey put together a group of professional players who played under the Joplin, Missouri name, and soon they would be in Texas.

Players could only make a small living playing ball, and most headed back to their jobs when the baseball season ended. However, by barnstorming, they could pick up extra cash, keep on playing ball, and avoid real work altogether. McCloskey and his boys were scheduled to play what some were saying was the best semi-professional team in Texas, Ward's Fort Worth Panthers.

A new park was hastily built in the southern edge of the business district, holding at least 1,000 fans. That was the announced attendance for the October 31th game.

Joplin, Missouri versus the Fort Worth Panthers, October 30, 31st and November 1st. This was the first time the ball fans of the Texas city had seen a team from outside of its boundaries. Fort Worth as a town was only 38 years old in 1887, and its extraordinary growth revolved around cattle and the railroads. The city attracted cattlemen from all over the state, and in a few years would have the largest number of cattle pens in the state. Hell's Half Acre, with its myriad of brothels, saloons, and gambling houses, kept the cowboys' money in town, as well as attracting outlaws and boys looking for fun. The money was too lucrative, and so the churches tolerated this infamous part of town. No doubt a large number of gamblers out of the Acres would be enticing the local fans to bet on their hometown boys when Joplin arrived.

Three games. By the third game, the Panthers were ready to cry uncle. Humiliation. But at least it was Joplin and not Dallas. The Panthers discovered that against professional talent, they were not even competitive: the Gazette reporter noted *Fort Worth's club would stand little chance of winning a game from these Missouri sphere manipulators*. In the first game, three times Joplin hit the ball over the left field wall on their way to a 14-2. The other two games were similar in outcomes. It was time for the state teams to turn professional. The following spring that wish became so. The Texas League chartered cities for its inaugural season. Bill Ward was there to pay his dues to bring professional baseball to Fort Worth.

Fort Worth's Second Park
JULY 26, 1889
THE SPRING PALACE GROUNDS

On July 26, 1889 the Panthers opened their new park on the grounds of the Spring Palace. The famous 1891 painting of the "Bird's Eye View of Fort Worth" by Henry Weggle does not include a depiction of the baseball field, probably due in from the fact that Mr. Weggle used his 1886 painting as a model for the updated print, and since the park was not built until 1889, neither view of the city included the home of the Panthers.

One year after the Eiffel Tower opened in Paris, Fort Worth introduced the Texas Spring Palace to the United States as "an educational, cultural and entertainment center for Texas residence." More than fifty counties in Texas took part in providing a wide variety of Texas products for the exhibition. The exhibition hall was gigantic, with its dome second only to the national capital in Washington in size.

Left: Henry Wiggle's illustration of the Texas Spring Palace published in 1891, one year after it had been destroyed by fire: The painting had been done in 1886, and so the Panther's Park was not included in the published picture

The Panther's ball park was dwarfed by the huge edifice, not only in size but by prestige, and given the park's location near the exhibition hall the newspapers and fans began to refer to the baseball stadium as the *Spring Palace Grounds*. There is no evidence that any formal naming of the park ever occurred. The name just became into fact through common usage.

Then on May 31, 1890, the Texas Spring Palace was destroyed by fire, which started while several thousand people milled about its interior. Incredibly only one person died in its burning, creating a Fort Worth hero for the millennium. Al S. Hayne perished when he went to the rescue of a woman and several children. The grateful citizens of Fort Worth honored their fallen hero with a monument that today still graces the south end of Fort Worth's business district east of Main Street near the railroad underpass.

Even though the structure that gave the ball park its name no longer existed, the name continued until a new landmark began to dominate the south end of the business district. The construction of the magnificent T&P Building brought a new sense of pride to that part of the city, and soon the ball field gained a new name, again based upon its proximity to a prominent structure. The ball field was now called the **T&P Grounds,** also sometimes referred to as *The Reservation,* in deference to the area set aside for the railroad reservation.

From 1889 until 1902, the Spring Palace (or T&P Grounds, or The Reservation) was the primary site for professional, semi-professional, and amateur baseball in Fort Worth. With the opening of the new park in 1902, most of the games went to that location, but the old ball park remained, used by amateurs and Negro League games until at least 1905.

FORT WORTH'S NEW PARK: SPRING PALACE GROUNDS OPEN JULY 26, 1889

The account of the first game ever at the Spring Palace Grounds detailed by the Fort Worth Gazette

This may be the only time éclat and bilious were used in the same article describing a baseball game

THE FORT WORTH GAZETTE: JULY 27, 1889

ONE FOR THE PANTHERS

They Baptize Their New Grounds in the Blood of the Wacos-A Pretty Game

The new base ball park on the Spring Palace grounds was initiated yesterday by a game between the Panthers and the Waco team. The Fireman's Band and the two teams in hacks paraded the streets prior to the game, and the opening of the place with éclat. The heavy rains had rendered the grounds quite muddy, a fact that made the game quite slow, and detracted somewhat from its enjoyment. To-day, however, they will be in fine condition, and a rattling good game is anticipated.

Yesterday's game was a-good on, baring the interference of the mud, and was won for Fort Worth by the superior all around playing of the team. Derrick was in the box for the visitors, and although he showed great speed and good curves with fine command of the ball, the home team sized him up for twelve hits, three of which were corking two baggers. France did the dynamo work for the Panthers and seemed to have the Indians completely at his mercy. Five singles were secured off of him, but they were so scattering as to be unproductive of results. One of them was a wonderful scratch hit, the ball striking about a foot in front of the plate and being stopped by the soft ground. Eight men fanned out to fruitless endeavors to line him out.

The first run was secured in the second inning. After Lemons and Welsh had been retired at first Motz was give a life by Bright's error, and immediately came home on Pike's slashing two bagger into deep center. France ended the inning with three strikes.

In the fifth Motz hit for a base, went to second on a passed ball, to third on a wild pitch, and home on another wild pitch. Pike got to first on balls, made second and third on wild pitches, and scored on Franc's safe one over third. McVey's fly was then nipped by Pettiford. Hassamaer pulled down one that Crogan popped up, and Mullally got Hill's short bunt and threw him out at the plate.

In the sixth Fogarty smashed the ball over into right for two bases. Then Lemons hit a red hot liner into left,which O'Neil failed to hold, and Fogarty scored. Lemons went to second on a passed ball. Welsh got four bad balls and went to first. Then after Motz fly ball had been gathered in by O'Neil, Pike made a second safe hit, bringing Lemons home and sending Welsh to second. Welsh went to third on Creeley error and was nipped at the plate when Rose field France's ground to McCormick. Pike making it to third meantime. With McVey at the bat and Pike

on third, France stole second. Playing off the base, Derrick threw to Bright to cut him off, and Pike started home. Bright threw the ball to McCormick, and he retired the side by touching Pike out, one of the prettiest plays of the game.

In the Seventh McVey hit for bag, stole second and went to third on Crogan's sacrifice . He scored on Hill's safe one. Hill stone second, Fogarty made first on Hassamaer's error, and he and Hill would both advance one bag by a wild pitch. Then Lemon sacrificed and Hill scored. Welsh retired the side by a fly to Creely

The last run was made in the eighth. After Motz had struck out,Pike was hit with a ball and sent to first. He went to second on France's hit, to third on McVey's sacrifice, and home on Crogan's safe hit. France tried to score on the same hit, and was caught at the plate, retiring the side.

It looked like several times as though Waco would score. In the first Pettiford was the first man at the bat, got to first on balls, to second on O'Neil's sacrifice. But Mullally struck out, and France threw out Bright at first base, and the first chance to score was gone.

In the fifth after Ellsworth struck out, Hassamaer hit safe and went around to third after wild throw. It began to look bilious for the Panthers, but Frances got down to knitting and Rose and Derrick struck out in order.

In the eighth after Rose and Derrick were out, O'Neil was hit with the ball and given first. Then bright hit a corker out to left. O'Neil made third all right and started home. By one of those circus throws of which he is capable McVey shot the ball into Pike. O'Neil turned back to third, but Pike got there ahead of him and he was touched out.

The greatest feature of the game was a double play by Motz unassisted in the second inning. Ellsworth was on first and Hassamaer made a hit that looked good for a two bagger. By a great one handed catch, Motz pulled it down and put it on Ellsworth before he could touch first.

NOTES OF THE GAME:

Pike played a great game yesterday. He caught without an error, and facing Derrick four times, was given a base on balls, was hit once, made a single and a two-bagger. Motz great double play brought down the grand stand. McVey's long distance throwing is something marvelous. A number of sluggers for the Indian village on the Brazos are in a badly crippled condition. Hassamaer's playing a plucky game with a sore finger. The way the Panthers used the ball yesterday was a caution. Crogan, the reliable, muffed a fly yesterday, but made up for it a moments after by a brilliant catch of a long drive from Rose's bat. Lemons slugged the ball in great shape yesterday. Derrick is a good pitcher, but yesterday was Fort Worth's day for hits. France has the prettiest delivery of any pitcher in the league. **Ft.Worth Gazette July 27, 1889**

Texas League 1889 final standings

Houston	54	44	.551 ---
Dallas	49	42	.538
Austin	50	46	.521
Galveston	50	48	.510
Ft. Worth	45	51	.469
Waco	33	50	.398

OPENING GAME LINEUP FOR THE FIRST GAME EVER PLAYED AT THE SPRING PALACE GROUNDS IN FORT WORTH

Fort Worth

Carl McVey, lf
Jack Crogan, cf
Wiley Hill, 3b
John Fogarty, rf
Harry Lemon, ss
Paddy Welsh,2b*
Frank Motz.1b
Unknown Pike, c
O.B. France, p

*CAPTAIN Paddy Welsh

Waco

Jack Pettiford, cf*
C. A. O'Neal, lf
M McCormick, c
E J Mullaly,c
GeorgeBright,2b
Gus Creely,ss
C. W Ellsworth, lf*
William Hassamaer,1b
Robert Rose,3b
Jess Derrick,p

*CAPTAINS Pettiford/Ellsworth

LINE SCORE JULY 26, 1889

Ft Worth 010 022 210 - 8
Waco   000 000 000 - 0

Fort Worth's Third Park
HAINES PARK (Home of the Panthers in 1906)
1902: The Texas League Resumes Operations

In 1902 owners revived the league and once again there was professional baseball in Texas. Corsicana, Fort Worth, Dallas, Waco, Paris, and Sherman-Denison became the first six members of the league in the new century, although two teams, Waco and Sherman-Dennison, withdrew from the league after playing only 60 games. The league's new president was John L. Ward, brother of Fort Worth owner William (Bill) Ward.

As the start of the renewed Texas League season loomed near, Bill Ward examined the T&P Park (a.k.a. Spring Palace Grounds), finding that the old ball park had greatly deteriorated and was no longer suitable for professional baseball. Fort Worth was a much larger city than it had been thirteen years earlier when the park was built.

The Texas Northern Traction Company had expanded greatly under the leadership of F. M. Haines. The company not only operated the local trolley cars, but had initiated the Interurban, which eventually connected many of the large and small towns of north central Texas.

When the company's General Superintendent learned that the Panthers were looking to build a new home, he offered the team land located on his company's property, a place that would serve both parties, giving the fans the convenience of the trolley on game day, and of course increasing the number of people using the trolley line.

Bill Ward accepted the offer from **Frank M. Haines**, and just prior to the opening of the 1902 season; a new park was constructed at the corner of Pacific and Pine Streets, just south of Front Street (today called Lancaster). The Texas Northern Traction Company and the Fort Worth Panthers were formal partners. The new park expanded the seating capacity from the one thousand who could fit in the old park, to a more spacious 2,000 who could find seating in the new stands.

During the construction of the new park, the Panthers continued play at the T&P Grounds during the preseason. However, once they left, the park continued to be a viable part of the city, used for several more years for both amateur games as well as Negro League games. In 1905 an article in the local paper referred to an upcoming game to be played at the *Spring Palace Grounds*. Fifteen years had passed since the great fire, but apparently one writer for the paper never ceased using the old name.

At the beginning of the 1902 season, the field located on the trolley company property was simply referred to as *the new park*. Then in June, the local papers began using the name HAINES PARK. And while there seems to have been no formal ceremony naming of the park, it was apparent that the baseball stadium park had an official name, *Haines Park*. The newly named park would host professional baseball from 1902 until the end of the 1910 season, at which time the Northern Traction Company informed the Panthers that they wished to reclaim their land for the purpose of the trolley company. The following year the Panthers moved north, to a location just west of North Main Street.

Haines Park became a footnote in Fort Worth history, and it was not until years later that there was much interest in the history of the old stadium. When local historians uncovered the name *Haines Park,* many made the easy assumption that the old park had been named in honor of the Spring Palace Hero Al Hayne. There was some logic in thinking that Fort Worth had named its park after the fallen hero, but it was a flawed logic. The first obvious problem was the spelling of the two names, one with an *"i"* and the other with a "y". There was also a gap in time. Al Hayne died in 1890, and the new park was not built until 1902, and besides the city had already constructed a monument in his honor. Obscured in time was the basis for the naming the stadium *Haines Park.*

AN HISTORIAN'S MYSTERY:
WAS HAINES PARK NAMED IN HONOR OF FORT WORTH HERO AL S. HAYNE?

Al S. Hayne Fountain and
Memorial, Constructed 1893
South Main Street

Texas Spring Palace 1890

An early Fort Worth
Fan

May 18, 1910:
The Northern Traction Company had informed the Panthers that they were reclaiming the land occupied by Haines Park, and so on this date the local papers announced: Ground has been broken for the Panthers' new park open for the 1911 season. (The new park was first called Morris Park, later Panther Park)

FRANK MARCH HAINES: 1854-1905

Frank M. Haines, a native of Boston, Massachusetts, came to Fort Worth in 1899. He had graduated from M.I.T. as a civil engineer, and his talents were put to use in 1900 by an expanding trolley car company, when Mr. Haines was named Second Vice-President and General Manager of the Texas Northern Traction Company.

It was under his imaginative leadership that the 1902 gift of land provided the Fort Worth Panthers a spot to build new stadium convenient to the business district. However, it was not until after the start of the 1902 season that the park received its new official name, *Haines Park* in gratitude for the use of the land, and in honor of Frank March Haines.

Mr. Haines' life was cut short by typhoid fever in 1905. Despite his involvement in numerous Fort Worth business endeavors, including the Fairmont Land Company, his family returned his body to Boston for burial.

Frank March Haines is largely forgotten despite his contributions to Fort Worth. However, Al S. Hayne's statue still graces the same spot it has occupied since 1893.

THE FORT WORTH PANTHERS AT HAINES PARK ON THE PROPERTY OF THE TEXAS NORTHERN TRACTION COMPANY, LOCATED JUST SOUTH OF FRONT STREET (Lancaster Street) ON THE CORNER OF PINE AND PACIFIC (These two streets no longer intersect)

FRANK MARCH HAINES

March 1862 – June 1, 1905

..it was under his supervision that the interurban line was constructed from Fort Worth to Dallas...

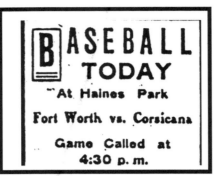

Frank March Haines was taken back to Boston, Massachusetts for burial.

Main Street Fort Worth

FRANK MARCH HAINES CAME TO FORT WORTH IN 1899 AS THE SUPERINTENDENT OF THE NORTHERN TRACTION COMPANY. IN 1902 HE PROVIDED LAND FOR FORT WORTH'S NEW BALL PARK.

Fort Worth's New Park
The Evolution of Haines Park as Reported in the Local Papers:

THE FORT WORTH REGISTER:

April 12, 1902, Page 8: "..new park not yet finished….."

April 13, 1902, page 8: " ..new park to be opened…"

April 14, 1902, page 5 " about two hundred brave souls ventured out to the new park"
(Story about exhibition game with Frisco)

April 26, 1902, First official game at the new ball park

June 3, 1902, page 8: "..the Colts, the crack colored team of this city won their game
yesterday with the Hot Springs colored team 7-3…"

June 16, 1902…"…fans at the south end of the grand stands say they need and are
entitled to some protection from the sun. A plank or two more
along the west side of the stands is their suggestion…"

June 22,1902: Front Page Headlines:

> **BASEBALL:**
> **DALLAS vs. FORT WORTH**
> **NEW PARK TODAY**
> **GAME CALLED AT 4:30**

July 5th, 1902: The park is now being referred to as HAINES PARK
There were no details regarding the selection of the name.

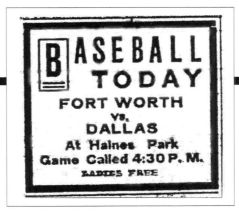

DALLAS: *Gaston Park*

In 1906 the Dallas Giants were neighbors of the State Fair of Texas, playing in Gaston Park, adjacent to the fair grounds, and like Haines Park, conveniently located on the trolley line. As a matter of fact, Fort Worth fans could, and often did, board the Interurban and arrive an hour later at the Dallas ball park, whose name honored one of the most powerful business leader in early Dallas history.

Captain William H. Gaston, known more commonly as Billy Gaston, became a significant city leader in the 1870's, organizing fairs, helping to bring about an iron bridge over the Trinity River, along with the arrival of a street car, he helped bring the railroad to Dallas. However, he is best remembered for his contribution in providing the State Fair of Texas its current location. As several leaders struggled to find a suitable place for the fair, Gaston used his considerable influence to sway the selection to land he would purchase and sell back to the Fair for stock.

For a short while, two state fairs in Dallas competed for survival, but eventually it was Gaston's location that prevailed. His tactics were not popular with a number of other prominent men of the area, but in the end, Gaston won the battle, and the Fair Grounds were firmly established on land he had selected, and remains so today.

After the State Fair was secured on the Gaston property, the Captain personally maintained a 14 acre tract adjacent to the fair grounds. It was there that the Gaston family operated an amusement park, and had ownership of Gaston Park, home of the Dallas professional baseball club.

The earliest Texas-Oklahoma football games were played in the same park, and it was not until 1921 that a new structure was built for the annual football event.

By 1913 the Fair Grounds were no longer adequate in size to host the ever expanding annual event. Just to the southwest was the 14 acre tract still owned by the Gaston family. The city offered the family $60,000 for the land, including the amusement park and baseball diamond. However, the owner of the Dallas Giants, J. W. Gardner held a lease on the stadium through 1916, and refused the city's offer of $10,000 for his rights to the park. He demanded $12,000 and the negotiations stalled.

When Billy Gaston arrived in Dallas after the Civil War, it was a community of about 2,000. He soon became one of the prominent businessman and civic leaders, playing a significant role in the development in the State Fair of Texas. His 14 acres amusement park adjacent to the Fair Grounds included Gaston Park, home of the Dallas Texas League baseball club.

The family sold their land to the Fair, but by 1914 only one payment had been made to the Gaston family. The wealthy family members graciously forgave the debt, and the property changed hands. With the land now in their name, Fair officials voted to provide $2,000 to buy out Gardner's lease, and at last the State Fair was able to make significant expansion plans.

The site of Gaston Park is near the Music Hall on the grounds of the State Fair.

The Site of Gaston Park is still visible in this picture taken around 1940. Gaston Park was located at intersection of Parry and Second Street

THE FAIR GROUNDS DALLAS TEXAS SITE OF GASTON PARK
Ca. 1940

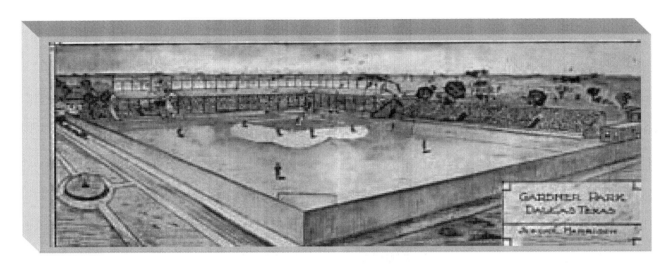

EARLY POST CARD PICTURE OF GARDNER PARK IN DALLAS

Picnic Party, arriving at Lake Erie, on The Interurban Line between Ft. Worth and Dallas.

THE INTERURBAN CONNECTING DALLAS AND FORT WORTH

TEMPLE
FREEMAN HEIGHTS

In April, 1905 local businessmen put up $750 to build the city a stadium in the Freeman Heights section of town. Roberts moved his franchise from Corsicana, and brought with him the contracts of a group of outstanding minor league players. The team had an outstanding season, but lost an important series with the Fort Worth Panthers, falling short one game of the 1905 Texas League pennant.

THE TEMPLE BOLL WEEVILS, 1905

Despite of the success of his club on the field, Doak Roberts lost money with his 1905 Temple venture, and so in 1906 once again moved his interest, this time taking his club and personal player contracts to Cleburne.

There was enough interest in keeping a team in Temple that Ewing Edens of Corsicana and a former partner of Roberts, assumed ownership of the Temple franchise for the 1906 season. Edens would soon sell his interest to several local businessmen. The biggest problem facing the new Temple team would be finding players, since Roberts took most of the '05 team to Cleburne. There was trouble ahead. When the Greenville Hunters folded in June of '06, and withdrew from the league, Temple, the southern most cities in the league, was also dropped in order to keep an even number of teams on the schedule. The Temple owners were bitter about the league's decision, and took their case to court, but it was to no avail. Their 1906 season ended the last day of June.

When the Texas League and South Texas League merged in 1907, Temple was a charter member of what was the first season of the modern Texas League. The Boll Weevils finished last that season as, and the city's days as a member of the league ended.

GREENVILLE: *Cotton Belt Park*

The Greenville Hunters wore garish green uniforms as might have been expected, and their nickname played off of the name of Hunt County, of which Greenville was the county seat. In 1906 Joseph Gardner, owner of the Dallas Giants, secretly funded the Hunters in order that the Texas League could operate as a six team circuit. Arch Bailey operated the club, and no doubt Gardner hoped that attendance would be sufficient to keep his losses at a minimum. However, with a population of less than 14,000, and being prohibited from playing Sunday ball, the club became a financial disaster. For a few weeks the team operated on the edge, but finally, unable to pay its players, the team threw in the towel, and ended the city's association with the Texas League

Greenville, Texas Early 1900's

GREENVILLE HUNTERS PLAYERS:

The Greenville Hunters' garish green uniforms pre-date the Oakland Athletics by several decades, but what other color could the team be? **ABOVE: _Billy Doyle, spit-baller_**

| Walter Snedden, 3B | Charles Reed, Catcher | Billy Doyle, Pitcher |

Greenville's lone appearance in the Texas League represents one of J.W. Gardner's efforts to prove syndicated baseball practicable, the then Dallas owner placed a team in the Hunt County metropolis in 1906 to round out a six club circuit. The veteran Texas League umpire A. P. "Pie" Bailey handled the franchise while Don Curtis managed the club on the field. H.B.Mock was also a business Official of the club. Although a strong team was placed on the field and succeeded in playing .500 winning baseball, Greenville lost money for Gardner and with Temple was dropped from the league at the end of the first half on June 30th. It has not since been represented in this circuit, though a familiar entry in strong Northeast Texas leagues. **History of the Texas League of Professional Baseball Clubs,1888-1951, William Ruggles, p. 221**

Greenville Hunters Roster:

Pitchers: Frank "Farmer" Moore, Doyle, Tom Huddleston, Jackson, Charles Spencer, **Catchers:** Stephens, Reed, **Infielders:** Raley, Maag, Snedden, Louden, Stouval, **Outfielders:** McIver, Jackson, Curtis, Phillips, Baumgardner.

WACO: *Katy Park*

WACO's KATY PARK HOSTED TEXAS LEAGUE BASEBALL FOR 27 YEARS

Waco's Katy Park played host to 27 years of Texas League baseball. Waco first entered the league in 1889, and in most of the early campaigns, the city was one of the mainstays of the circuit. Katy Park was adjacent to the Cotton Palace Fair Grounds, and just north of the old Baylor Stadium. During the depression Lights were added to the ball park, and on August 6, 1930 the first night baseball game was played in the Texas League. In 1906 the Waco Navigators were the only team that was not competitive, but the owners held on for the entire season.

In May of 1906 Doak Roberts scouted an amateur game in Corsicana. One team was the semi-professional Nicholson-Watson Store. A left-handed pitcher, who also handled the bat quite well, caught the attention of the owner of the Cleburne Railroaders. He offered the youngster a chance to sign with his Texas League club, and the following day, the 18 year old lad arrived in Waco, announcing his prowess to a skeptical Ben Shelton, captain of the Railroaders. Later that day **Tris Speaker made his professional debut at Katy Park.** *Thirty – two years later he was inducted into the Baseball Hall of Fame.*

Fourth Street Waco, Texas

WACO'S FAMOUS IRON BRIGE SPANNING THE BRAZOS

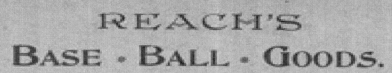

V

WINTER of '05   SPRING of '06
DEATH AT GORMAN PARK

JANUARY 17, 1906
EXECUTIVE MEETING: WHITE ELEPHANT RESTAURANT
Plans for the 1906 Season Finalized

THE 1906 TEXAS LEAGUE SCHEDULE

CLUBS.	AT FORT WORTH.	AT DALLAS.	AT WACO.	AT GREENVILLE.	AT CLEBURNE.	AT TEMPLE.
PORT WORTH	TEXAS	May 24, 25, 26. June 27, 28, 29, 30. July 19, 20, 21. Aug. 9, 10, 11.	May 16, 17, 18, 19. June 21, 22, 23. July 29, 30, 31. Aug. 17, 18, 19.	April 25, 26, 27. May 30, 31, June 1, 2. July 26, 27, 28. Aug. 24, 25, 26.	May 10, 11, 12. June 15, 16, 17. July 10, 11, 12. Aug. 27, 28, 29, 30.	May 20, 21, 22, 23. June 18, 19, 20. July 13, 14, 15. Aug. 2, 3, 4.
DALLAS	May 1, 2, 3. June 12, 13, 14. July 16, 17, 18. Aug. 20, 21, 22, 23.	LEAGUE	May 13, 14, 15. June 18, 19, 20. July 19, 11, 12. Aug. 27, 28, 29, 30.	May 30, 31, 22, 23. July 4, 5, 6. July 29, 30, 31. Sept. 1, 2, 3.	April 25, 26, 27. May 27, 28, 29. July 7, 8, 9. Aug. 6, 6, 7, 8.	May 16, 17, 18, 19. June 21, 22, 23. July 26, 27, 28. Aug. 24, 25, 26.
WACO	May 7, 8, 9. June 6, 7, 8. June 24, 25, 26. Aug. 12, 13, 14, 15.	May 10, 11, 12. May 30, 31, June 1, 2. June 9, 10, 11. Aug. 2, 3, 4.	SEASON	May 24, 25, 26. June 7, 28, 29, 30. July 19, 20, 21. Aug. 21, 22, 23.	May 1, 2, 3. June 5, 6, 8. July 22, 23, 24, 25. Aug. 24, 25, 26.	April 25, 26, 27. May 27, 28, 29. July 16, 17, 18. Aug. 31, Sept. 1, 2, 3.
GREENVILLE	May 13, 14, 15. May 27, 28, 29. July 1, 2, 3. Aug. 5, 6, 7, 8.	April 28, 29, 30. June 3, 4, 5. June 15, 19, 17. July 22, 23, 24, 25.	May 4, 5, 6. June 12, 13, 14. July 7, 8, 9. July 13, 14, 15.	BEGINS	May 16, 17, 18. June 6, 7, 8. June 21, 22, 23. Aug. 2, 3, 4.	May 1, 2, 3. June 9, 10, 11. July 10, 11, 12. Aug. 16, 17, 18, 19.
CLEBURNE	April 23, 29, 30. June 9, 10, 11. July 4, 5, 6. Aug. 31, Sept. 1, 2, 3.	May 4, 5, 6. June 24, 25, 26. July 13, 14, 15. Aug. 16, 17, 18, 19.	July 1, 2, 3. July 7, 8, 9. Aug. 9, 10, 11.	May 30, 21, 22, 23. June 18, 19, 20. July 19, 20, 21. Aug. 12, 13, 14, 15.	THIS	May 13, 14, 15. June 12, 13, 14. July 29, 30, 31, Aug. 1. Aug. 21, 22, 23.
TEMPLE	May 4, 5, 6. June 3, 4, 5. July 7, 8, 9. July 22, 23, 24, 25.	May 7, 8, 9. June 6, 7, 8. July 1, 2, 3. Aug. 12, 13, 14, 15.	April 28, 29, 30. June 15, 16, 17. July 4, 5, 6. Aug. 5, 6, 7, 8.	May 10, 11, 12. June 24, 25, 26. Aug. 9, 10, 11. Aug. 27, 28, 29, 30.	May 24, 25, 26. May 31, June 1, 2. June 27, 28, 29, 30. July 19, 20, 21.	WEEK

THE TEXAS LEAGUE SCHEDULE AS PUBLISHED IN NEWSPAPERS   JAN 1906

On a cold Wednesday, January 17, 1906, Bill Ward opened his famous White Elephant Restaurant for the winter meeting of the Texas League executives, who were optimistic about the upcoming season, featuring two new cities, Cleburne and Greenville. Cleburne was headed up by Doak Roberts, who also served as the president of the league. Greenville was being secretly funded by J.W. Gardner of Dallas. The star attraction of the meeting was the presence of C. D. White of the Spalding Company, who, the owners hoped might help them upgrade the classification of the Texas League from its present "D" league status to the more prestigious "C" standard. The designation would provide the owners with higher compensation when they sold player contracts to other leagues. The primary scheduling problem dealt around the fact that three towns, Temple, Cleburne, and Greenville, were prohibited from playing Sunday ball, resulting into a scheduling *that had some rough edges to it,* but the league officials agreed that *if at any time a club might be getting the worst of it, the schedule could be adjusted to take care of any inequities that might arise.* The 1906 schedule called for a 120 game season, beginning April 25, and concluding on Labor Day.

White Elephant Restaurant
604 and 606 MAIN.

Lake Trout, Spanish Mackerel, Black Bass, Gulf Trout, Lobsters, Red Fish, Pickerel, etc.
Stop Here for Good Dinner or Lunch

WILLAIM (BILL) WARD OPERATED FT. WORTH'S FAMOUS WHITE ELEPHANT RESTAURANT IN THE 600 BLOCK OF MAIN STREET

WHERE IS HOME?

On Thursday, January 18, The Cleburne Daily Enterprise published the 1906 Texas League schedule, which included Cleburne opening the season at home, but where would home be? Cleburne had a team with no place to play, and the clock was ticking. Roberts and Thacker seemed unfazed by the tight time frame, with Roberts promising preseason games would start in March.

On January 26th it was announced that grounds had been leased from the Trinity and Brazos Valley Railroad for a period of three years, with work to begin at once on building the fences, grand stand and in beautifying the park, making it ready for the opening of the baseball season. *It is understood that this park is to be used for all outdoor pleasures by the people of Cleburne...anytime the grounds are not in used by the baseball team it can be used for picnic occasions..*

WORK HAS BEGUN ON BASEBALL PARK

GROUND BROKEN AND SURVEYS BEING MADE PERPARATORY TO ERECTING FENCES, GRANDSTAND, AND OTHER IMPROVEMENTS.

Work has been begun on the Cleburne baseball park. Ground was broken today and the ground will be leveled up and graded so as to construct a perfect field for the players.

Messer. A.L. Chase, J.R. Nail and R. J. Corson, with others, have been at work laying off the ground, surveying and measuring the bounds, and making preparation for erection of the fences, grandstand, bleacher, etc., with all modern improvements necessary, which work will be begun at once.

It will require probably 25 to 30 days to complete all the improvements, and it confidently stated by those having the matter in charge, that the grounds will be in readiness for the training games scheduled during the later part of March and the first half of April. The players are to report here to go into training the 15th of March, and it is thought everything will be ready for them by that time.

The Cleburne Enterprise, Feb 17, 1906

PERSONNEL OF THE BASE BALL PLAYERS

While the Cleburne Railroaders had to scramble to get a field ready for play by March, the personnel of the team was not as much of a concern, since Doak Roberts already had most of the players from the 1905 Temple team under a personal contract with him. The 1906 Cleburne team would look much like the previous season's Temple ball club. The preseason would begin with the following line-up:

Powell, Catcher *
Dickson, Criss, Pitchers
Shelton, first base
Wright, second base
Shellenberger, third base*
Akin, shortstop **
Poindexter, left field
Ransom, center field *
Waite, right field*

*players in bold would lose their position during the season; Akin was moved to third

The grandstand is receiving the chief attention of the builders at present, but the fence will be put under way at once and this together with the bleachers and other improvements contemplated will be finished within the next week or ten days, provided the necessary men can be had to do the work.

The Cleburne Enterprise ...March 13, 1906

THE COTTON BELT CONTROVERSY

By the middle of March, Gorman Park was ready for the *ante-season*, practice, exhibition, preseason games. While the games would not be a part of the season standings, they nevertheless offered the teams a chance to pick up some extra money to offset costs.

Doak Roberts had been in baseball long enough to realize that fans would see the games as pointless. Not a good sell. In March he hoped to spark the interest of the Cleburne fans with a series of exhibition games that would feature two of the major league teams in Texas for spring training. Roberts had known John J. McCloskey since the early day of the Texas League. He was now the manager of the St. Louis Cardinals. The Cincinnati Reds were also working out nearby, and he hoped that at least one, if not both teams, would come to Cleburne, an excellent chance for the Johnson County fans to see major league baseball.

The Cincinnati Reds came to Texas for spring training in 1906. The major league club played with local minor league and college teams for practice. Doak Roberts attempted to get the Reds to Gorman Park but the two teams were not able to work out a schedule.

As it turned out, neither team was able to find an opening in their training schedule to come to Texas. Without a game with one of the major league teams, Roberts turned to another gimmick that might draw interest. He met with his old friend and follow Corsicana businessman Ewing Edens. Edens would be operating the Temple club in 1906. Roberts proposed a 15 game series in which the winner would gain sole possession of the Cotton Belt Cup.

The Cotton Belt Cup was first awarded in 1904 when Pine Bluff, champions of the Cotton States League challenged Corsicana, winner of the 1904 Texas League pennant to a best of 13 series., the winner being awarded the impressive $340 trophy, in the shape of a baseball held above the ivory base by three silver bats. The engraving was describes as elaborate and extensive.

The 1904 Corsicana team, jointly owned by Edens and Roberts, took the series by seven games to two. The two men assumed joint ownership of the cup. Then in 1906 they agree that a series between Temple and Cleburne would establish single ownership. It seemed simple enough. The cup would be on display for the fans to see and want for their team. The trophy would transform otherwise meaningless games into an exciting series. And so the announcement was made. Then came controversy.

Arch Pie Bailey, the man who had opposed Roberts' election to the presidency of the Texas League, and now current manager of the Greenville Hunters, protested the legality of Roberts' claim to the trophy. Bailey and General Manager Green of the Cotton Belt Railroad claimed that the cup was under the control of the rail line that bore its name. And furthermore, the two men were disgusted by the claim of two teams *not even on the Cotton Belt Route could expect to compete for the Cotton Belt Trophy.* (Note that Greenville was on the Cotton Belt line).

However, J. P. Lehane, General Freight and Passenger Agent for the Cotton Belt with headquarters in Fort Worth, added his own opinion regarding the dispute. Mr. Lehane supported Roberts' right to play for the cup, and took exception to the protest of Bailey and Green: *the cup is not the property of the railroad, but was in fact offered personally by him. The original intent of the cup was to be limited to amateur clubs along the Cotton Belt Route, and that it would become the property of a team only after it had won two years in succession by one team. Since I personally presented the award, I have the right to determine the rightful owner of the cup.*

Edens shrugged off the challenges of Lehane, Bailey and Green as no more than an attempt to gain free newspaper space for their railroad. To Edens there was no doubt as to the rightful owner of the cup, citing the inscription on the trophy showing that it had been awarded to J.D. Roberts of Corsicana, and there were no restrictions or conditions attached to its ownership.

The first game of the Cotton Belt Trophy series was held on Wednesday, March 21, inaugurating Cleburne's new park, referred to as The Athletic Park. As Roberts prepared the team for the first game, he told the Morning News and Daily Enterprise reports that *this is one of the nicest little parks in the entire state of Texas.*

The first game in Cleburne, be it only an exhibition game, nonetheless was an occasion of great celebration. The merchants of Cleburne donated merchandise that would be given to players for specific accomplishments:

Bradford Brothers offered a fine new Stetson hat for the first home run, and they also offered a pair of Halan's shoes for the man with the most stolen bases.

The Graham Dry Goods Company promised a fine new cream white vest, trimmed in black braids for the player with the most hits...*it's a hummer*...valued at $5!

J. H. Douglass, a dealer in *Gent's Furnishings,* located on East Henderson Street, offered a fine R&W sweater for the first Cleburne player getting a triple.

Charles Thacker, who owned a sporting goods store, offered a fine bat to the first man hitting a homer.

A sizeable crowd made their way to the park for the first game, but left disappointed when Temple pulled out a 7-6 win over the Railroaders.

If you read the report of the game the next day in the Cleburne Morning Review, you might have scratched your head a bit at the writer's recounting of the eighth inning when Cleburne scored 6 runs....*The appeal of Harriet Beecher Stowe's favorite son of Ham, in the eighth inning, brought forth results that were a terror to the pikers and a spasm of ecstasy for Cleburne.*

By March 30th the series had advanced to the seventh game, Cleburne having won the latest game 13-7, taking a four to three lead in the series. Cleburne was handicapped when Charles Moran was called back to Nashville, Tennessee to look after his wife who had taken ill.

Eventually the series went to 17 games, with Cleburne winning nine games to eight for Temple.

The Trophy was in Doak Roberts' possession. The history of the Cotton Belt Trophy went behind the dark vale of history.

This is a rare look at a country ball game in progress . . . the man in the foreground has retrieved a foul ball

Young men off the farms and ranches got together as often as possible to play some "country ball". Communities like Greenbrier and Blum in Hill County would match talents on a flat piece of land. Seldom would anyone outside of the community know the results, but the games were taken seriously, and occasionally a youngster would be spotted and signed by a local semi-pro team, which in some cases led the player to a minor league team.

GORMAN PARK ON A STORMY DAY

Cleburne's opening day game was less than two weeks away, but there was still much to be done. Roberts was still looking at various ball players hoping to make their way onto the 1906 roster. Lawrence Walker, a friend of local businessman Russ Hart, came in from Jefferson to play right field, and after getting a couple of extra base hits in a March 25 exhibition game with Temple, looked like a possible outfielder, but he was soon gone for reasons never revealed. No doubt the local writers were relieved when a left fielder by the name of Schumleffeld played only a few exhibition games before disappearing from the baseball scene. Other names appeared ever so briefly in the preseason box scores for the Cleburne Railroaders. There was a Waite, and a Welsh. And they too were gone.

By April 12, the opening day lineup was ever closer to completion. Dude Ransom playing third, Roy Akin at short, William Powell in center field. However, Doak Roberts was looking at better talent. He had wired Charlie Moran a contract, but with no immediate answer assumed the legendary Moran had signed with another team. His plans were to put the versatile athlete at third, although Charlie had proven he could play every position, including pitching.

At the end of March he received a telegram from Nashville. It was from Charles B. Moran. His wife had been ill and confined to an infirmary, but she was healing, and soon he would be heading to Cleburne to reunite with his good friend Doak Roberts. He wrote that he would be traveling with Fisher, also thought to be a *crack player*.

And there was one other player Roberts was negotiating with. Corsicana man Zena Clayton was with Houston, but there were rumors of dissatisfaction between the club and Zena. Roberts was feeling good about enticing Clayton to Cleburne. It looked more and more like the Railroaders were in shape to give both Fort Worth and Dallas a good run for the pennant.

After the long series with Temple, Roberts was anxious to mix it up with other clubs to get a better feel for the upcoming season. He had hoped to entice the Cincinnati Red Legs to Cleburne, but the two teams were never able to work out a good convenient schedule. On Thursday, April 12, the San Antonio Broncos were to appear at Gorman Park for an ante-season game.

The wood from which Gorman Park sprang was still fresh, the field sanded, leveled, the spring grass green and mowed, all awaiting the Broncos of the South Texas league. There was yet nothing worked out, but some plans were made for a possible post season (known at the time as *saw-off*) games between the Texas League champs and the South Texas League champions.

Scheduled to pitch that afternoon for Cleburne was their sensational rookie, six foot-two Dode Criss, signed off the sandlots of Wichita Falls, where, in 1905, he had starred for the semi-pro team known as the Cremos, sponsored by the Cremo Cigar Company. In addition to his left-handed pitching prowess Criss was a hard hitting batsman, a trait much valued in this era of limited rosters. The team would only be carrying 13 players, and a pitcher who could hit was a tremendous addition to a team. So impressed was Roberts with the young man's ability, he was willing to cut one of his better pitchers from his '05 Temple squad. Roy Mitchell was in the midst of a long and illustrious career as a Texas League pitcher, as well as stints in the major leagues with the St. Louis Browns and Cincinnati.

Dode Criss

The Wichita Falls Cremos, 1905.

GUSTY WINDS and DEATH
BEFORE THE FIRST OFFICIAL GAME IS EVER PLAYED TRAGEDY STRIKES
April 12, 1906

On this spring afternoon, Dode Criss was everything that he was billed to be, dominating San Antonio, and through the fourth inning had not given up a single hit. Unfortunately his own club was not having much more success at the plate, the score 0-0. But in the 5th the home town fans screamed and yelled in excitement as their club scored three times, which with the strong effort of the rookie pitcher seemed to ensure victory.

It was spring time in Texas, the time of the greatest number of storms. Skies over Cleburne were indeed changing. Dark clouds to the southwest were an almost certain sign that rain was coming, and likely in a stormy fashion. Gentle rains in the spring are not the custom in this part of the country. A gusty cool wind accompanied by lightning and thunder caused those who chose to stay at the ball park to scamper for the protection of the grandstand roof.

At the end of the sixth inning, umpire Collins waved the players off the field and Charles Thacker sounded the gong, an indication that the game was officially halted by rain. The field was quickly turning into a mud pit.

Then it hit. A vicious wind, some called a cyclone. Gusting to well above 90 mph, the fans were being drenched by the blowing rain, and then alarmed when the wooden roof could no longer resist the horrendous gusts. Panic set in as the roof disappeared completely from the grand stands, landing onto Buffalo Street viciously scattering timbers for several hundred feet.

Roberts watched helplessly as a twenty dollar bill blew away from the money till.

Then almost as quickly as it had started, the winds dropped to a gentle breeze and the rain took on a gentle character. Thacker looked around at his little park, stunned by the abrupt destruction. At first, despite the damaged, it appeared that no one was hurt, but that assumption proved to be premature. Mr. B. B. Hand sustained a bruise on his arm, while a young boy suffered a cut on his left arm. One player was slightly hurt.

As everyone milled about, some looking for hats blown away, one young man was found unconscious. William G. Dalton had been struck by a large board, breaking his shoulder and collarbone, as well as inflicting a severe blow to his head, rendering him helpless. A hack was summoned to take him to his home at the corner of Buffalo and College Street. A doctor hurried to his bedside. There was no hospital in the city in 1906. Eventually he could be taken to the Santa Fe Hospital in Temple, or perhaps to St. Joseph, or the recently opened All-Saints hospital in Fort Worth.

Throughout the county there were reports of widespread damage and injuries, including Will Hanson and Frank Weathered. The cotton compress reported having a wall blown down, while the round house in the Santa Fe Yards suffered damage when several cars in for repair were toppled. Dr. Strickland's office was reported to have been severely damaged.

Death relieved him....
The following Monday, at 2am Will Dalton died...*death came to relieve him from suffering.* The Morning Review reporter noted that he had received careful nursing and medical treatment. Walton was a member of the Cross Timbers Camp of No.4 W.O.W. (Woodmen of the World) and would receive $5,000 from a policy from the Travelers' Accident Association. His funeral was held at 10am, Tuesday.

The damage to the park was estimated at $500, about 40% of its original cost. The community joined together to help raise money for the repair of the park. A local roller rink offered one-half of its ticket sales towards the repair funds.

BENEFIT GAME...*Poorly attended*

A benefit game to help raise repair money, featuring Charles Thacker on the mound, against a team that included owner Doak Roberts, pitching, as well as Joe C. Hubbard and W.W.Murphy. Thacker's team won 8-7. The local paper noted the play of the local businessmen stating they *kept their positions in the game in a fairly commendable manner.* Only about 100 fans turned out to see the game. No mention of the amount of money raised by the charitable efforts.

Doak Roberts and Charles Thacker looked at the gaping hole in the fence, and the missing grandstand roof with the realization that the Texas League season opener was a little over a week away. There was much to be done before the first pitch.

IS GORMAN PARK

April 24, 1906
Mr. Charles H. Thacker, Secretary of the Cleburne Athletic Association some time ago wrote to Mr. M. Sweeney, General Manager of the Trinity and Brazos Valley Railroad, indicating to him a desire on part of the Association to name the Cleburne base ball park, which is erected on land leased from the company, in his honor. Mr. Sweeny answered the letter in appreciative terms and suggested that the park be named in honor of the ex-General Superintendent, P.A.Gorman, under whose regime the deal for the land was made. Acting on the suggestion the park has been christened *Gorman Park,* and the many friends of Mr. Gorman made while he was here will appreciate the courtesy of the Athletic Association. Mr. Gorman is one of the best and best known railroad me in Texas, and the Cleburne people remember him with a friendly remembrance. *Cleburne Morning News*
April 24, 1906

After the April 12 damage to Gorman Park, the City Rink dedicated ½ of its receipts to the emergency repair funds

The storm that devastated Cleburne on April 12, 1906, first struck Briggs, Texas in Bell County. Joe Williams took this amazing picture of the tornados' destruction that April day

AT AN ALARMING RATE: 1906 Report on Civil War Vets
…..veterans reunions

It was now the 20th century and the old ways and the old men who knew those ways were dying off. The most significant event of the previous century was the American Civil War (1861-1865), a war that engaged hundreds of thousands of men. By 1906 they were becoming old men who remembered the war with a strange fondness.

The six remaining veterans from the Battle of San Jacinto met for the last time in 1906, seven decades after the historical battle that brought independence to Texas. That same year, thousands of Civil War veterans gathered in New Orleans, both Confederate and Yankee. Men once intent upon killing the other forty years earlier reminisced about the great war. Reporters gathered to cover the story, noted that the annual gathering was dropping significantly in number: *the old veterans are dying off in alarming numbers.* While thousands were dying on an annual basis, the last veteran lasted until 1959.

In Cleburne, many of the old vets gathered around the courthouse square to play cards and checkers, and to anyone willing to listen, or anyone who had heard their tales less than a dozen times, the men would talk about their trek to war.

Men like Phil Allin, the mayor of Cleburne, and the son of a war hero, as well as Doak Roberts, were often called Colonels out of deference to the memory of the conflagration. The country was at peace, but the memory of the conflict raged long.

Civil War veterans, who suffered through the hated war, stood tall and proud during annual reunions that were being held around the country. In 1906 the convention was held in New Orleans, and the reporters could not help but to notice that the numbers of survivors was shrinking at an alarming rate. Men intent on killing one another now shared stories of misery and valor. As the time grew longer since the war, young boys would shake hands with the old vets, and would brag that they had shaken hands with history.

A Group of Unknown Civil War Vets at Attention

TEXAS LEAGUE UMPIRES:
1906 Season

A Pie Bailey
W. J. Backly
S. A. Collins
Tom Hoffman
Aaron Eldridge
Ed Macky
Wirt Spencer
William C "Lucky"
           Wright
Frank Richards
Harry Tackaberry
Ed Stewart

**TEXAS LEAGUE
UMPIRES, 1906**

In 1906 umpiring was a solitary profession both in the minor leagues as well as in the majors. The job involved severe abuse from players and fans, constant traveling, all for $75 a month. Working the game alone increased the number of incorrect calls, especially when multiple runners were on base. Foul/fair calls, always difficult, were especially hard to make when the umpire had positioned himself behind the pitcher. One of the driving forces behind encouraging an increase of female attendance was to mitigate the use of loud and foul language, more often than not directed at the umpire.

It was not uncommon for the umpire to either not show up, perhaps having missed a train, or more likely in fear of his life based on an incident from the previous day. When it was determined that the assigned umpire would not be showing up for his assignment, teams were required to take someone from their roster, give them the umpire's shirt, and hope that they could call the game impartially. At other times, one man from each squad was put into the arbitrator's position. Ironically, there were almost no incidents of outrageous behavior when the team's player became the game's umpire.

One of the endearing traits of Owen "Chief" Wilson of the Fort Worth Panthers was his total honesty. Later he would star for the Pittsburgh Pirates, but in 1906 he was in the outfield for Fort Worth. When there was doubt about a close call, often the umpire would consult with Wilson, who could be counted on giving an honest answer, even at the cost of his own Fort Worth team.

The Umpire Calls out the starting lineup to the fans

Almost all of the umpires assigned to Texas League games were former players still interested in being a part of the league, but they soon discovered the camaraderie that they had loved so much as a member of a club was absent when they took on the umpire's garb. Most did not stay around long in the position. The constant haggling was too much to long endure.

Umpires have always been invisible on the field, and likewise the newspapers largely ignore them. However, in April of 1906, The Cleburne Daily Enterprise ran this short article about S. A. Collins, considered one of the most controversial umpires in the league, noted for his loud, commanding voice:

COLLINS CAME HOME

Umpire Collins didn't go with the boys to the Bayou City, but came home, arriving on the early train this morning. He will remain here until the opening and will call the results for the first series here. After which he goes to Fort Worth and Tackaberry will come here. The disposition of umpires for the first month of the seasons gives Collins assignments at Fort Worth, Dallas, Greenville, and Cleburne, but does not send him to Temple and Waco. He is to be in these cities later in the season, however, when the assignments for next month are made out. ....*The Daily Enterprise*

...In 1889 the question was put to the league regarding the umpire's positioning during the game. Charles H. Thacker, the 1889 Texas League Secretary issued that edict that allowed the arbiter to stand behind the pitcher in order to give him a better vantage point for runners on the bases.

The officials of the Texas League issued a statement before the 1906 season began reminding the players that the umpire was the ultimate authority during games, and it was their duty to keep the game in line. In reality the umpires did not always receive the strongest support from the league office, which at times made a difficult job almost impossible.

In addition to their $75 monthly salary, they were paid train fare and expense money, working and traveling alone.

Some worked exclusively behind the plate, while others would start behind the plate, then move behind the pitcher when runners reached base. They had double duty, not only calling the game, they too were expected to announce the starting lineup and changes to the lineup. In small parks, using a megaphone, they generally could be heard. There were no electronic speakers, nor did the scoreboard have much more information than the running run totals.

Two umpires that garnered most the headlines in 1906 was S.A. Collins, and Wirt Spencer, generally considered the most respected umps in the league that year. Collins' toughest assignment occurred in 1905, when he called a 17 inning game in San Antonio.

Like most of the umpires of his day, Spencer was an ex-player who had begun his career in 1891 as a pitcher, having played for John J. McCloskey and Mike O'Connor. He began his stint as an umpire when the Texas League was revised in 1902, working as well in the South Texas League. He was credited in finding several outstanding ball players, including Cleburne's Rick Adams, who played for Washington in 1905.

During the winter preceding the 1906 season Spencer had the unusual experience of going to the Yucatan to umpire a series of exhibition games between players from the South Texas League and the Southern League. A wealthy Yucatan citizen had induced the players to make the trip, and once there Wirt was surprised to discover that the park in Merida was very similar to the stadiums in Dallas and Houston. The American players were surprised and delighted at the support the games received, noting that $2800 was taken in for each of the first two games.

In addition to the Southern League, the South Texas team played a native team twice, winning 25-3 and 15-6. Later an all-Cuban team arrived, and they too were defeated by the American team.

Wirt Spencer reveled in the fact that the local Yucatan fans supported the umpire. When the captains raised a fuss, the fans reacted towards the player in favor of the ump. In one incident, Ed Luson, managing the Alabama squad, began raising a ruckus after a call at the plate. Luson suddenly found himself confronted by the local police, who threatened to take him to town to be locked up if he continued his tirade. The Captain backed off, and abstained from any other protest for the duration of the series.

The players were rewarded with a payment of $75 to $100 per month in gold, plus their expenses. Such was the success of the exhibition series that Spencer began mapping out plans to return the following winter to establish a four team league composed of both American and Cuban players.

Wirt Spencer, it might be noted, was the coach of the Texas A&M baseball club from 1904-1908. Ironically, when he left A&M he was replaced by Charles Moran, who in 1906 was a utility player for the Cleburne Railroaders.

FAVORITE UMPIRE's ANTICS WEARS THIN
S.A. Collins

1906 would be S.A. Collin's first year umpiring in the Texas League, bringing with him a tough reputation. In the previous year, while working in Missouri, the management of the club attempted to bar him from working a game by preventing his entrance to the park at the gate. The pugnacious Collins climbed over the fence and presented himself at the plate, and announced the time for the beginning of the game, and if the home team failed to take the field, he would declare a forfeit. The game began at the prescribed time with Collins working as the indicator.

In 1906 he brought this style to Texas. Every call was an *event*, as he gestured in a style more common to the stage than to a baseball field. He was short to listen to the complaints from the players, and in a voice that could be heard all over most stadiums, he made certain that everyone understood that he was the man in charge. He would scream "Oi am the boss here!" as he pointed his finger at the breast of any player who was not willing to accept his umpired judgments in silence.

Early in the season he was the darling of the newspapermen, who were not bashful in printing their biased views, lauding his ability's to call a game. The other umpires, included Wirt Spencer, quietly went about their business with as little fuss as possible, but Collins preferred the notoriety his antics created.

Within a few weeks after the season opener, his style was wearing thin, and too many people were being offended by his style. The President of the Texas League was forced to make a tough decision regarding Collins' affiliation with the league. Collins soon learned he had been relieved of his duties with the league.

Affidavits have been made against Mr. Collins to the effect that
he had pledged him to be unfair to certain players, by reason of
dissatisfactions created by these players. I like Mr. Collins personally
but to keep harmony in the league, he had to be let go. I invited Mr.

Collins to come to Cleburne today to hear his side, but he has not shown up. He is a good umpire and will not have any trouble getting on at other points.

However, Roberts within a few days S.A. Collins met with Roberts and successfully argued that the charges against him were unfounded, and the feisty umpire was reinstated.

His return was not well received, and he continued to meet a lot of resistance, continued bickering, and within a few weeks left of his own accord. 1906 was his only year in the Texas League. He completed the year with the South Texas League.

This blurry shot from long ago captured Charley Moran calling a play at home plate.

Charles Moran and Wirt Spencer not only served as umpires they were both football coaches at Texas A&M. Moran would umpire in the National League for 22 years.

Defending Champions:
The 1905 Fort Worth Panthers
Down to the Wire: The League's Closest Race

The Texas league began the 1905 season as a six team league, which included Doak Roberts, elected president, and operating a team in Temple. Legendary Mike O'Connor headed up a team in Austin. Corsicana continued, as they had since 1902, as a member of the league, but for the first time without the involvement of native son Doak Roberts.

By June 1st, without Roberts guidance and more importantly without the inflow of money from his other businesses, the Corsicana owners surrendered their team to the Texas League, which operated the team for about a week before throwing in the towel. The Austin team was also having financial problems. Both clubs were dropped from the remainder of the schedule.

The league decided not to split the season, but to continue the current schedule, modified to the four remaining teams, resulting in a rather odd final standings. The four clubs that finished the season all ended up with winning records, with the Panthers claiming the flag with a lowly .545 winning percentage.

Temple concluded its home schedule on August 29th with six to go, four games ahead of Fort Worth in second place. The red hot Panthers streaked past the Boll Weevils, claiming the flag. Details of the Temple's lost pennant are recounted below.

As the 1906 opened, Fort Worth carried the flag. Most of the Temple players who had suffered through the final week of 1905 were now on the Cleburne Railroader's roster. A new roster of players awaiting the 1906 Temple fans, and Greenville replaced Corsicana. There was new grass, a new season, and a new flag to be won. Fort Worth was the defending champion.

NOW FOR THE PENNANT.

The Fort Worth Panthers had the 1905 flag in hand, ready to defend their trophy in the upcoming 1906 season, but it was the Dallas Giants who figured to be the winner in 1906.

A LOOK BACK AT THE END OF THE 1905 TEXAS LEAGUE RACE:
How Fort Worth Became the Defending Champions in 1906: Incredible finish

Doak Roberts entered the Texas League with the Corsicana Oilers of 1902, operating the team in that city in '03, and '04 before transferring his interest to Temple for the 1905 season.

Despite operating in the smallest city the in the circuit, Roberts team was poised to claim the pennant with a week remaining in the season. The 1905 season began with six teams. but by June two cities, Corsicana and Austin were having financial difficulties, and were dropped from the remainder of the schedule. At that point, the Texas League decided to continue the season with the games against Corsicana and Austin counting in the standings.

With four teams remaining to battle it out for the pennant, the season ended with the closest race in the short history of the league. The last week is captured below, game by game, as the Panthers put together an extraordinary season ending winning streak to take the season trophy.

The following accounting is taken from the contemporary standings as printed in the local newspapers:

On August 30th the Fort Worth papers printed the standings of the Texas League:

Standings at the beginning of the Day   **Games played that day**

Standings Published August 30, 1905

	GP	W	L	Pct.	GB
Temple	123	69	54	.561	---
Ft.Worth	125	68	59	.528	4
Waco	122	64	58	.525	4 ½
Dallas	123	60	63	.488	9

Game Played August 30

Ft.Worth	2	Ft.Worth	8
Temple	1	Temple	2 *Note Roy Mitchell lost both
Dallas	5	Dallas	7
Waco	1	Waco	0

Standings Published August 31, 1905   **Games Played August 31, 1905**

	GP	W	L	Pct.	GB
Temple	125	69	56	.552	----
Ft.Worth	127	68	59	.535	2
Waco	124	64	60	.516	4 ½
Dallas	125	62	63	.496	7

Ft.Worth	7	
Temple	1	
Dallas 5	7	
Waco 3	3	

Standings Published September 1, 1905   **Games Played September 1, 1905**

	GP	W	L	Pct.	GB
Temple	126	69	57	.548	---
Ft.Worth	128	69	59	.539	1
Waco	126	64	62	.508	5
Dallas	127	64	63	.504	5 ½

Ft.Worth	8
Temple	1
Dallas	3
Waco	4

Standings Published September 2, 1905   **Games Played September 2, 1905**

	GP	W	L	Pct.	GB
Temple	127	69	58	.5431	----
Ft.Worth	129	70	59	.5426	----
Waco	127	65	62	.512	4
Dallas	128	64	64	.500	5 ½

Ft.Worth 4 (ninth straight win)
Waco   3
Temple vs Dallas Rained Out

With two days remaining on the schedule, Temple and Fort Worth were separated by .0005 of a percentage point, the Panthers having played two more games than the Boll Weevils. The rainout on September 2nd required Temple to schedule a double header the following day, and thus Temple had 3 games remaining while Fort Worth would play Waco twice. The Texas League could not have asked for a better scenario: the championship would like be decided on the last game of the season, played on Labor Day. Large crowds were expected for both games.

On September 3rd, all looked well for the prospects of a double header between Temple and Dallas, assuring a satisfactory conclusion to the season.

The standings on September 3, 1905:

Ft. Worth	130	71	59	.547	
Temple	127	69	58	.543	½
Waco	128	65	63	.508	5
Dallas	128	64	64	.500	6

The Fort Worth Panthers defeated Waco 6-5, for their 10th win in a row. In Dallas, Temple kept up the pace opening with a 5-3 win over the Giants, but game two was a heartbreaker, as they lost by the narrow 2-1 margin:

LABOR DAY 1905:

Owing to their victory, and Temple's loss, the Panthers woke to find themselves in first place by a full game going into the final game of the season:

	Won	Lost	Pct.	GB
Ft. Worth	131	72	59	.550	----
Temple	129	70	59	.543	1
Waco	129	65	64	.504	6
Dallas	130	65	65	.500	6 ½

Thanks to the fact that the Panthers had played two more games than Temple, and had won both of the extra games, Fort Worth was in the position to control their own destiny: win the final game, and they would be the pennant winners. However, as a results of the inequity of the league schedule, a Fort Worth loss and Temple win would result in the Boll Weevils taking the championship by .0007 percentage points. If the Panthers were to win their 11th straight, they would be crowned.

With 2,000 fans in the park, Temple edged Dallas 3-2 for their 71st win of the season. Now it was time to wait for the phone to ring with the results from Ft. Worth, where 2,100 fans had crowded into Haines Park. Then the call: for Temple, it would be *wait until next year*.

As the victorious Boll Weevils gathered to hear the results from Fort Worth, their heart sunk, the Panthers had defeated the Navigators 5-4 for their 11th straight and pennant winning game. The Fort Worth Panthers had roared their way into first place and into Texas League history.

This may be the closest race in the history of the league. Ironically, the Temple team, because of financial issues, would move in large part to Cleburne for the 1906 season. Temple would have a team in 1906, but the personnel who had given them a fun ride in 1905 would be gone.

TEXAS LEAGUE STANDINGS BASED UPON CONTEMPORARY NEWSPAPERS
Published September 5, 1905

	Games Played		Won	Lost	Pct.	Games Behind
Ft.Worth	132	73	59	.553	---------
Temple	130	71	59	.546	1
Waco	130	65	65	.500	7
Dallas	131	65	66	.496	7 ½

THE FORT WORTH PANTHERS PUT TOGETHER A SEASON ENDING 11 GAME WINNING STREAK TO OVERCOME THE TEMPLE BOLL WEEVILS TO CLAIM THE 1905 TEXAS LEAGUE FLAG.

William Ruggles, the long time historian of the Texas League, published the official standings of the 1905 season, which differs slightly from the 1905 newspaper accounts of the day. The numbers vary, but the results are the same, Fort Worth claimed the 1905 league flag.

WILLIAM RUGGLES FINAL STANDING FOR THE 1905 TEXAS LEAGUE SEASON:

TEAM	Won	Lost	Pct.	GB
Fort Worth	72	60	.545	----
Temple	70	59	.543	½
Dallas	65	64	.504	5 ½
Waco	65	64	.504	5 ½
Austin	17	22	.436	*
Corsicana	9	29	.370	*

*dropped out of the league June1905

Why the discrepancy between the published and the official standings?
... Fort Worth had meanwhile taken three straights from Waco and Temple lost its only opportunity to win a Texas League flag. Fort Worth's victory was by two (percentage) points, and ½ game, and at the close there was a question over a game forfeited to the Panthers, but Doak Roberts was quoted in the newspaper interview as saying Fort Worth had won, and so the results stood.
The History of the Texas League of Professional Baseball Clubs, 1888-1951, William Ruggles. p.98

THE DEFENDING CHAMPIONS
FORT WORTH PANTHERS AT HAINES PARK

Top Row: D. Cavender L.F. – Leo Walsh P. – Mike Erwin C. – Owen Wilson R.F. – Ed Hanlon P. – Ed Wicker P.
Middle Row: Rich. Scheniwinek P. – Tom Huddleston P. – Heavy Wills 1st B. – Ollie Ghroeten C.F. –
Bottom Row: Rob Christman P. – Pat Waugh C. – George Markay 3rd B. – Walter Boles SS. – A. Pennell 2nd B.
1905 PENNANT WINNERS.

In the first six years of the 20th century, the United States had experienced the devastation of the Galveston hurricane of 1900, the assassination American President William McKinley, and now in April of 1906 San Francisco first suffered a severe earthquake, soon followed by a fire of epic proportions, the likes of which had not been seen since the great Chicago fire in 1871.

 The Dallas Morning News.

EXTRA
11:00 P. M.
VOL. XXI.

DALLAS, TEXAS, WEDNESDAY, APRIL 18, 1906

EXTRA
11:00 P. M.
NO. 192

SAN FRANCISCO IN RUINS

Thousands of Houses Wrecked by Earthquake Shock and Business Section of City Destroyed---Fire Follows and Water Supply Is Cut Off.

THOUSANDS OF LIVES MAY BE LOST

Telegraphic Communication With the Stricken City Completely Shut Off---Large Area Is Affected by the Seismic Disturbance---Many Are Killed in the Ruins of Falling Buildings.

A CLEBURNE
BASE BALL
PITCHER

D. Criss

Wins a Suit in

Monte Haley's

Suit Club,

3rd Drawing.

LUCKY NO.

31.

Fitting a suit to Dode's 6'2" frame may have presented a challenged to the Cleburne haberdasher.

THE CLEBURNE HOTEL: where visiting teams stayed

For the Cleburne fans who wished to travel to Fort Worth to see the Railroaders play the Panthers, Santa Fe advertised "Excursion Round Trips" which varied in cost from 85 cents to one dollar.

MAJOR LEAGUE BASEBALL IN TEXAS

CHICAGO WHITE SOX IN MARLIN, TEXAS
SPRING TRAINING IN TEXAS
Picture: Rare amateur Photo taken In Marlin, Texas of the White Sox in Spring Training

Long before Florida and Arizona became the spring training Mecca of major league teams, Texas hosted several clubs that left the cold north for warmer weather, and a place to keep the players away from distractions. Run more like boot camps, the teams trained hard and long, playing local professional, college, semi-pro teams, as well as amateurs around their training centers.

In 1906 both St. Louis teams, the Cardinals and the Browns, trained in the Dallas area, while Cincinnati played in Marlin. Doak Roberts sought to bring the Reds to Gorman Park for a few exhibition games, but was never able to work out a good date, and so the major league team never got to Cleburne.

In 1911 The Chicago White finally made it to Gorman Park to play the local Texas-Oklahoma League team.

In 1906 baseball was the national game. No other sport came close to rivaling the national game. Football was still a game for high schools and colleges. Basketball was struggling to find an audience. If you wanted to play pro sports, baseball was practically the only option for young men.

Semi-pro and amateur teams abound all across the nation. It seemed every town, no matter how small, had a local team. Some played to a schedule, while other teams consisted of local farm boys who donned their regular work clothes to take on teams from nearby communities, played before a handful of fans.

VI
THE 1906 SEASON BEGINS
APRIL 25, 1906
PROFESSIONAL BASEBALL COMES TO
CLEBURNE, TEXAS GORMAN PARK
CLEBURNE RAILROADERS   vs   DALLAS GIANTS

SCORE BOOK FOR DALLAS

Brice Hoskins, the Dallas official scorer, has issued the new score book for the season, and it contains much information that will interest the fan and be an aid to him during the game. Complete instructions for tabulated scoring, the line-up of the teams and batting positions, with table for scoring are given in the book. It also contains a biographical sketch of each player on the Dallas team. A full page picture of the whole team is published in the book. The book contains the 1906 Texas League season. *..Dallas Morning News*

APRIL 25, 1906

OPENING GAME OF THE 1906 TEXAS LEAGUE SEASON
WEDNESDAY, APRIL 25, 1906
DALLAS vs CLEBURNE: GORMAN PARK, CLEBURNE TEXAS

Not since 1898, when murderer John Shaw was hanged, had there been this much excitement in Cleburne. Hundreds of Johnson County citizens took a short vacation from their jobs and farms to venture into the city line the streets to watch, what the Morning Review called a *credible parade,* winding around the square, then proceeding down Main Street towards *the finest little park in Texas*, where the Railroaders and pre-season pick Dallas were to open the 1906 Texas League season. For the first time there was professional baseball in Johnson County.

Mayor Phil Allin, the son of a Civil War hero and President of the Cleburne Athletic Association, was the Grand Marshall. Gaskill's Hungarian Military Band, which happened to be in town with the circus, provided marching music. The players from both teams were cheered, waving from the horse drawn wagons, all heading to the park for the four pm starting time.

Mayor Allin had been asked to throw out the first pitch. As the crowd cheered, umpire Collins screamed in his distinctive voice…*Stee…riiike!* It was time to get the 1906 Texas League season underway.

The Cleburne team had a large number of men who had come close to winning the 1905 league pennant as members of the Temple team, but it was Dallas that was picked to win it all in 1906. Cleburne hoped to embarrass the baseball sages who saw Dallas as the best team.

Phil Allin was now mayor of a "League" city, one of only eleven such cities in the entire state of Texas.

The 11 Cities included:
Texas League:
> Dallas-Ft.Worth-Waco
> Temple-Greenville-
> Cleburne

South Texas League:
> Houston-Galveston-
> Austin-San Antonio-
> Beaumont

The South Texas League included one non-Texas town
- 12th city: Lake Charles, La.

Cleburne had arrived! Wednesday, April 25, 1906. The Texas League was less than two decades old, and now Johnson County had a league team, a wonderful ball park, men in new baseball uniforms with a block maroon **"C"** proudly sewn into the upper left chest. The few hundred fans that gathered that day were witnessing history, but many of the details of that day are lacking. Did the team issue a score card? What kinds of condiments were sold at the park? Exactly how many fans gathered in Gorman Park that day?

The Railroader team that took to the field was still a work in progress. Zena Clayton at third would soon be lost to Houston in a legal dispute. Cal Earthman started the season in centerfield, but would lose his job when Dee Poindexter became available. The legendary signing of Tris Speaker would not take place for another month. Parker Arbogast would replace Powell behind the plate.

Joe Gardner, the Dallas owner, had signed several strong players that made the Giants likely team to beat for the pennant. The defending champion Fort Worth Panthers was still a strong team. The odd teams out appeared to be Temple, Greenville, and Waco.

UPSIDE DOWN

While it was accustomed for the home team to bat last, Cleburne opted to bat first. And so for the first game ever to be played in Johnson County, the line score would be turned upside down, with Cleburne on top, and Dallas on the bottom.

FIRST PROFESSIONAL GAME IN CLEBURNE:
APRIL 25, 1906: INNING BY INNING DETAILS OF THE GAME

STARTING PITCHERS: Charles Pruiett (Dallas) vs. Walter Dickson (Cleburne)
Captains: Curley Maloney (Dallas), Ben Shelton (Cleburne) **Umpire:** S.A. Collins
Official Scorer: Charles H. Thacker **NOTE:** As home team Cleburne elected to bat first

BATTER BY BATTER SUMMARY OF GAME:
Cleburne, 1st: Roy Akin makes first out, fouls out to catcher; Zena Clayton base-on-balls; Ben Shelton strikes out, Criss fouls out 3B
Dallas: 1st: Sullivan grounds out, second to first; Maloney get the first hit, singles to right; Fink strikes out; Ragsdale at bat, Maloney caught stealing.

Cleburne 2nd: Powell flies out to center; Poindexter strikes out; Earthman pops out to second
Dallas 2nd: Ragsdale grounds out third to first; Meyers out, second to first; Ury grounds pitcher to first

Cleburne 3rd: Wright strikes out; Dickson strikes out; Akin singles; Clayton grounds out to first
Dallas 3rd: Burleson gets infield single; Bigbie flies out to center; Burleson steals 2nd; Pruitt doubles, Burleson scores (1-0); Sullivan ground out to first, Pruitt goes to 3rd; Maloney singles to right, Pruitt scores, (2-0); Fink strikes out

Cleburne 4th: Shelton grounds to first; Criss pops out to second; Powel singles; Poindexter grounds to second, safe on error; Earthman hits ball back to pitcher, out at first
Dallas 4th: Ragsdale singles; Meyer hits to short, Ragsdale forced at 2nd; Meyers steals 2nd; Ury singles, Meyer scores (3-0); Ury caught stealing; Burleson pops out to catcher

Cleburne 5th: Wright base-on-balls; Dickson bunt singles; Akin grounds out to first, runners advance; Clayton called out on strikes; Shelton strikes out swinging

Dallas 5th: Bigbie base-on-balls; Pruitt bunts, Bigbie thrown out at 2nd; Sullivan singles, Pruitt goes to 3rd; Malone at bat: double steal, Sullivan is thrown out at 2nd, Pruitt scores (4-0); Maloney strikes out

Cleburne 6th Criss grounds second to first; Powell out short to first; Poindexter grounds to third, safe on error; Earthman, pitcher to first
Dallas 6th Fink grounds out to first; Ragsdale out on long fly ball to center; Meyer base-on-balls, Meyer steals 2nd; Ury flies to center

Cleburne 7th: Bobby Wright long fly to left; Dickson grounds to first; Akin singles to right field; Clayton third to first
Dallas 7th: Burleson, chopper to the pitcher, out at first; Bigbie grounds second to first; Pruitt grounds pitcher to first

Cleburne 8th: Shelton singles past second baseman; Criss singles to center; Powell bunts ,close play at first, called out, runners advance; Poindexter base-on-balls (bases loaded); Earthman strikes out; Wright grounds to short, Poindexter forced at 2nd
Dallas 8th: Sullivan flies out to left; Maloney grounds short to first; Fink pops out to 3rd

Cleburne 9th: Dickson pops out to short; Akin grounds to first; Clayton singles; Shelton grounds second to first
Dallas 9th: DID NOT BAT, Wins 4-0

Cleburne Railroaders:

	AB	R	H	PO	A	E	RBI
Akin, SS	5	0	2	2	2	0	0
Clayton, 3b	4	0	1	0	2	0	0
Shelton, 1b	5	0	1	11	0	0	0
Criss, RF	4	0	1	1	0	0	0
Powell, c	4	0	1	4	2	0	0
Poindexter, LF	3	0	0	1	0	0	0
Earthman, CF	4	0	0	2	0	0	0
Wright, 2b	3	0	0	3	4	0	0
Dickson, p	4	0	1	0	5	0	0
	36	0	7	24	15	0	0

Dallas Giants

	AB	R	H	PO	A	E	RBI
Sullivan, LF	4	0	1	1	0	0	1
Maloney, CF	4	0	2	1	0	0	0
Fink, 2b	4	0	0	3	4	1	0
Ragsdale, c	3	0	1	8	0	0	0
Meyers, RF	2	1	0	0	0	0	0
Ury, 1b	3	0	1	12	0	0	1
Burleson, 3b	3	1	1	1	2	1	0
Bigbie, ss	2	0	0	1	2	0	0
Pruitt, p	3	2	1	0	3	0	1
	28	4	7	27	11	2	3

Cleburne: 000 000 000 - 0 7 0
Dallas: 002 110 00x - 4 7 2
Summary of Game: Earned Runs: Dallas 4, Cleburne 0
*Stolen Bases: **Dallas 3, Cleburne 0** SB: **Pruitt, Meyers, Burleson**, CS: **Ury, Sullivan, Maloney***
*Strike Out: **By Pruitt- 7; by Dickson –2***
*Base On Balls: **off Pruitt; 3; off Dickson 2** Extra Base Hits: 2B; **Pruitt(1)***
*Sacrifice Hits: **Dallas 1, Cleburne 2** Errors: **Fink(1), Burleson (1)***
*Time of Game: **1:50** Umpire: **Collins** Attendance: **Not Announced***

87

THE LUCKY KID IS BRIGHAM, WHOSE PAPA IS A MORMON ELDER. HE HAS TEN GRANDMOTHERS, ALL OF WHOM WILL NO DOUBT 'PASS AWAY' ON THE DAYS WHEN THE FORT WORTH PANTHERS ARE SCHEDULED TO PLAY HOME GAMES.

New Players...New Sports Writers
...End Fielders and Box Scores

When the Texas League arrived in Johnson County in 1906, the two Cleburne papers were suddenly thrust into the baseball reporting business. This was a city that had seen little more than a handful of scattered amateur games, with few, if any formal box scores, and little more reporting than generalized statements. Now with a team in town, the papers would not only have their usual readership to report to, they would be expected to wire summaries of the games all around the state. One of the primary driving factors for securing the team was the lure of the state wide publicity that the club would bring to Cleburne. It was understood that the newspapers would play their important role in disseminating details of the game, which would be included in hundreds of papers all over the state of Texas.

The papers did a surprisingly good job most of the time, and while they fell somewhat short of the Fort Worth and Dallas papers, nonetheless, there was enough detail for most fans, and certainly enough for the casual fan.

There was one slight breakdown early in the season, with the Cleburne Morning Review man referred to one of the Railroaders as an *END FIELDER,* although likely he blamed the copy editor for the obvious mistake.

TYPICAL BOX SCORE PUBLISHED 1906
*Note lack of Column for RBI

Dallas..

	AB	R	H	PO	A	E
Meyer, rf	4	0	1	1	0	0
Maag, 2b	4	0	0	5	4	1
Ury, 1b	4	0	3	13	1	0
Louden, ss	4	0	0	1	6	0
Sullivan, lf	3	0	0	1	0	0
Fink, 3b	3	1	0	1	2	1
Maloney, cf	3	0	1	1	0	0
Stevens, c	4	0	2	3	0	0
Garrett, p	3	0	0	1	1	1
* Pruitt, ph	1	0	0	0	0	0
Totals	33	1	6	27	14	3

Pruitt batted for Garrett in the 9th inning

Cleburne

	AB	R	H	PO	A	E
Aiken, 3b	5	0	2	1	2	0
Coyle, 2b	4	0	0	1	1	0
Powell, c	4	0	2	9	2	0
Shelfton, 1b	4	0	1	8	0	0
Whiteman, cf	4	1	1	5	0	0
Poindexter, lf	3	1	2	2	0	0
Speaker, rf	3	0	0	1	0	0
Wright, ss	3	0	0	0	1	0
Dickson, p	4	0	0	0	2	0
Totals	33	2	8	27	8	0

Score by Innings—
Dallas .... 010 000 000 – 1   [note: Dallas is listed at top in line score, but batted last]
Cleburne .... 010 100 000 - 2

Summary:
Two-base hits: Shelton, Maloney, Stevens; sacrifice hits: Poindexter, Speaker; left on base by Dallas 7, by Cleburne 9; Struck out by Garrett 2, by Dickson 9; double plays: Lounden to Maag to Ury, Fink to Maag to Ury; stolen bases Fink, Poindexter; Batter hit: Coyle; Time of Game: 1 Hour and 55 minutes. Umpire: Dunham

BALL PLAYER KILLS RABBITS

♣

Practices on Bunnies to Keep in Training and Throws Straight
Special to the News

Temple, Tex., May 26 – Catcher Kelsey of the Temple baseball team has been out of the game for the last two weeks nursing a broken digit. Kelsey has chafed under the forced vacation, and has been burning with anxiety to get back into service. In order to keep in shape and not lose out in throwing, he hit upon a novel expedient.

Close to the city is a large gravel pit and near by are farms ripe with golden fruit, the fields being thickly peopled with rabbits. Kelsey selected some hundred round pebbles about the weight of a baseball and began to practice on killing rabbits. After the first few days he recovered his proficiency and every day for the last week he has walked back into town with plenty of game swinging on his shoulder.

Up to date he has killed forty-two rabbits. Every rabbit killed has been winged on the run, the catcher scorning to try for one sitting still, and every one so far killed shows to have been struck fairly in the back of the head, testifying eloquently to the precision of aim attained by the catcher. It is thought that this record will excel that of Pitcher Criss of Cleburne, who recently killed thirty-seven birds, with the assistance of a gun and several obliging friends. Kelsey feels proud of his success and has the pelt of every rabbit to show for itself.

-----The Dallas Morning News May 27, 1906

GHOST TOWN TEAM
THURBER MINERS
SEPTEMBER 9, 1906

One of the famous ghost towns of Texas was a thriving community in 1906, including its own baseball team, appropriately called the Thurber Miners, since in fact the town was a coal mining town about 60 miles west of Fort Worth. Millions of bricks still being used today were manufactured in Thurber using the bituminous coal to fire one of the largest brick operations in the United States.

THE THURBER MINERS: 1906

Dan J. Shaughnessy, Manager
Robert McKinnon, Second Base
Charles Lowe, Captain, Catcher
James Tweed, Pitcher
Guy Wilkins, Third Base
Moran Rosse, Right Field
Bennie Campbell, First Base
Frank Francis, Center Field
William Stanton, Left Field
Sam Gordon, Shortstop
Gar Snapps, Backup Catcher

POST CARDS FROM THURBER

ZENA CLAYTON….Houston Bound

THE RED SNAPPER KID: Controversy at Third

Zena Clayton played for Doak Roberts in 1905 at Temple, where he led the league in doubles, while earning honors as the top fielding third baseman. As might be expected, Roberts was anxious to sign his all-star infielder to a 1906 contract as a member of the Cleburne Railroaders.

Unfortunately Clayton signed with the Houston club of the South Texas League, forcing Captain Ben Shelton to try a number of players at third base, including Dude Ransom, and a player with an unbelievable name of Scharmelefeld. None of the players proved satisfactory, and so Roberts called Clayton to offer him a new contract in Cleburne. Zena sent back a positive reply, and so Doak sent $20 to Houston to cover the third baseman's cost of transportation.

His arrival strengthened the team considerably, and after several preseason games, Zena Clayton was in uniform for the opening game at Gorman Park. However, Houston soon protested, reclaiming Clayton. Roberts argued but when Houston threatened legal action, the Cleburne owner decided not to prolong the process and released his prized player to Houston.

His departure left Cleburne with a gaping hole at third, and for several weeks Shelton tried to find a suitable player for the hot box. Finally at the end of May, Roy Akin moved from short to third, Bobby Wright took over at short, and Mickey Coyle became the regular second baseman.

Zena Clayton was from Corsicana, where he worked in a fish market in the off season. As the fans are want to do, he earned a nickname from some leather-lunged fan, who screamed *here comes the red snapper kid,* and the moniker stuck, to Zena's chagrin.

His career started with Austin College, but shortly afterwards he signed a pro contract with Ardmore's Texas League team in 1904. The following year he moved to Temple with Roberts.

In 1910 and 1911 he returned to Austin College as its coach, and finished his professional baseball career once again with Doak Roberts, this time in Houston in 1910. The next year he moved on to play with the Fort Worth Panthers.

Did the Cleburne fans sing "Take Me Out to the Ball Game" at Gorman Park? Not likely since Jack Norworth did not write the lyrics to the song until 1908. Did the fans buy Cracker Jack at their park? Perhaps. In 1896 the process for keeping the molasses clad kernels from sticking together had been perfected, making packaging possible.

TRIS SPEAKER
CLEVELAND " A. L.

VII

May 1906
TRIS SPEAKER SIGNED
DOAK ROBERTS' GREATEST FIND

MYTH AND MAN

THE CONTRACT:

On Sunday, May 20, 1906 Doak Roberts hitched his horse to his fine new buggy for the short ride to Corsicana's ball park, where the Nicholson-Watson Store team was gathering to play. Roberts took every chance to scout amateur and semi-professional teams for fresh talent, and over the years he signed hundreds of young men to personal services contacts. On this spring day in Navarro County, the owner of the Cleburne Railroaders would make the find of his illustrious baseball career.

The two men involved in the transaction that day varied in their recollection of the event. From Doak's perspective it was an eventful moment, to be recalled almost with reverence, one of the greatest days in his storied life. On the other hand, Speaker tended to view his life, especially those days as a youngster, in a flippant, carefree manner, adding a humorist twist whenever he could. Both men loved baseball, but Speaker viewed his profession more in "ah-shucks Texas modesty", often making himself the butt of the story. Despite his celebrated career on the big stage, Speaker kept his humble Hubbard roots up until the day of his death in 1958.

Roberts would eventually sell Speaker's contract "to higher company", but he never stopped marveling at the talent that brought immortality to the kid he inked in 1906. One of Doak Roberts' favorite souvenirs was Speaker's first contract for $50 a month.

.

SIGNED AND FINED: May 20, 1906

Doak Roberts tied his buggy up outside of the ball park, walked to his favorite spot in the stands to watch the semi-professional baseball club take to the field.

One of the legends of that day claimed that Roberts was there to scout another young man. If anyone remembers who that player might have been, his name has been lost to the ravages of time. There are no newspaper reports from that day in Corsicana. A fire years later destroyed the only copies of that city's newspapers from 1906.

Tris Speaker was a natural athlete who had starred on the sandlots in Hubbard before going to Polytechnic College in Fort Worth. Earlier in the year, at the end of the collegiate season, Speaker had written to every Texas and South Texas League team begging for a tryout, but his return trips to the mailbox were futile. No club responded to his requests. Needing both a job, and wanting to play baseball, Speaker landed on the Nicholson-Watson Store team, hired primarily as a player, as was the custom of the day. He had been a pitcher for the Polytechnic Parrots, but other times had played a variety of positions, including shortstop, a testament to his athletic ability.

Speaker was on the mound that day for the amateur Corsicana club. With Criss hurt, Cleburne needed pitching. Roberts watched Speaker's work as a pitcher, seemingly adequate, at least to the point that perhaps Cleburne could use him for an interim period, at least until Criss regained his full health. The key to the deal came from Speaker's appearances at the plate. A pitcher who could hit! An invaluable commodity! Pitcher Criss was a hitter, now with two pitchers on the squad that handle the bat would give Cleburne a huge advantage.

Polytechnic College Fort Worth where Tris Speaker majored in business while playing shortstop and pitching for the Parrots.

Tris Speaker's mother was opposed to him signing a baseball contract, which would allow him to be sold like a head of cattle.

After the game Doak Roberts invited Speaker to join him in his buggy to discuss playing for his Cleburne Texas League team. Still in his uniform, the promising young player climbed aboard the carriage to discuss his future. Roberts had in hand his standard contract, terms were simple. Compensation was fifty dollar a month, and the contract was a personal services contract to Roberts. It allowed him to trade his players at his own wishes. Tris Speaker was a delighted, excited young man, quickly agreeing to the terms, promising to report immediately to Ben Shelton, the Captain of the Railroaders. After signing the contract, Speaker leaped from the buggy to share his good fortune with his teammates.

As Roberts headed back home, he noticed that Speaker's cleats had left a permanent scratched on his prized vehicle. When Speaker received his first month's pay, it was $10 short of the $50 promised. The ten dollars was a "fine" imposed to pay for the repair cost of the buggy.

Tris Speaker's mother was not pleased with the prospect of her son being sold like a head of cattle. It had been her earnest desire to get him through college so that he could get a respectable job indoors. She should have known her son better. He hated the inside of a room, and was far too restless to endure the collegiate life. Baseball! It was his calling, and he would not be denied! With his signature on the contract, there was no stopping his ambition.

THE DOLLAR NOT SPENT

The Cleburne club was on the road in Waco, some 50 miles from Corsicana. Doak gave Tris a silver dollar to pay his train fare to Waco. Tris thanked the owner, but he was not about to buy a ticket when he could hop a freight for free. That afternoon, with fame and stardom in his future, Tris Speaker risked injury and danger to save a dollar, a hard to come by commodity. He called his mother, told her of his good fortune and headed to Waco.

And there came a rapping, a tap tapping at my door....

And now we have the recollection of Captain Ben Shelton's first encounter with Tris Speaker. It was early Monday morning, May 21, 1906. Sleeping soundly, he was not pleased by the loud banging at his door. (Rick Adams claims the time of the knock at 6:30 in the morning!) Ball players played in the daytime, the nights were theirs. Sleeping late was one of the luxuries of being a professional ballplayer, and any interruption of that ritual was not kindly accepted. Crawling out of bed to answer the door, Ben was greeted by an enthusiastic young man singing his own praises.

The old veteran Shelton was not impressed by seeing an 18 year at his door at this time of the morning. He let out a string of profanity, letting Speaker know that he would discuss baseball with him at a time of his choosing. Tris quickly retreated with his tail between his legs to await a more opportune time to impress his new boss.

One rookie to another....

Next to remember meeting Speaker that spring day was rookie pitcher Dode Criss, who had not pitched since May 1st because of injuries. Speaker was a left handed pitcher with a fresh arm. Criss encouraged Shelton to take a look at the young man who had just arrived. Criss needed rest, and so Ben Shelton watched the Hubbard youngster warm-up and was sufficiently impressed to put him in the pitcher's box that very afternoon. Speaker had arrived with almost no equipment, but Criss was quick to offer his cleats, pleased to share them in exchange for some much needed rest and time off to recover.

GAME ONE, A PITCHER

Monday, May 21, 4pm, Tristam E. Speaker took his first step in baseball, a journey that would culminate in his induction into baseball's Hall of Fame. Throwing from the mound for the first time as a professional, he faced the Waco Navigators. He looked good, giving up only four hits, impressing the Cleburne newspaper writers, who eventually took to calling him *our little Speaker*. In that first game, he lost the game 4-1, but he was not overwhelmed by the professional players. That afternoon he was a pitcher, but that would soon change. His true talent would be as a hitter and an outfielder.

....Dude Ransom's tragic end to his short baseball career

Dude Ransom was a 19 year old youngster from Corsicana, and over the years would develop a deep friendship with Doak Roberts. On this day, he was the team's regular right fielder. Speaker was sitting on the bench still learning the ropes of being a teammate on a league team. It was Wednesday afternoon, May 23. A crowd of about 300 had gathered at Katy Park for the finale of the Cleburne series. Dude Ransom stepped to the plate in the third inning against Lindy Hiett. Lindy was a thin, right handed pitcher. He sized up Dude, started into his windup, and let go a high, inside pitch. Wearing nothing more than his ball cap, Ransom ducked to avoid an errant pitch. He reacted an instant too late. The crush of the ball hitting his head echoed sickeningly through Katy Park, bringing a silence to the stands, both benches rushing to his aid. As he lay silently stilled by the ball, every player felt an appalling sensation. Each knew that it could have been them at the plate, their worst fear, and for Dude Ransom, it had become reality.

The young man was severely injured, disoriented. The game was stopped. A hack was summoned to speed him to the hospital. The horror-stricken players watched as the cab left the park, but there was still a game to be played. Umpire Spencer ordered the teams to their positions. Hiett was clearly shaken up by the mishap. Shelton needed a right fielder.

The young, brash Tris Speaker began yelling for the Captain to put him in. Speaker's enthusiasm at the chance of getting into the game offended his teammates. Still shaken at the sight of their friend lying on the ground, unconscious and bleeding, it was not the time for jubilation, even if you were a rookie getting a chance to play in the field for the first time.

Ben Shelton agreed to let him play, in large part because he did not have very many other options. Speaker took his glove and headed to right field. Ransom was hurt and a youngster the other players hardly knew was having a hard time hiding his excitement. His teammates were offended, especially one.

Mickey Coyle, playing second base, was particularly upset at the brazen young man's lack of respect to their fallen buddy, and took a strong dislike for Tris, so much so that the next morning he met the train carrying Doak Roberts to Waco.

Roberts had barely left then train before Coyle began to berate him, demanding that Tris Speaker be discharged from the team and be sent back to Corsicana.

Doak Roberts had been around hundreds of baseball players over the years and understood their volatile tempers as well as their cockiness, the later a trait he liked. It was not easy being a ball player on any level and those who succeeded more often than not had a heavy dose of moxie. He was not about to fire a young player full of promise no matter how obnoxious he was, at least not until he had discussed the issue with Ben Shelton.

Mickey Coyle, who was described in the day as a "feisty Irishman" took his disdain for Speaker to the club house. Speaker took the abuse as long as he could. The Railroaders were next scheduled to play Temple. Tris was one of the first players to board the train, and as he sat next to an open window, he saw Coyle walking by. Leaning from the window, he sucker punched the second baseman. Mickey Coyle had met his match.

Mickey Coyle was furious with the brash Speaker's insensitivity to Ransom's plight.

Ransom was rushed to Waco's Providence Hospital following the blow to his head.

96

Three days after making his first start, the rookie was back on the mound against Temple. His performance actually failed to match his initial outing, but circumstances being what they were, the lefty won the game, his first win against one loss. In two games Speaker had given up 11 hits and 6 runs, but disturbing to Shelton was the fact that he had walked 11 men. However, the other side of the coin was the young man's plate appearances. In his first 10 at-bats, he had 4 hits.

Shelton put the Hubbard boy on the bench for the next four days, putting him back on the mound against the mighty Dallas Giants on May 28th. The 18 year old pitcher soon discovered he was no match for J.W. Gardner's outstanding collection of hitters. Shelton left his pitcher in for the entire game, watching painfully with Dallas pounding out 12 hits, scoring 10 runs, and adding insult to injury, Speaker tossed five wild pitchers. The only positive that came out of the game was Tris Speaker's torrid hitting. With 2 more hits in four at-bats, his batting average at the end of the Dallas game was a lofty .429. Both Captain Shelton and owner Roberts were pleased in at least one aspect of the rookie's game.

After a day's rest from his exhausting pitching performance in Dallas, Shelton put his pitcher into right field in hopes of taking advantage of his bat. However, with five at bats the youngster failed to connect. After that day, he would not play again for almost 2 weeks. On June 9th Speaker was put back in the lineup against Fort Worth. His hitting returned to form, and along with his 3 hits was his first extra base hit, a double. At this point, with 9 hits in 24 appearances at the plate that day, the cocky pitcher-turned-outfielder was amongst the leaders in league with a .375 average, although 24 at-bats hardly qualified him for any title. Still, Shelton and Roberts could not help but to take notice.

Roberts was the more impressed of the two. Shelton saw no future for the lefty on the mound, but his hitting and natural athletic ability were obvious. The two men debated the future of their young star until June 14th, when at last Tris Speaker earned a regular spot in the lineup as the Cleburne Railroaders' right fielder. From that day forward he saw his future in baseball as a hitter and fielder. Once Tris had been inserted into the lineup as an outfielder, he had little enthusiasm for the mound, partly because of his other talents, but in larger part because he simply was not very good as a pitcher. His ego rejected failure.

However, because of fatigue, injury and double headers scheduled close together, Shelton called upon Speaker several more times to pitch. Of his 85 games for the Railroaders, Tris appeared in right field 75 times. Eleven times he took to the mound, finishing with a record of 2 wins and 7 losses, with two non-decision relief appearances.

Tris Speaker spent two years in the Texas League: 1906 in Cleburne, before going to Houston in 1907.

NEWSPAPER ACCOUNT OF SPEAKER'S PROFESSIONAL DEBUT

The sports columnist for the Waco Daily Times Harold was afforded the opportunity to be the first reporter to write about the future American League super star. Below is the article that the Waco fans read about Tris Speaker's first professional game:

May 22, 1906.........

KEEPS UP THE RECORD
When Navigators Took Another Game From the Cleburne Railroaders
A PITCHERS' BATTLE

Another pretty victory for the Dawkinites yesterday raised them in the estimation of Waco fandom high in the scale of ball players, and pitcher Dunbar, who allowed the Railroaders only three hits and but one until the ninth inning, made himself sold with every Indian in the village. It was a contest worthy of the followers of Dawkins and those lovers of the best sport in the world, who failed to see the game, missed a chance they might not have again.

It was a pitchers' battle, and while Dunbar got decidedly the best of it, Speaker, the new pitcher for Cleburne, did fine work. His one trouble was locating the plate, and as a consequence he issued five passes, but in handing the Skippers elusive curves, he was an excruciating success. They only found four of them and the same number were struck out.

Moran threatened to puncture Dunbar's reputation in the first inning and singled after Wright had popped out to Dawkins, but Shelton was a victim of a long fly ball to Hickey and Powell perished Bero to Hoffman.

Hoffman scored the first hit off Speaker in the third, but could not be stretched into a run. These were only hits until the last half of the sixth, when the Navigators made a dash for a landing further up the Brazos. Dawkins singled and drew second on Wright's error. Bero measured one for two sacks, but had not counted enough for Whiteman's sprinting and retired.

Barry grounded one to the pitcher, who threw quickly to second for a double, but Wright dropped the ball, and Barry and Dawkins were both safe.

Hickey popped a fly to the infield and Speaker and Coyle executed the Gaston and Alphonse with professional perfection, but as it was an infield fly, first and second bases were occupied, and only one man was out, so under the rules, Hickey was out. But Dawkins had advanced to third and Barry to second. Murphy came to bat and was greeted with cheers. He did not disappoint his confident admirers. A clean hit brought Dawkins and Barry home on a singled that enabled him to take home on a throw home, which was designed to catch Hoffman, but which arrived too late. Dunbar went out Wright to Shelton.

This ended the scoring until the ninth, Wright led off in the last inning with a two bagger and scored on Moran's duplicate. Shelton, Powell, and Poindexter each flied out to Barry, ending the game.
......**Waco Daily Times Harold,**
May 22,1906

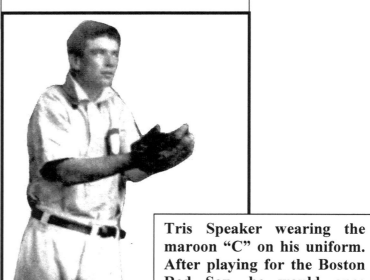

Tris Speaker wearing the maroon "C" on his uniform. After playing for the Boston Red Sox, he would once again wear a "C", this time for Cleveland.

NEGRO LEAGUE: Texas 1906
The Amazing One-armed Left Fielder

Stories of lynchings far outweighed any positive images of African-Americans in 1906, when *separate but equal* was the law of the land, be it *separate* was in reality the driving word. However, once in the summer of 1906, the local Cleburne papers carried an account of two *colored* teams that were to meet at Gorman Park. Cleburne took on the Temple in a double header on June 12, 1906.

Cleburne defeated Temple in both games, 6-5, and 10-5, with, as noted by the Cleburne Morning News, *the game was attended by a great many whites.* The story continued on: *the whites were awed by the one-armed left fielder for Cleburne.* The one armed Cleburne player was Oscar Frame, nicknamed *Fudge* by his teammates.

OSCAR FRAME.
ONE ARMED LEFT FIELDER

STARTING LINEUPS JUNE 12, 1906

TEMPLE:
D.M. SPENCER, FIRST BASE
A.L. ROBERTS, SHORTSTOP
C.L. COFFEY, SECOND BASE
R.L. GRIFFIN, THIRD BASE
J. SIMPSON, CATCHER
J. JOHNSON, LEFT FIELD
S. KELLEY, RIGHT FIELD
J.H. MOORE, CENTER FIELD
M. BROWN, PITCHER

CLEBURNE:
R. MATTHEWS, FIRST BASE
R. GRANBURY, SECOND BASE
J. LIGGIN, THIRD BASE
H. LEWIS, SHORT STOP
D. HERON, CENTER FIELD
O. FRAME, LEFT FIELD
HENDERSON AND SIMPSON,
 PITCHERS
M. FOSTER, CATCHER

UMPIRE:
KATHAN TOWNSELL

One-Armed Baseball Heroes

The story of Pete Gray is one of baseball's truly amazing stories, a one armed man who lived out his dream to play in the major leagues, when on April 17, 1945, he made his debut with the St. Louis Browns.

Long before Gray showed that a one-armed man could play baseball, Cleburne had its own one-armed baseball man, Oscar Frame.

When he turned fourteen, his father gave him a shotgun for his birthday. But the event was soon marred by a blast from the gun that cost Oscar his arm, and nearly his life. Young Frame was resilient, recovered from the accident, and was soon back with his friends skipping over the Johnson County countryside. Baseball was his sport of choice, and Oscar refused to succumb to the handicap of having only one arm. He taught himself to quickly shed his glove in order to throw the ball back into the infield in one smooth motion. His strength and dexterity allowed him to hold his own at the plate.

Oscar Frame, according to family tradition, later played in the major Negro Leagues. Unfortunately, his appearances in those leagues elude official records, leaving only oral memory as proof of his baseball career in the major Negro Leagues.

Baseball wasn't his only talent. Frame had a wonderful baritone voice, accompanied himself on the piano with his single hand.

Oscar from died in Houston, Texas on March 26, 1973. He was brought back to Cleburne for burial in the Chamber Memorial Cemetery. His sister Hortense Williams was, for many years, the principal for the Cleburne black high school.

Cleburne produced several other players who went on to the Negro Leagues, including the Maxwell brothers, Aaron and Zearlee, who was variously known as Knapp and Jiggs. Zearlee played for the Memphis Red Sox in 1938 as well as the Monroe Monarchs of the Negro Southern League.

This amateur photo from the late 1940's was taken in the "Negro Section" of La Grave Field, located far down the right field line.

For several years the Texas League operated under the Louisiana Rule. African-American players were not allowed to play in Shreveport, thus teams with black players were allowed to carry extra players insuring that they would have an equal number of players when the teams played in the Louisiana city.

Maury Wills broke the color-line in Fort Worth in 1954.

VIII

THE FIRST HALF CHAMPIONS
THE FORT WORTH PANTHERS

THE STORY OF THE MOST AMAZING AND EXCITING SERIES EVER
PLAYED BETWEEN FORT WORTH AND DALLAS
JUNE 27TH, 28TH, 29TH, 30TH 1906
GASTON PARK: DALLAS, TEXAS

A RIVALRY UNRIVALED
Fort Worth vs. Dallas

Say *Windy City* and you immediately think of Chicago. Say *Cowtown* and Fort Worth comes to mind. Say *Panther City,* and unless you are from Fort Worth, no city is likely to come to mind. But indeed Fort Worth is also Panther City, a name born of rivalry.

Long ago before the city fathers adopted the *Cowtown* moniker, Fort Worth referred to itself as *Panther City*, which doesn't make sense unless you know the origin of the reason for the adaptation of this nickname. Fort Worth is not a likely considered panther territory. The oft-told tale was a result of a Dallas writer seeking to insult his neighbor to the west. Dallas, much larger, and heaven knows much more sophisticated, was more apt to poke gentle fun of Fort Worth in lieu of any praise the smaller town might deserve.

Fort Worth it is said is such a sleepy dusty town that a panther was seen sleeping on its Main Street. Out of the insult was born a new image, so ingrained that in 1887 Bill Ward called his semi-professional team *The Panthers*, a nickname that has prevailed throughout the city's baseball history. Today the minor league team at the new La Grave Field is known as the *Cats*, a diminutive form of Panthers, created by newspapers in the '30s to save print space. Eventually the club's official name was changed from Panthers to Cats.

The rivalry between Fort Worth and Dallas was best expressed on the sporting fields, and for most of its history, on the baseball diamond. Both cities were charter members of the Texas League, and during the first 20 years, the heaviest gambling was done when the two cities met, be it either a routine regular season game, or especially when the clubs were battling for the pennant.

An unexpected playoff series....

In a series long forgotten, the Panthers were scheduled to play the last four games in June at Gaston Park in Dallas. When the season began, the four games were a part of the long season, but as often happened in the first two decades of the Texas League, cities dropped out of the league because of financial reasons. In 1906, Greenville began the decline, and Temple soon followed. The Texas league went from six cities to four. The owners decided for the sake of competition to divide the season into two halves, with the two winners meeting at the end of the season in a series of games to determine the league champion.

The repercussion of that decision thrust importance on that four game series, turning the routine set of games into a first-half championship playoff.

The Giants, picked to win the 1906 Texas League, was poised to take the first-half title, holding a commanding 1 ½ game lead over the Panthers going into those last four games. Split the series and they were the champs. However, Fort Worth still held its fate in its own hands. If they could win three of the four games, they would claim the unofficial first half flag, assuring themselves of a spot in the post season playoffs.

Dallas and its fans were cocky, in first place, and expected to remain so. The city was ready for the arrival of hundreds of Fort Worth fans, who planned to take the Interurban, a regional trolley-car line operated by the Northern Traction Company of Fort Worth. Gaston Park would be packed, with the additional 300-400 Fort Worth gentlemen there to root for their team…..a perhaps a few bets on the side to make the series *interesting.*

The four games played on June 27th, 28th, 29th, and Saturday, June 30th, may be the most exciting games ever played in this part of Texas, if only anyone remembered.

Dallas had not won the Texas League pennant since 1903, but owner Joe Gardner put together a collection of players that became the overwhelming pick to take the 1906 flag. Two pitchers were the backbone of the team, including Eddie Rodebaugh, and Charles Pruiett. Led by Captain Curly Malone, and hitters like Lon Ury, Clarence Fink, and Luther Burleson, the Giants appeared to have every other team in the league overmatched.

Maloney's team opened the season as advertised, winning the opening three game series in Cleburne, winning 7 of their first 8 games, and 20 of their first 25. Dallas was devouring the league. By May 23, barely a month into the season, Dallas was 6 games ahead of second place Greenville, and 7 ahead of Fort Worth.

While Gardner's team was marching through the Texas League season, there was trouble at hand. Every season, it seemed, since the inception of the league in 1888, at least one or two teams fell apart financially. In 1906 it was the Greenville Hunters, who despite their excellent field record, was failing to draw fans in sufficient numbers to pay the bills.

Greenville was one of the smallest, if not the smallest, city in the league with a population of around 12,000, a figure likely inflated by the city leaders. There simply was not a large enough fan base to support the club. Greenville, like Cleburne and Temple was not a *Sunday* town, and any chance of having large crowds on that day sunk any chance the Hunters might have had to succeed.

NO LONGER IN THE HUNT

The ugly situation came to public light on June 6th when the Greenville players refused to take the field against Cleburne unless they were compensated. The umpire declared a forfeit and awarded the game to the Railroaders 9-0. For a short while, the situation seemed to be resolved when the players were given a promise that they would be paid.

Eventually it came to light that Joe Gardner was secretly bank rolling the team in order to assure a six team could be fielded for the 1906 season. With poor attendance and cost mounting, Gardner became more reluctant to send money to Hunt County. By June 24th it was apparent that Greenville would go bankrupt and would be returning the franchise back to the league.

On that day the despondent Greenville Hunters took to the field against the Temple Boll Weevils. Their disgust with the situation led to a mockery of the game of baseball. Scheduled to play a double header, Greenville lost the first game by the weird score of 16-15. The attitude continued into the second game, and by the sixth inning they were trailing Temple 24-2. Before the start of the 7th inning, the players refused to continue the game, and the official result was a forfeit to Temple.

The league officials called an emergency meeting. It became apparent that there was no desire by the league to continue to operate the Greenville franchise. At times other leagues would assign the folded franchise as a perpetual road team in order to complete the season. For the Texas League owners, this was much too expensive for their taste.

Dropping Greenville would create a five team league, not impossible, but an awkward scheduling situation. The most satisfactory resolution was to drop the fifth team, and continue the season with four teams. The league would have to determine what team had drawn the short straw.

The choice came down to Cleburne or Temple.

Doak Roberts, as President of the League, was put into a difficult position with a conflict of interest, since he also operated the Cleburne franchise. His contract with the Cleburne Athletic Association was a double edged sword. The Association had guaranteed the finances of the club based on several specifics, one of which was to conclude the season. Dropping Cleburne would put Roberts personally at financial risk. Obviously his public position had to avoid the appearance of bias, and he had an excellent argument.

The Greenville Hunter's mascot was, as might have been expected, a bird dog. After 60 games in the Texas League, the team was dissolved for financial reasons, leaving the dog in mourning, and the players anxious about their professional future. The team went quietly, in large part because funding was primarily from the Dallas owner Joe Gardner.

Temple, ostensibly since they were located furthest away, was dropped from the league because of scheduling issues. However, the Temple players and owners were not willing to go away without a strong fight.

Temple was back in the league in 1907, while Greenville never again fielded a Texas League baseball club.

Temple was the southernmost city, the city farthest away, which in terms the other owners understood, meant higher travel cost. Fort Worth could travel a mere 30 miles to Cleburne, as opposed to over 100 to Temple. Visiting teams were only guaranteed $50, so a substantial savings in travel cost made sense.

Temple was dropped, but they refused to go quietly. Their owners threatened law suits, and at first the players showed up at the city on their schedule, demanding to play. It was all for naught. The Texas League would start the new schedule without Temple.

The league wanted to avoid problems that resulted from a similar situation in 1905. In the previous year when the league was forced to complete the season with only four teams, the decision was to continue the schedule, with all games counting in the standings. Those four clubs all finished above .500, creating a rather odd looking won-lost standings, since the two team that had been dropped no longer appeared in the standings.

In 1906 the owners decided a more satisfactory solution would be to split the season into two halves. The first half of the season would conclude June 30, with July 1st in essence becoming the opening date of the new season. The team in first place on June 30 would be declared the first half champions, and would meet the winner of the second half for the full season championship cup.

With the league's decision to split the season, the Dallas and Fort Worth players suddenly realized that their four game series had taken on a sense of urgency. It was the good fortune of the league that the first and second place teams just happened to be scheduled for the final four games of the first half. June 27th, 28th, 29th, 30th.

COST of OPERATING A TEXAS LEAGUE TEAM

Not a lot of information survives about the cost of operating a minor league franchise during the early days of the twentieth century. Teams were almost entirely dependent upon ticket sales for income. Of course there was no television or radio money, or little in the way of advertising, a few signs on the outfield walls, but little else. The teams needed butts in seats.

In August of 1904 Bill Ward was tired of the criticism he received as an owner, and decided to open his books for examination. The 1904 season was divided into halves, with Corsicana winning the first half with a record of 32-20, but the Panthers roared past everyone in the second, capturing the second half race with an incredible 40-10 record. Corsicana had won only 18 of their 49 second half games, and decided to add many of the better players from the Dallas team, while Bill Ward sold off star players from his club, leaving the Panthers vulnerable to the Corsicana team.

The fans and newspapers screamed loud and long at the Fort Worth owner, accusing him of giving the pennant away for a handful of money. The fans and paper even vented anger towards legendary Mike O'Connor, who was umpiring the post season series. Mike became so discouraged, he resigned during the series.

Bill Ward laid open the finances of his club and the league. He noted that by July of 1904 the Paris Reds club was abandoned by its management, the players finding themselves stranded at the White Elephant Restaurant in Fort Worth. Ward wanted to keep the Texas League viable and promised the players that he would bankroll the team until the end of the season. As a result, he was forced to sell some of the players to recoup his losses.

On August 24, 1904, Bill Ward released this information to the newspapers.

EXPENSES RELATED TO BASEBALL OPERATIONS: AUGUST 1 –AUGUST 24 1904	
PAYROLL	$1100.40
RAILROAD FARE	$104.00
HOTEL CORSICANA	
ARDMORE, DALLAS	$145.65
PRINTING/ADVERTISE	$45.00
EXTRA MEN	$27.00
GLOVE & CHEST PROTECT	$7.50
INCIDENTAL EXPENSES	$30.00
SCORER	$13.00
WAGON & SIGN	$13.00
UMPIRE	$55.00
LEAGUE DUES	$25.00
BALLS	$15.00
½ of AMOUNT SALARIES PARIS	$185.50
TOTAL EXPENSES	$1766.05
− TOTAL RECEIPTS	$1313.95
DEFICIT:	**($452.10) (loss)**

WITH GREENVILLE AND TEMPLE REMOVED FROM THE SCHEDULE THE TEXAS LEAGUE DECIDED TO DIVIDE ITS SEASON INTO TWO PARTS. THE FIRST HALF SCHEDULE WAS SCHEDULED TO END JUNE 30. FT. WORTH WAS 1 ½ GAMES BEHIND DALLAS WITH FOUR GAMES LEFT. BY THE FORTUNE OF THE SCHEDULE THE LAST FOUR GAMES IN JUNE WOULD AMOUNT TO A PLAYOFF SERIES FOR THE FIRST HALF PENNANT.

FOUR GAME SERIES NOW A PLAYOFF SERIES: JUNE 27-30th
FORT WORTH vs DALLAS: GASTON PARK

Dallas had started fast, but the Panthers had hung close by, and with only four games, their chances were slim, yet they still had a chance. Trailing the Giants by 1 ½ games, they would have to win 3 of the 4 games to land in first place on June 30th

.

TEAM	WON	LOST	GB
TEXAS LEAGUE STANDINGS JUNE 26, 1906			
Dallas	42	19	----
Ft.Worth	39	19	1 ½
Cleburne	34	24	6 ½
Greenville	27	30	13
Temple	20	39	21
Waco	14	45	28

The series created tremendous interest in the two cities, especially in Fort Worth. All four games were scheduled for Gaston Park, but thanks to the Fort Worth Pike, the dusty, bumpy road to Dallas, and the Northern Traction Interurban, a large number of Panther fans would be traveling to Dallas. The largest weekday crowd in the history of the league was expected.

For those Fort Worth fans who could not attend the games in person, they had two options to keep up with the game. The Fort Worth Star-Telegram operated a large scoreboard which would be updated throughout the game thanks to the telegraph. For the fans who needed more up to date information, they could gather in the 600 block of Main inside of Bill Ward's Restaurant, or just stand outside the door. Using the long distance phone, an employee of the restaurant would relay the results to the awaiting crowd.

The Northern Traction Company planned on adding additional cars to handle the expected crowd heading to Gaston Park in Dallas. The newspapers estimated as many as 300-400 Fort Worth fans would be going to Dallas.

FORT WORTH FANS LINEUP TO SEE THE RESULTS FROM GASTON PARK

GAME ONE: Jarvis vs Garrett

The series was almost over before it began. Jess Garrett brought a 6-3 record into the first game, opposing Ft. Worth's Red Jarvis at 6-2. The game had the makings of a pitchers' duel and both men were tough in the box. When it was over, Dallas had won, 3-1. Their lead over their archrivals was nearly insurmountable: 2 ½ games with but three to go. The Fort Worth fans headed back home despondent.

Fort Worth's Red Jarvis brought a 6-2 record into the first game of the four game series in Dallas

Lon Ury,
Dallas
First Base

GAME TWO: Dupree vs Pruiett

The Dallas pitching staff was a remarkable collection of men. Game 2 game would feature a future major leaguer, Charles Pruiett, who at this point was 11-4. However Fort Worth had a weapon of its own, Alex Dupree, with a sparkling 12-1 record. Again it was going to be a tough day for the hitters. However, as was common in the summer of 1906, rain threatened to kill the game, but it slacked off just before time for the first pitch. The two tense clubs took to the field, with Wirt Spencer calling the game.

Dallas needed only one more victory to wrap up the first half title, assuring themselves of a spot in the playoffs at the end of the season. Alex Dupree was expected to put up a tough battle, but he was being hit hard by the Giants, managing to hold the Giants to 2 runs in the first three innings. The two teams were tied at 2-2. Dallas ace Pruiett had allowed runs in the first and third innings, but appeared to be more in command than his counterpart on the mound.

Charles struck out the first two men he faced in the fifth, but then fell apart for the star pitcher. Fort Worth shortstop Walter Boles singled, and then was brought home by heavy hitting Walter Salm, who slammed a triple into left center. Owen Wilson was up next and singled, bringing Salm home for the second run of the inning. Both runs scoring after two were out. Pruiett held the hitters scoreless the rest of the way. The final score, 4-2. Once again Fort Worth was within 1 ½ game, with two remaining. The math was simple: to win the first half, the Panthers would have to win both of the remaining games.

STARTING PITCHERS

In the 5th Walter Boles singled, then scored when Walter Salm tripled, giving the Panthers the lead.

Walter Boles (L)

Charles Pruiett(R)

Again dominating pitchers got the call. Leo Walsh was 11-5 while Rodebaugh could best that number, with a 13-2 won/lost record. The Dallas fans were still quite confident. They had the better record, were at home, and had the ace of their staff on the mound. The intensity of the series brought out large crowds, and an equally large number of gamblers, openly plying their trade, without so much as a glance by the Dallas police. One writer at the Dallas Morning News decided to take a public stand against the law breakers.

The Dallas Morning News: [Hey! Guys, Let's Don't Gamble, or Cuss!]... *not actual headline*

The boisterousness has far exceeded that which sane people indulge, even at a base ball game, and the time is at hand when strong measures should be adopted to check it. ...furthermore, some of the players who have participated in these games should be given to understand without delay that profanity will not be tolerated hereafter..... it seems proper to devote some attention to a few practices at Gaston Park, which should be stopped without delay. One of these is that of betting on games. Since base ball became the National sport, the promoters have frowned down such things as this and frequently have had recourse to the plan of ejecting betters from the grandstands, for it is contended nothing more will speedily kill the sport....Dallas Morning News, June 30, 1906

The truth was that the league was not yet in the position to discourage betting. It was good for attendance and the league needed as many people in the stands as possible.

In Ft. Worth a large number of fans gathered Main Street. The White Elephant was crowded with fans lucky enough to have gotten inside, while the remainder stood along the side walk, all straining to hear reports of the game relayed from descriptions sent to Fort Worth via the telephone. As the trolley cars made their way up and down Main Street, they were forced to go slowly in front of the White Elephant Saloon, least they run over a baseball fan standing near the tracks.

For seven innings there was little to report. The two pitchers were in total command of their game, resulting in a 0-0 tie after seven. Then in the eighth there was that one dramatic moment that for years to come would be etched in the minds of those fans either in Gorman Park, or being entertained at the White Elephant. In Dallas there was a moan and silence. At the Bill Ward's place the roar was so loud that one trolley driver momentarily abandoned his passengers, rushing toward the noise to discover what had happened. He learned to his delight that Walter Salm had blasted the ball over the right centerfield wall. The Panthers had gained the lead, ever so precarious, 1-0. Before his mighty blow, Salm had struck out three consecutive times. Then with his dramatic homerun, the Fort Worth fans were ready to retrieve the homerun ball and hang it around the neck of the John Peter Smith monument. For Walsh the 1 run was enough.

Salm's homer had given Fort Worth the lead, but Dallas had one more chance to pull the game out. Sullivan led off the ninth by grounding out to first, but Curly Maloney revived hope with a single. With the Dallas fans standing and screaming, Luther Burleson grounded into a fielder's choice, Maloney out at second. Two outs, a runner at first. Right fielder J.G.Hackney carried a heavy burden on his shoulders as he stepped to the plate. He took a hard swing, but the ball popped into the air for an easy out. Dallas was now 43-21, while Fort Worth improved to a 41-20 record. After falling a distant 2 ½ games back, the team had put itself into a position to win the first half race.

Walter Salm, First Baseman

SALM   PHOTO BY BRYANT

Walter Salm's real name was Salmburger. He played in 15 Texas League seasons, appearing in 1,114 games during his illustrious career as a first baseman.

Leo Walsh compiled a 26-26 record as a left-handed Texas League Pitcher

Dallas pitcher *Eddie Rodebaugh* returned during the off season to Pennsylvania, where he was a coal miner.

TEXAS LEAGUE: June 29, 1906

	WON	LOST	PCT.	GB
Ft.Worth	41	20	.6721	½
Dallas	43	21	.6719	---
Cleburne	36	24	.600	5
Greenville	29	31	.483	12
Temple	20	41	.327	21 ½
Waco	15	47	.246	27

Going into the last game of the first half, the Texas League standings had the bizarre situation in which the first place team based on percentage was ½ a game behind second place Dallas. But it was all coming down to the last game. The winner would claim the flag.

Even though the season would only be half over, there was great satisfaction in beating the team that seemed so certain of a championship season, especially since that team was Dallas. Bill Ward could still remember those early days of the rivalry, back to the days of amateur ball, 1887. Now two decades later, Fort Worth still toiled under the perception that they were inferior to their sister city. But on this day, there was no doubt what city was best, and it had two heroes to prove it…Salm and Walsh!

The Fort Worth Telegram writer was in a jubilant mood, and ready to poke fun at his Dallas counter point. The city, home to Hell's Half Acre, laughed at the Dallas newspaper anxious to rid the game of gambling.

If it is wicked to bet on ball games, then there were several hundred sinners at the Dallas grandstand Friday, and a few thousand dollars changed hands on account of the way Mr. Salm rapped Rodebaugh. Policemen and deputy sheriffs swarmed about the place. There were even police from Fort Worth present, but what can a Fort Worth cop do in Dallas?

Ft. Worth Telegram

A CHAMPIONSHIP GAME IN JUNE:
GAME FOUR: Red Jarvis vs Jess Garrett
SATURDAY, JUNE 30, 1906

The largest weekday crowd in the history of the league squeezed into Gaston Park, Saturday still being considered just another of the six work days in the week. In an era of small rosters, pitchers were expected to be on the mound every third day, and so once again Red Jarvis and Jess Garrett would face off. Red hoped to redeem himself. At this point he was the only Ft. Worth pitcher to lose a game in this important series with Dallas.

June 30, 1906 was a momentous day in the Texas League. Temple and Greenville were gone. At least Greenville. The Temple owners and players were not yet willing to give up.

In Cleburne, the Railroaders played a double header. Walter Dickson twirled a no-hitter, while Tris Speaker easily won the second game, 10-2 against Temple, in what was the Boll Weevil's last game of the season. Greenville said goodbye to the Texas League with a 10-7 win over Waco. To add to the gravity of the day, the Railroaders pulled off a triple play against Temple. But all that was lost to the interest of the game in Dallas. Gaston Park was the only game of significance on June 30th.

With 1,894 paid fans crowding the stands, Dallas, the home team, elected to bat first. Dallas drew first blood. In the second inning Dallas scored first when Hackney hit a ball deep to

111

first, which Salm fielded cleanly, but Jarvis committed a horrendous mental error by not covering first base. Hackney was safe. Luther Burleson executed a perfect sacrifice bunt, sending Hackney to second and in scoring position. Charlie Pruiett, normally a pitcher, but today playing right field, hit a double to right, Hackney easily scoring, giving Dallas a 1-0 lead.

In the fourth inning Fort Worth evened the score. Cavender hit a sharp single to left field, but when Hackney ran over the ball, Cavender went to second on the error. Walter Boles attempted to bunt his way on, but was thrown out, Cavender advancing to third. Salm walked. Owen Wilson hit a hard ball to third baseman Meyer. Cavender broke for home, but was caught in a run down. As he was tagged out, Salm went to third. Again a grounder was hit to third, but this time Meyer juggled the ball, allowing Salm to score. Owen Wilson attempted to make it to third, but was thrown out. The score 1-1.

Owen Wilson thrown out at 3rd.

Three years after playing right field for Fort Worth, Owen Chief Wilson became the first native born Texan to play in the World Series as the right fielder for the Pittsburgh Pirates in the newly opened Forbes Field.

Going into the top of the ninth, the score remained 1-1. Remember that Dallas was batting at the top of the inning. Dallas looked as if they might take the lead. Hackney singled to right, and again Luther Burleson laid down a perfect sacrifice bunt, sending his teammate to second, with only one out. Then Carlin at third bobbled a ground ball, putting runners at first and third, one out. Catcher Ragsdale stepped into the batter's box. He hit the ball sharply, and for a moment the crowd leaped, but shortstop Boles leaped high into the air, snagged the ball, then threw to first, doubling up Pruiett at first. Red Jarvis had dodged a bullet.

The Panthers came to bat in the bottom of the ninth. For decades this would be one of the most remembered innings in the history of the Texas League. In the process, one man's career was destroyed. Men who had watched Texas baseball since 1888 agreed that the one deciding play in that inning was the single costliest play in the history of the league.

THE COSTLIEST PLAY IN THE HISTORY OF THE LEAGUE:
Luther Burleson, the Goat of 1906: Ft. Worth at Bat 9th Inning

Dred Cavender was up first. He hit a ball to deep short, Luther Burleson grabbed the ball and threw to first, but a step too late. Dred was safe. Jess Garrett suspecting that Cavender might attempt to steal second, attempted to keep him close to first, but an errant throw to first eluded first baseman Lon Ury, the ball going into right field. Right fielder Pruiett hustled to the ball, holding Cavender to second.

112

Walter Boles hit a ball back to Garrett. Dred Cavender broke for third base and drew a throw from the pitcher. The ball beat the runner, but Meyer failed to apply the tag. Now there were runners on the corners for Fort Worth with no outs.

Then it happened. A blunder of monumental status. Yesterday's hero, Walter Salm stepped to the plate. Garrett delivered the ball, which Salm slapped towards Luther Burleson at short. He bobbled the ball, but recovered. It would have been better if he had made a simple error, but what happened made him a goat for all time.

Instead of throwing the ball to the plate, as the slow Cavender lumbered down the third base line, Burleson instinctively threw to first. Salm was out, but of no consequence. The winning run touched home plate.

The Panthers jumped in jubilation, while the 300 Fort Worth fans went crazy. The hometown Dallas fans looked on in stunned silence, watching Luther Burleson as he bent over at his shortstop position, crying. The instant he let go of the ball, he realized the significance of his mental blunder. He didn't want to look, to have to face his teammates, or the 2,000 fans.

Watching his distraught shortstop, Captain Curly Maloney raced to console his young player. The disappointment of losing the game seemed the pale in Burleson's inconsolable agony. Curly Maloney had never seen a player so distraught. It was just a game, but to the players it felt like a death in the family.

Joe Gardner, the team owner, met with the sport writers after the game:

Poor Burleson. He is completely broken up over it and says he is going back home. He's quitting baseball.

Post Game Interview:

The writers may have had some sympathy for Luther, but still had to call the play as it was: *it was a dumb play...the costliest play..the likes of which has never been seen before in the Texas League.*

The Fort Worth fans may have had some sympathy, but were thankful for the blunder, which helped give them the flag. Fort Worth, winners. Dallas, losers. It had a nice ring back in Fort Worth.

The hundreds of fans watching the Telegram scoreboard, and those near the White Elephant saloon were jubilant. Liquor consumption was large that Saturday evening. Fort Worth: fans celebrating, their Dallas counterparts: drowning their sorrow.

Walter Salm was all grins following the Dallas series. His homerun Friday was the only run. Saturday he hit the ball that brought Dred Cavender home for the pennant winning run.

TRAGIC FIGURE OF 1906

LUTHER BURLESON

As Luther Burleson kneeled down at his shortstop position listening to the stunned silence of the Dallas crowd, and the cheering of the Fort Worth Panther fans that had traveled the 35 miles to Gaston Park, he swore that he would never play baseball again.

His career had started in 1904 as a part of Doak Roberts' Corsicana club. The next year he moved to Fort Worth, where he appeared in 64 games for the Panthers, even taking to the mound in one game.

In 1906 he was signed by Dallas as their third baseman, but by the end of June he had been moved to short. The fateful game was his 44th of 1906 and last game in professional baseball.

However, he did keep his hands in sports, and in 1908 was in Waco as the Baylor basketball coach.

In 1914 he had mellowed to the extent that he managed the Waxahachie Buffaloes of the Central Texas League. The following year he moved to Temple to manage their minor league team, the Temple Governors of the Middle Texas League (class D).

In 1909 Luther must have been deeply sympathetic to Fred "Bonehead" Merkle. They both suffered from mental errors committed in a crucial baseball game.

Picture of Dallas from their 1906 Scorecard

1, Pruitt; 2, Farris; 3, Williams; 4, Stovall; 5, Rodebaugh; 6, Ury
7, Fink; 8, Burleson; 9, Maloney, Mgr.; 10, Sullivan; 11, Bigbie
12, Metz; 13, Stephins; 14, Ragsdale; 15, Meyer.   Photo by Church.
DALLAS (TEX.) TEAM—TEXAS LEAGUE.

**FIRST HALF CHAMPIONS OF 1906
THE FORT WORTH PANTHERS**

During the summer of 1906, as the Railroaders battled their way to the Texas League pennant, one of the great players and characters of the game came into this world. On July 7, 1906 Leroy Robert Paige was born in Mobile, Alabama. Baseball fans would know him as Satchel, and mourned his death on June 8, 1982

SUNDAY: JULY 1,1906
SECOND HALF SCHEDULED RELEASED

THE DAILY ENTERPRISE, CLEBURNE, TEXAS

TEXAS LEAGUE BASEBALL SCHEDULE.
SECOND SEASON.

	CLEBURNE. At Home.	WACO. At Home.	DALLAS. At Home.	FORT WORTH. At Home.
CLEBURNE, abr'd	READ DAILY	July 7, 8, 9. July 29,30,31. Aug 1 Aug. 28, 29, 30, 31.	July 4 (2 games)5, 6 July 14, 15, 16. Aug. 17, 18, 19, 20	July 1, 2,3. July 21, 22, 23, 24 Aug. 9, 10, 11, 12.
WACO, abroad	July 17, 18, 19, 20. August 2, 3, 4. Aug. 21, 22, 23, 24.	ENTERPRISE	July 1, 2, 3. July 21, 22, 23, 24 Aug. 13, 14, 15, 16	July 4(2games)5, 6 July 14, 15, 16. Aug. 17, 18, 19, 20
DALLAS, abroad.	July 10, 11, 12, 13. August 5, 6, 7, 8. August 25, 26, 27.	July 25, 26, 27, 28. Aug. 9, 10, 11, 12. September 1, 2, 3.	FOR BASE-	July 7, 8, 9 Aug. 1, 2, 3, 4. Aug. 28, 29, 30, 31
FT. WORTH, abr,d	July 25, 26, 27, 28. Aug. 13, 14, 15, 16. September 1, 2, 3.	July 10, 11, 12, 13. Aug. 5, 6, 7, 8. Aug. 25, 26, 27.	July 17, 18, 19, 20. July 29, 30, 31. Aug. 21, 22, 23, 24	BALL NEWS

116

SHOCK IN DALLAS: Fire Sale

On July 2nd Dallas owner Joe Gardner, still stinging over his loss to Fort Worth, announced shocking news to the fans of Dallas that popular pitcher Charlie Pruiett had been sold to St. Paul of the American Association. A second player was also sold to the American Association team under the condition that Captain Curley Maloney could find a replacement for Clarence Fink. Gardner would later claim that he was forced to sell off his players to recoup some of the losses he incurred operating the Greenville franchise, and the drop in attendance following the disappointing Fort Worth series. The Greenville franchise had folded, Temple, before being dropped from the league, struggled financially, and in Cleburne the entire season was played behind a backdrop of monetary issues.

Clarence Fink should be reported to the Dallas Police Department for loitering during yesterday's game.
The Dallas Morning News June 12, 1906

SALARY
Tris Speaker signed on to play for Cleburne at a rate of $50 a month. How did that compare with salaries outside of baseball? Below is an article from the spring of 1906 that listed the salary for the street foreman in Cleburne.

RECOMMEDATION
$65 Per Month
We would recommend that the present fire chief, Mr. John Cashion, be appointed foreman of the street work, to whom the street working forces can look to for detailed instructions, and to whom the mayor and the general council and street committee can look to for results, and in view of such responsibilities we recommend a salary of $65 per month be paid him, and that an extra driver be employed to work the team that Mr. Cashion now Drives.
Cleburne Enterprise, April 28, 1906

A PLAYER'S DAY: 1906
Schedule

8am	Breakfast
9am	Write & Receive Letters
10-12	Recreation
Noon	Lunch
1-2pm	Dress for Game
2:30	Warm-up
4pm	Game Called
6:30	Dinner
7:30-9:30	Recreation

A $$$$TRUGGLE IN CLEBURNE

Problems Start Early: Roberts Threatens to Move the Team Back to Corsicana: May1,2,3

When the Cleburne Athletic Association signed its contract with J. Doak Roberts, they in fact were signing on with a secret partner in the deal. Behind the scene was Lola Roberts, Mrs. Doak Roberts. She had patiently watched her husband sink good money into his baseball hobby, first in Corsicana, then Temple. Having failed to halt the bleeding of money in Temple, it was for that reason that Roberts was lured into Cleburne. His old friend Charles Thacker had assured him that the Association would underwrite any losses he might incur operating the team in Cleburne. Otherwise, why would he have brought the team to this small hamlet? Lola was putting pressure on Doak to stop throwing good money after bad.

It was not from lack of trying or good faith, the reality was that Cleburne was very small. The published census was 14,000, but that was a chamber of commerce number. The city was likely barely over 9,000 in population, and it was mostly a blue collar community, with the Santa Fe yards, being the largest employer. Night baseball was still only a concept. Games started at 4pm all across the league, and attendees were in large part from the business community, except on holidays and Sundays when the working men were off and could attend. Cleburne did not have Sunday ball, and there were not enough holidays to make a dent in the attendance figures.

The 1906 season was barely into the first week when Owner Roberts announced that he was taking the team to Corsicana for a three game series with Waco. In what should have been its finest hour, opening week, Cleburne's attendance had been woeful. It was not necessarily totally the fault of the city. At the very time that baseball was in town, it had to compete for the entertainment dollar with a huge circus and carnival. Baseball would be in town for the whole summer, while the carnival would be in town for less than a week.

Doak Roberts' announcement to move three home dates infuriated many of the members of the Cleburne Athletic Association. It was clearly a breach of the contract between the organization and Roberts. The association clearly felt embarrassed by Roberts' action. From Temple there were disparaging reports from their businessmen, *who would never have allowed their team's home games to be moved.* Their snide remarks were likely based upon the resentment of having lost much of their 1905 personnel to Cleburne.

The move to Corsicana had deprived the local Cleburne fans from seeing their team's first win of the season, a 7-1 lopsided win over Waco. However, Roberts released information that the transfer had been successful. The game in Corsicana had brought in $113 to the register. The Cleburne businessmen were both incensed and humiliated; first that the move had taken place and that the Corsicana fans had turned out in larger numbers than in Cleburne.

118

THREE BALL GAMES AT CORSICANA THIS WEEK

Manager Roberts Will Take the Cleburne Team to Corsicana this Week to Play Waco.

Manager Roberts was here Monday morning getting ready to go to Corsicana, where he had been offered a $300 bonus to play the three games with Waco. Since Cleburne has had so many carnivals and shows of every kind he thought it would be a good scheme to try and change luck by playing the games there and at the same time give the Cleburne fans time to catch up on sleep and get ready for the return of the team. The team will go to Dallas on Friday and will play there Friday, Saturday and Sunday afternoons. On Sunday a big crowd is going up from here to see the game. The Cleburne team will then go to Greenville for three games and will be back here on May 10th to try and take three straights from Waco. The Cleburne team is only taken to Corsicana to try and catch up on a little shortage, that has crept into the exchequer since the opening of the season.

The Cleburne team is taken to Corsicana to try and catch up on a little shortage that has crept into the exchequer since the opening of the season…Daily Enterprise 5/1/1906

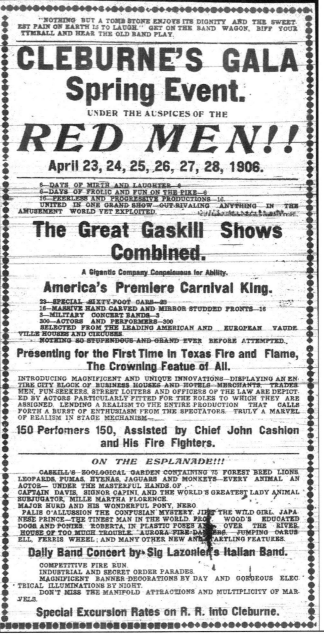

There was not a lot of money to be spent on entertainment in 1906. During opening week of the new baseball season, the big circus came to town, severely impacting attendance at Gorman Park.
An ad from Cleburne Morning Review April 1906

COST OF OPERATING A TEAM FOR ONE GAME:

Doak Roberts had been involved with Texas League baseball long enough to well understand the financial risk he was undertaking when in 1902 he took control of the Corsicana franchise. From its inception in 1888 until the demise in 1899, the league struggled every year to complete a season schedule. When the league was revised in '02, Roberts was a successful businessman who could, and often did, reach into his own pockets to keep his club financially viable.

By 1905 his patience with the financial ledger had grown thin, and it was only with the promises made by the association of businessmen in Cleburne that had persuaded him to move his operations to Johnson County. Despite the urgings of Charles Thacker, the Athletic Association was finding the reality of writing checks was far more difficult than making preseason promises.

Thin attendance at Gorman Park was making it evident that the Cleburne gentlemen were going to be obligated to move their personal funds into the operations of the Cleburne Railroaders. Despite the agreement between the city and Roberts, the Corsicana citizen was still being forced to use his own personal assets to make payroll. This was not what he had bargained for when he moved his team from Temple.

Tension mounted all through the first half of May, with threats of moving the team permanently to Corsicana. From an article that appeared in the Dallas Morning News, Roberts announced that he had been given permission by the league *to follow his own pleasure in the matter of transferring the Cleburne franchise to some other town.*

Still threatening the city, Doak stated that the three game series with Dallas May 4th, 5th, and 6th would be played in Cleburne *for the purpose of making another attempt to ascertain if the games will pay expense.*

Roberts was in no mood to continue to support his team from his coal and wood businesses. The meetings with the Association were cantankerous and to the point. If they wanted to keep their team, the organization would have to match their rhetoric, guarantee the money, or lose the team.

Swagger and pride prevailed with the businessmen publically announcing: *...as the season had been commenced here, it would never do to allow Manager Roberts to feel dissatisfied, and for that reason the Association has an obligation to guarantee him against any loss, either in rainy or fair weather.* The double header scheduled in Cleburne on May 6th was rained out. Rainouts and lack of Sunday games were taking their financial toll.

Cleburne was not the only town in financial trouble. On May 19th Ewing Edens, also from Corsicana, announced he was selling his franchise to the local Temple businessmen.

It was a tough time for Texas League baseball. Greenville, Temple, and Cleburne were all in serious financial trouble.

Despite the promises by the local business association to keep the Railroaders in Cleburne, the feeling of unease about the solvency of the team prevailed throughout the season. Would they stay, be moved, or simply be dissolved? Roberts was constantly aware of this situation throughout the season.

On July 18th, Tim O'Rourke, the old St. Louis Brown player, and one of the more renowned baseball scouts of the time, came to town, making the local Cleburne newspapermen nervous about the impact he would have on their team: *he has his eagle eye on several players for a week. He is looking at Criss and Moran, and perhaps Dickson. St.Paul is willing to pay a bonus for them, and the players would be getting bigger salaries and of course are anxious to advance.* O'Rourke's appearance added more alarm to the status of the Railroader franchise.

About that time, rumors began circulating that the team would be sold to a group of businessmen for $2,000. The only businessman who supported this notation was Joe Hubbard, declaring he would take $50 worth of the team stock. But nothing else about the potential sale was forthcoming: *last night a Review man mixed among the fans but nothing newsy could be picked up.*

Cleburne Daily Review, July 17, 1906.

Attendance figures were seldom given in 1906. Sometimes there would be a vague reference to the stands: *a large crowd, greatly attended by ladies.... a sparse crowd... etc.* On June 29th, perhaps at the goading of Doak Roberts, the local paper decried the lack of attendance, noting that the take was only $70 for the game. At a quarter a ticket, based on $70, the attendance would have been about 280, short of the 400 to 500 needed to make the game a break even proposition. With expenses running about $105 per game, income was 30% below what it should have been. Despite warnings from Roberts, attendance at Cleburne continued to lag.

Lured by the Association's promise, Roberts kept the Cleburne Railroaders in Gorman Park for the remainder of the season. By this time Roberts had despaired about his ability to carry on and continue his association with the Texas League. He had to go home to Lola and explain it all to her.

THIS ROOSTER CROWS FOR CLEBURNE

CLEBURNE WINS FROM WACO—EASY WINNING—7—TO 1

3 CLEBURNE HOME GAMES MOVED TO CORSICANA

The start of the 1906 season was disastrous for Cleburne. Three straight losses to Dallas, then three more to Fort Worth left the team 0-6. Then there was the discouraging news that Roberts was transferring the next three scheduled home games to Corsicana. With the Railroaders *at home* in Corsicana, the team finally won its first game of the season over Waco by 7-1.

The Cleburne papers treated this first win as if

On May 1 Cleburne won its first game. It was a "home" game that had been moved to Corsicana.

LOLA ROBERTS: Years later, when Doak Roberts was associated with Houston and no longer faced the constant financial struggles of his earlier days, Lola Roberts remained frugal. Dode Criss shared stories with his family about her legendary miserly ways. Lola had seen too much money lost to her husband's baseball franchises, and could never overcome the fear of his continued association with baseball. Despite his wife's objection's Doak prevailed. He died a baseball man.

121

"BIG MOIKE IS DEAD"
Mike O'Connor
One of the Famous Characters of Texas Baseball History
June 17, 1906

Back in 1887 Bill Ward decided to take baseball seriously in order to defeat the much hated Dallas team, he shelled out the dollars it took to sign Mike O'Connor, who brought a huge frame into the game, 6'5", intimating, and described as *Celtic pugnacious*. In 18 years in the Texas League, he played for and managed eleven different teams. In 1894 he batted .401.

When Mike was added to the team, he was selected as the captain of Bill Ward's Fort Worth Panthers. However, his most successful season came fourteen years later when he piloted the Corsicana Oil City team to an incredible 88-23 record, a .791 percentage. Only one other professional team has topped that winning percentage. On that 1902 was the 1906 Cleburne Captain, Ben Shelton, along with Curley Maloney, the Dallas leader. Future Fort Worth manager Walter Morris was at short for O'Connor's team.

On June 15, 1902, Texarkana was scheduled to play Corsicana in their park, but because of the Sunday blue laws Mike's team was forced to go to nearby Ennis to play the game. Site of the game that day was truly a bandbox, with the right field reportedly 210 feet from home plate. The 1902 Corsicana newspapers were destroyed by a fire and so little remains of that game from a contemporary standpoint. Historians have had to rely on memory, and as evidenced when facts are obtainable, memory is a poor substitute for the mundane reporting by a local newspaperman.

In one version, the owner of the Texarkana Casketmakers sent his son to Ennis to pitch. Cy Mulkey, Captain of the visiting team, was so disgusted with the meddling, that he left C. B. Dewitt in the game for its entirety, as he watch Corsicana win by the incredible score of 51-3. Justin "Nig" Clarke made history that day by slamming eight, yes "8" homeruns over the short right field wall.

The Texas League split the 1902 season, with Corsicana winning both halves, (30-14) and (58-9). There was little doubt as to the champions of 1902.

Mike worked in the off season as a railroad man.

In 1905 his health began to decline, and without long term health facilities, he was placed into the state hospital for the insane. When he died, his body was shipped to Marion, Ohio for burial alongside his mother and two sisters.

Upon hearing of his death, Manager Curley Maloney declared: "Mr. O'Connor was the greatest baseball strategist in Texas."

A Remarkable Stunt
NINETEEN INNING GAME: JULY 23, 1906
THE STORY OF ONE OF THE MOST AMAZING GAMES
IN THE LONG HISTORY OF THE LEAGUE

Sunday, July 22

In 1906 it was the custom for only one umpire to work Texas League games, and, at times, the $75 a month salary hardly seemed worth the constant abuse the lone arbitrator had to endure. One such day of ill-treatment occurred on a blistering Sunday afternoon game in July. On that day the starting time at Haines Park was 3:30, in the heart of the heat of the day.

Rather than to continue fighting the scorching heat, the fans began to drift down onto the field, in foul territory down the right field line. There was a bit of shade offered by the stands as the sun began its descent.

Being that close to the action, the fans verbal abuse of Umpire Dunham became more threatening. Had the fans alone been the source of the bickering, Durham would have easily handled the situation, but Captain Dred Cavender along with pitcher Charles Merkel, yelped at every call that went against the Panthers.

Captain Dred Cavender

Through seven innings the hometown supporters were, while loud, not out of control. But then in the eighth inning all of that changed. Cleburne began to rally, thanks in large part to a very controversial call by the umpire.

Parker Arbogast, Cleburne's catcher, walked. Rick Adams hit a ball to Clayton at second. In his haste, the second baseman threw wide of first and the ball landed in the midst of the fans sitting in foul territory along the first base line. Walter Salm could not get to the ball, lost amongst the fans, allowing Parker to race all the way home from first, as Adams hustled to third.

Captain Cavender and first baseman Salm were livid. They yelled that the ball should have been called "a blocked ball." *"You saw those fans sitting there. You should have established a ground rule in case a ball landed there."*

Had Dunham invoked such a rule, then the runners could have advanced only one base. The umpire screamed back: *There is no such rule. If you were worried about the fans, then it was up to the Fort Worth officials to see that the fans were kept clear of the field.* Dunham stood by his ruling, and when Adams later scored from third, the Railroaders took the lead, and eventually held on for a 2-1 victory.

When the last out was recorded, the Fort Worth fans began an alarming diatribe directed at the frightened Dunham. As the umpire attempted to walk towards the exit, a large number of fans gathered at the gate, gesturing menacingly. The umpire feared he would not escape unharmed.

Charlie Moran, the Cleburne utility man, who himself had at different times umpired, and well understood the difficulties of officiating, slung a bat over his shoulder. He walked to the side of Durham, and as the two men approached the gate, in a voice that no one could mistake, Moran screamed: *If anyone wants to start a ruckus, be prepared to get your coconut cracked!* The crowd hastily backed down, and the umpire left as quickly as he could.

Durham returned to his hotel room, and quietly checked out, taking the first available train out of Fort Worth. At this point, he did not care that he was scheduled to work the next game on Monday.

Charles B. Moran would later umpire in the National League for 22 years, but on this Sunday afternoon he was just a utility player for Cleburne intent on keeping Umpire Dunham from bodily harm.

If anyone wants to start a ruckus, be prepared to get your coconut cracked!

		R	H	E
Cleburne Railroaders	000 000 000 000 000 000 0 - 0	9	4
Fort Worth Panthers	000 000 000 000 000 000 0 - 0	6	2

Monday, July 23rd

The hostilities of Sunday were mostly forgotten the following day. Perhaps it was the unexpected cool night, with temperatures uncharacteristically dropping into the 50's, a pleasant change of pace for the Texas summer.

At 4:30, Monday, July 23rd, 1906, under threatening skies, Cleburne and Fort Worth once again prepared to do battle on the diamond. However, not quite 24 hours since Durham had faced mortal danger, he was not to be seen. There was no umpire available for the game. The teams would have to huddle and find a solution. The game would be played with or without Umpire Durham.

The Panthers planned to pitch Alex Dupree, one of the premier pitchers in the Texas League. He would finish the season with a 24-8 record, including two no-hitters. Ordinarily Ross Emil *Mike* Erwin would complete the battery for Fort Worth. But on this Monday, he was injured, and his spot behind the plate was deferred an old timer, Emmet Rodgers, who, in 1906, was the only player in the Texas League still playing who had played in the league's first season in 1888. Rodgers was on his last leg, while Irwin was just beginning his fabulous career that would end with him playing for Brooklyn of the National League. However, on this Monday, on what would prove to be a *remarkable stunt*, the spotlight would belong to the old hind-catcher.

Cleburne's battery was no slouch. In the box for the Railroaders was Walter *Hickory* Dickson, who himself had pitched a no-hitter when he shut down Temple on June 30th.

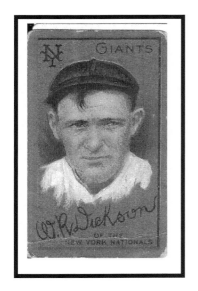

The two managers got together, and in place of the missing umpire, they selected one man from each squad to share the umpiring duties. Ironically, the man who had escorted Durham from danger, Charles Moran, was one of the men selected to call the game. The Fort Worth representative was catcher Mike Irwin. Moran would be behind the plate, and when he took the megaphone to announce *Play Ball*, much of the intensity of the previous afternoon seemed to be missing. Part due in fact to the very small crowd that had gathered. The threat of rain no doubt had played a large part in the deterrence of the crowd.

The first two innings were quickly gone. In the third, in what would prove to be an ominous decision, and what might well have started an angry reaction, went by with hardly any protest. Big Walter Salm hit what appeared to be a triple down the third base line. But, while standing on third, umpire Moran called Salm out for failing to touch the first base bag. There was a small fuss, but the bickering was short lived.

Soon the fourth, fifth and sixth innings passed with no scoring. Then the seventh, eighth and ninth innings went by without a run. The game would now go into extra innings. The Panther fans screamed for a score, so that they could go home to supper with a victory under their belt. But to no avail. Walter Dickson saw to it that Fort Worth was held scoreless. Alex Dupree continued to do likewise.

After the eleventh more zeros were added to the scoreboard. One newspaperman yelled, "Let me borrow somebody's cuff... I've just run out of paper!" The eleventh seemed likely to see an end to the deadlock. Future St. Louis Brown star Dode Criss, used his entire six-foot two frame to slug a deep double to centerfield. George Whiteman, the ex-Panther, sacrificed Criss to third, but Poindexter up next failed to get Criss home. Youngster Tris Speaker was in the on-deck circle. Captain Ben Shelton, anxious to get the game over with, decided to call back his right fielder, and inserted himself as a pinch hitter. Years later, looking back on this decision, Shelton would chuckle. Eventually Speaker would go to the major leagues and compile a lifetime .344 average. Shelton would marvel at his audacity to have pulled Speaker. But on this July day in Texas, the Railroader Captain, took his spot at home. The umpire announced to the crowd: *Pinch hitting for Tris Speaker.....*

Shelton hit a sharp drive between third and short. Walter Boles stretched out, knocked the ball down, and in a close play at first, he threw out Shelton. The game would continue at 0-0.

In the fifteenth inning it was Fort Worth's turn to threaten. Pitcher Alex Dupree walked, was sacrificed to second by Boles. Ollie Gfroerer hit a high pop up to Wright at second Owen Wilson, who still holds the major league record for triples in one season, batted next. He lined a hard shot to center. It bounced once and centerfielder George Whiteman was able to field it cleanly and fired a strike to home, where Dupree was out sliding.

The exhausted Dupree then had to walk to the mound to start the sixteenth. George Whiteman yelled out, bringing wails of laughter from the fans and the players as well: *We will break this up when the moon rises!*

But Whiteman had bragged too early. The seventeenth, eighteenth, and nineteenth innings passed still without a score. In the bottom of the nineteenth it looked again as if the game might finally end. Dred Cavender drew a walk, stole second, and then went to third on an error by Pitcher Dickson. With two outs, the winning run at third, it came down to pitcher-versus-pitcher as Alex Dupree came to bat. Dupree hit a grounder to Mickey Coyle at second, who fielded it cleanly, and threw out the runner at first.

And with that out, umpire Charlie Moran threw his hands into the air, and declared, "Game called: **Darkness!**"

Nineteen innings, without a score. It seemed fitting that the game should end in a tie. Neither team deserved to lose. Both starting pitchers were there for the final out.

Nineteen innings! The game had lasted two hours and fifty minutes!

DON'T YOU WISH YOU HAD BEEN THERE!

Earlier that afternoon, about 4 o'clock an 11 year old boy saw the banner on Main Street advertising the game between the Panthers and the Railroaders. He was an avid fan, knew the players, even the visiting team members. He considered going, but there were dark clouds lurking about. The day had been heavy with the threat of rain, cool, an unusual Texas summer afternoon. It was a short ride from where he was by trolley car to Haines Park, but the nickel charge seemed an unlikely investment, what with the game likely to be rained out. He decided to keep the five cents, and headed home. There of course was no radio to broadcast the game. It would be the next morning before he would discover that not only had the game not been rained out, it was an historical game. Nineteen innings, 0-0. He clipped the game summary from the paper. Agonized over the last sentence…. *Don't you wish you had been there…..*and indeed did he wish he had been there! The missed opportunity haunted him until the day he died.

In 1950 55-year old Gardner was reading the Dallas Morning News, when he saw a reference to the famous 19 inning game played forty-four years earlier. The pain of having missed the game back then was still there. The memory of that missed opportunity was rubbed raw by the 1950 article. Just as he had clipped an article about the game when he was 11, he repeated his actions when he was 55. He cut the Dallas Morning News article out of the papers. He sent the clipped article to a relative of Walter Dickson, one of the two pitchers who toiled those 19 innings without giving up a run.

Forty-four years after he decided not to spend his nickel for the ride to Haines Park, Gardner Godwin still bemoaned his decision that day, having missed the historical 19 inning 0-0 game between Cleburne and Fort Worth.

Gardner penned the following letter to Virginia Bond, whose aunt was married to Walter Dickson's brother:

W. G. Godwin

July 24, 1950

Dear Virginia:

Thought you might like to send the enclosed clipping to your aunt. Even though I was only eleven years old when Hickory pitched the greatest game in the history of the Texas League, I well remember the day. I was downtown and started to hop a street car, one of the open summer kind, but it was cloudy and rain threatened, so decided at the last moment not to go. I have always regretted it. In that game was the Great Tris Speaker, one of base ball's immortals. Also Dode Criss who later led the American League in batting. Both on the Cleburne team. Fort Worth had Owen Wilson who later was a sensation at Pittsburgh, and even to this day holds the record of having made more three base hits than any man in the history of the game.

I had a newspaper account of the game which I treasured, but let a man read it, and never saw it again. Just proves that if we have anything we treasure, we should never let it out of our hands.

Gardner

***Gardner saved a nickel
then spent the rest of his life in regret.***

Fort Worth Panthers	AB	R	BH	PO	A	E
Boles, ss	7	0	1	2	4	1
Gfroerer, cf	6	0	0	4	0	0
Wilson, rf	6	0	1	6	0	0
Salm, 1b	7	0	1	24	0	0
Carlin, 3b	7	0	3	4	5	1
Cavender, lf	5	0	0	7	0	0
Rodgers, c	7	0	0	9	2	0
Clayton, 2b	7	0	0	1	6	0
Dupree, p	5	0	0	0	4	0
Totals......	57	0	6	57	21	2

Cleburne Railroaders	AB	R	BH	PO	A	E
Aiken, 3b	8	0	1	0	1	1
Coyle, 2b	8	0	0	3	10	0
Criss, 1b	8	0	4	25	0	0
Whiteman, cf	8	0	2	3	1	0
Poindexter, lf	8	0	0	2	0	0
Speaker, rf	6	0	0	3	2	0
Shelton, rf	2	0	0	0	0	0
Arbogast, c	8	0	0	9	2	0
Wright, ss	7	0	1	11	9	2
Dickson, p	7	0	1	1	7	1
Totals.........	70	0	9	57	32	4

Score by innings:

Cleburne	000	000	000	000	000	000	0	- 0	9	4
Ft.Worth	000	000	000	000	000	000	0	- 0	6	2

Summary:- Stolen bases: off Arbogast 4; two base hits: Criss, Whiteman, Salm; double plays: Dickson to Wright, Speaker to Arbogast to Wright; Struck out: by Dupree 9; by Dickson 7; Bases on balls: off Dickson 2; Wild pitches: Dickson; Batter hit: Dickson; Passed balls: by Arbogast 1; by Rodgers, 1; Sacrifice hits: Boles, Grfoerer. Time of Game: Two hours and fifty minutes. Umpires-Moran and Erwin.

Eleven and Ten Year Old Boys

Gardner was 11 in 1906. That year a ten year old youngster lived just a mile north of the modern day site of LaGrave Field, home to the Fort Worth Cats since 1925. Rogers Hornsby lived at 1304 North Commerce. In a few years he would become one of the games' greatest hitters.

DAY FOR PITCHING…..

Walter Dickson and Alex Dupree were masters that Monday in July:

Ben Shelton removed Tris Speaker from the game, went in as pinch hitter for the future batting star

Mike Erwin, injured Fort Worth catcher, shared umpiring duties with Charlie Moran

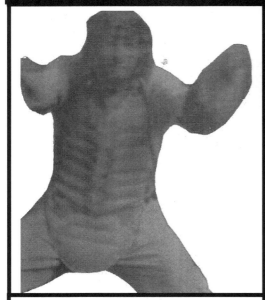

Parker Arbogast caught all 19 innings for Cleburne

With Erwin injured, Emmett Rodgers caught all 19 innings.. Rodgers was in his 18th year in baseball. First played for Fort Worth in 1888

Dode Criss was the hitting star; if there can be a hitting star in a 0-0 19 innings game. Criss had 4 of Cleburne's meager 7 hits.

In his letter, Gardner mentioned the great Owen Wilson, who was playing centerfield for the Panthers and would later set the major league record for triples (36) in 1912, a record that remains unbroken almost a century later. In 1908 Pittsburgh bought Wilson's contract. And as was the custom for rookies, his roommate on road trips was a veteran, the immortal J. Honus Wagner. He gave Wilson his nickname, Chief.

CRISS. p
St.Louis "BROWNS" American B. B. League.
BY H. M. BRIDGETONE 1318 CASS AV. ST.LOUIS

Ben Shelton removed Speaker from the game in lieu of a pinch hitter! By the time the picture to the left was taken in 1912, no one would ever think of pinch hitting for a man who would accrue a .344 lifetime batting average.

A Look Back: July 24, 1905: Ft. Worth vs. Dallas

Owen Wilson walked four times that day

There were a total of 19 walks in the game that day

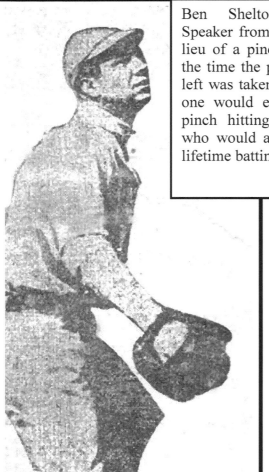

129

OWEN WILSON Panther Right Fielder had a single in six at-bats in the 19 inning 0-0

SHOT TO PIECES
August 9, 1906
Haines Park and Hells Half Acre

Tris Speaker began his professional baseball career in May of 1906 as an unwelcomed, brash, bordering on the edge of obnoxious, arrogant 18 year old with the Cleburne Railroaders of the Texas League. On the very day he joined the team in Waco, Tris managed to upset team captain Ben Shelton, along with several other players, who soon determined it would best serve the team to have him removed immediately from the roster.

The summers in Texas can be unbearably hot. Hotel rooms were insufferable, and most games began just as the heat of the day reached its zenith. The constant grind of daily games takes its toll. As glamorous as it looked to the fans, the player's life can be tough.

On August 9th the Cleburne Railroaders were in Fort Worth to take on the Panthers at Haines Park. Tris' enthusiasm for pitching had waned considerably by late summer, but injuries and fatigue forced Captain Shelton to schedule his youngster for mound duty. This would be his last pitching duty for Cleburne, and would, as time passed, be, unlikely as might have been, the source of one of his fondest memories of his days in the baseball and in the Texas League.

As Tris Speaker grew older, his hair whiter, his fame greater, he developed a way to deflect the praise that so often came his way. He liked to talk about the times in which he was not such a great ball player, and gleefully pointed to that August day in Fort Worth in 1906. His remembrance of that day and the facts that transpired were somewhat at odds. Tris' eyes would glisten as he began his version of that August 9th game. *Why that day, Fort Worth beat my head in...we lost the game 24-2. Captain Shelton looked at me and said: "Son, you're doing a great job today...Fort Worth doesn't have a single hit off of you...they're all doubles!"*

He could tell that story and laugh, after all he was an All-Star. One bad game in a season few remembered could hardly have brought shame to the great man.

Tris Speaker's humorous self-deprecation made for a story of a lifetime, but for the handful of Cleburne fans that who were there that day in August, it not viewed kindly, nor with any sense of humor. The visiting fans saw the game as a day of great shame, and their embarrassment was not limited to what they witnessed on the diamond. Indeed, it was a far deeper disgrace, and upon returning to Cleburne, the fans shared their disgust with the local Cleburne writers, who were quick to quote them in print. The people of Cleburne and Fort Worth were considerably different in character. Cleburne was a dry town. Fort Worth had Hell's Half Acre.

HELL'S Half ACRE

By the late 1870's Fort Worth earned a reputation as *the Paris of the Plains.* Saloons, gambling halls, dance halls, and prostitution reigned supreme in a section near the business district, famously referred to as Hell's Half Acre. This was the era of the city's most colorful sheriff, Longhair Jim Cartwright, whose casual acceptance of sin in the city was a comfort to the cowboys who came to town to drink away the dust from their mouth, while visiting gambling halls, and perhaps seeking the comfort of a willing soiled dove.

While there were many of the fine citizens who opposed the sinful activities along the southern part of Rusk Street, opposition was limited because of the financial impact the area had on the city's economy. Hard working cowboys were separated from their meager salaries by frivolity of the Acre, money which found its way into the legitimate businesses in the upper part of town. *Hell's Half Acre don't bother the churches..and the churches don't bother the Acre.* Sin and legitimacy reached a satisfactory truce, lubricated by the influx of money into the city.

Fort Worth's tolerance of the vices was not to be found in Cleburne, where, the citizenry deemed it a sin *merely in attending a baseball game on Sunday.* Hell had no acreage in Cleburne. The Railroaders played no home games on Sunday, contrasted to Fort Worth which was pleased to open Haines Park on Sundays, and indeed Sundays were generally the best attended games. Gambling at the game brought in many fans, who might have otherwise been indifferent as to the outcome. There was no gambling in Cleburne, and there was nowhere in Cleburne where a man could get a legitimate alcoholic drink, and certainly no bawdy houses.

It was probably not uncommon for visiting ball players to wander over to the Acre, but mostly it went unnoticed, the same likely for the Cleburne boys, except for that one time in August, when Tris and his buddies indulged a little too much. Hell's Half Acre was within walking distance of Haines Park, but from all appearance, the following day, ambulation of any kind was a challenge to the young men recovering from their nocturnal celebration. August 9, 1906, a date which would live in infamy in Cleburne, and would as long as he was alive, remain one of Speaker's favorite memories.

By the time the Railroaders visited Fort Worth's famous spot, there was considerably difference of opinion amongst the people in town, part because of the reputation the city wished to have. As the twentieth century brought an end to the days of the *Wild West*, Fort Worth preferred to keep its western heritage alive. Swift & Company next door to Amour & Company brought modernization to the cattle industry, but with its indoor rodeo and desire to maintain a distinct characteristic, especially in contrast with chief rival, Dallas, Fort Worth began to advertise itself as the place *Where the West Begins.* This desire to keep its perceived image as a place where the cowboy could come and feel at home, closing down its shadier side by the local Christian community was still being met with some resistance by the business leaders.

In 1906, Hell's Half Acre had shrunk in size, and if possible, in respectability. During the 1880's and 90's, the city tolerated the activities of the ranch hands, who had come to Fort Worth along the legendary Chisholm Trail, bringing cattle to the stock yards, before heading to Rusk Street with money to burn. As the new century brought progress to Fort Worth, it also witnessed deterioration to the Acre. There were still gambling halls, saloons, and bawdy houses, but it was attracting fewer outside visitors, with local derelicts becoming the mainstays. It was a place where both local boys as well as visitors often went bad.

Apparently during the evening of August 8, it was the Cleburne players who, even momentarily, went *there* and went bad. The lingering effects of the preceding evening forced them to struggle the next day in front of several hundred fans to do what they were paid to do: play baseball. The team did the best it could do, but it was not a pretty site. The boys with the hangovers lost 16-4, and from all accounts the game was not that close.

TRIS SPEAKER'S PITCHING CAREER ENDED AUGUST 9, 1906

Once Speaker established himself as a premier player in the American League, growing tired of the constant admiration heaped his way, Tris would turn to humor to bring himself back to his human side, and so he would tell stories of his foibles, both on and off the field. One of his favorite stories was of the August 9th game in Cleburne, when his career as a fledgling pitcher came to an end. His recollection of that game was always tinged with a bit of exaggeration. He always remembered the final score being 24-2, and his favorite line in the story was a quote from his field boss, Ben Shelton: *well son, you haven't given up a SINGLE hit.. they're all doubles....*

We don't have any quotes from Speaker on the actual game day, only years later did he chuckle about his performance. Besides battling the effects of a sinful night in Fort Worth, Speaker no longer had any interest in pitching. In the few short months since he had signed a contract, he transitioned himself as a batter and an outfielder. He was at best mediocre as a pitcher, and Speaker had no tolerance for failure. Captain Shelton was reluctant to put his youngster back on the mound, but numerous double headers, fatigue and injuries had played havoc with his three starters, and so Ben had few options other than to put Tris back on the mound.

Tris Speaker may have viewed the game with humor, but the serious church minded fans of Cleburne who had taken the Interurban to Fort Worth saw no humor, only disgust and horror at what they had witnessed. Those fans returned to Cleburne, expressing their collective opinions with the local papers, leading to a story that described the events in terms outside of ordinary bounds of most sports writers. The following line sums up the fans perception of the game:

...a howling farce. Given to the fact that there is no local ordinance to temptation, the entire Cleburne lineup was shot to pieces, leading to the ignominious defeat

THE CLEBURNE MORNING REVIEW, AUGUST 10, 1906

As Tris Speaker grew older, he often discussed the afternoon of August 9[th,] if he shared any of the sordid details about his evening in Hell's Half Acre, that information remains hidden from view. All is known about that day was the observation that the Cleburne boys, including Speaker, were *shot to pieces.*

The last vestiges of Hell's Half Acre did not disappear until the construction of the Fort Worth Convention Center in the early 1960's.

Off to the right (in this picture) of Main Street was Rusk Street, the southern end of which was site of Fort Worth's famous (infamous?) Hell's Half Acre, a place financially lucrative, if not somewhat naughty and dangerous to the citizenry of Fort Worth.

BILL WARD, THE WHITE ELPHANT SALOON, AND HELL'S HALF ACRE

The Lure of Baseball and Gambling

The famous White Elephant Saloon was never considered a part of Hell's Half Acre. It was first established in the 300 block of Main Street in Fort Worth in 1884. However, it gained its reputation through fine food and *top-of-the line gambling.* A young man by the name of John Ward ran the cigar apartment in the antechamber to the White Elephant. There he was able to greet and meet every customer who came through the front door. In 1885 owners Gabriel Burgower, Nathaniel Bornstein, and Samuel Berliner decided to sell the saloon. John Ward was interested, and, needing a partner, enticed his brother, William "Bill" Ward to help him raise the money to buy out the three Jewish gentlemen. Bill Ward was a railroad man, but once he and his brother took ownership, they worked on creating one of the finest gambling establishments in the city.

The White Elephant was opened with great flair, attracting the business leaders in the city. While promoting gambling, the White Elephant screened out the sort of men who would go to Hell's Half Acre. The billiard tables were moved to the back of the saloon, a cigar factory was set up, selling "Bill Ward's Cigars". Eventually John Ward left the White Elephant and joined the Texas League. In 1887, a year before the Texas League was set up, Bill Ward enticed John McCloskey to bring his Joplin team to Fort Worth Ward helped to finance an enclosed park, where admission was charged, and brought in Big Mike O'Connor all for the love of baseball....and gambling. In the world of sport, betting was pretty much limited to baseball and horse racing.

The White Elephant employed 25 gentlemen, some of whom were called "mixologist" who could, as the advertisement in the local papers proclaimed: *there is no known drink known to modern or ancient times they cannot concoct with all the latest improvements.*

Bill Ward wanted a high profile gambler to run his establishment. Luke Short came to Fort Worth with a reputation that *stretched from Tombstone to Dodge City.* He preferred to be known as a *gentleman gambler.* He was very much the stereotypical gambler, always armed. He was reported to have killed a man in Tombstone. Bill Ward needed an influx of capital, and so sold 1/3 of his interest to Short. Luke brought the game of keno to Fort Worth, while maintaining an establishment devoid of police raids, or any sort of rowdiness. Short's reputation attracted the likes of Bat Masterson, Wyatt Earp, and other famous and legendary western figures.

And then there was Timothy Cartwright, a former city marshal, better known as Longhair Jim. The two men developed an animosity that came to head on February 8, 1887. A drunken Cartwright called Short out, and the two men stepped out on Main Street. A gunfight erupted, leaving Cartwright dying in the 300 block of Main Street in Fort Worth. A coroner's inquiry ruled the killing self defense, and the matter was put at rest, and became a legendary moment in the history of Fort Worth.

In 1894 the White Elephant moved to the 600 block of Main Street, equipped with electric lights, telephones and indoor plumbing, with facilities for both men and women.

In 1908 John Lomax came to town with an Edison Recorder to record genuine American cowboy songs. By 1912 the Fort Worth public had grown weary of Hell's Half Acre and saloons in general. Taking advantage of the more conservative mood, another legendary figure in the history of Fort Worth began using the Anti-Saloon League of Texas for his own devices. J. Frank Norris was a fiery preacher in the pulpit of the First Baptist Church. Norris' life is a book unto itself. This brings us to yet another major figure in Fort Worth history, Winfield Scott, who had bought the White Elephant, but his death turned the deed over to his wife Elizabeth, who turned it into a chili parlor, then by 1913 the White Elephant Saloon was no more.

After selling the White Elephant, Bill Ward confined himself to baseball and the new movie industry.

When Bill Ward died in 1934, the people of Fort Worth had lost one a genuine historical man of the old west.

In 1919 baseball's cozy relationship with gamblers exploded onto the stage with the devastated Chicago Black Sox World Series scandal.

Fort Worth

	AB.	BH.	PO.	A.	E.
Boles, ss.	4	2	3	3	1
Gfroerer, cf.	3	0	1	0	0
Carlin, 3b.	4	1	1	4	2
Salm, 1b.	3	1	9	0	0
Wilson, rf.	5	3	3	0	0
Cavender, lf.	5	1	0	0	0
Erwin, c.	4	4	3	0	1
Clayton, 2b., 1b.	5	2	6	6	0
Merkle, p.	5	2	0	1	2
Rodgers, 1b.	1	1	1	0	0
Totals	39	17	27	14	6

Cleburne

	AB.	BH.	PO.	A.	E.
..lken, 3b.	5	0	1	2	2
..oyle, 2b.	4	1	1	1	1
..helton, ss.	4	1	3	0	0
..oran, c.	3	3	5	1	1
..hiteman, cf.	4	0	5	0	1
..oindexter, lf.	4	0	0	0	0
..eaker, p.	4	0	0	5	0
..rbogast, 1b.	4	2	9	1	0
..lams, rf.	4	1	0	1	1
Totals	36	8	24	11	6

Score by innings:

..rt Worth .....2 0 4 3 0 2 0 5 *—16
..eburne ....0 0 0 0 0 0 0 4 0— 4

Summary—Earned runs, Fort Worth
Cleburne 2; stolen bases, Carlin,
..win 2; two-base hits, Boles, Carlin,
..win, Moran; home run, Shelton;
..ck out, by Speaker 4, by Merkle
..ases on balls, off Speaker 3; bat-
..hit, Moran; passed balls, Moran 4;
..crifice hits, Gfroerer, Carlin. Time
..game—2 hours. Umpire—Spencer.

THIS IS THE BOX SCORE FROM SPEAKER'S FAVORITE STORY ABOUT THE DAY HE GAVE UP 24 RUNS… not true, but the one thing he was correct about..he was awful that afternoon..Aug 9, 1906

A LINEUP MESS:

The Cleburne lineup for the Thursday, August 9th game was a mess. Obviously Tris Speaker was not the only player affected by the preceding night's activities. Bobby Wright begged off, forcing Ben Shelton from first base to cover short. Utility man Moran was behind the plate, since the regular catcher Arbogast was asked to cover first base. Pitcher Rick Adams found himself in right field, while right fielder Speaker was put into the pitcher's box.

It was little wonder that the Railroaders were roughed up by the more sober team.

The Railroaders would like to have forgotten the game, but Cleburne businessmen attending the game brought back stories of their unbecoming activities.

Speaker spent a lifetime laughing about his performance in this game, but in Cleburne that August it was not considered a laughing matter.

Owen "Chief" Wilson

Fort Worth Right Fielder 1905, 1906
Sets Triples Record 1912

Two of the greatest outfielders to ever play baseball were in the Texas League in 1906.

Cleburne right fielder Tris Speaker was, within a couple years, a member of the Boston Red Sox. After a slow start in the major leagues he hit his stride, and eventually was considered only second to Ty Cobb during his era in the American League.

The other star outfielder playing that year was also a right fielder playing in his second year with the Panthers. He started his Texas League career in Austin, but when that team folded, Bill Ward quickly snatched him up for his Fort Worth squad. And rightly so. Wilson was one of the finest fielders in the league, with hitting prowess to match. He, like Tris, was on his way to stardom in the big leagues.

Owen Wilson became better known as *Chief Wilson* thanks to Honus Wagner. In Pittsburgh it was a tradition to match rookies up with veterans, and it was Wilson's good luck to room with the immortal Wagner on road trips. Learning that Owen was a Texan, his roommate began referring to him as Chief, and the name stuck.

In his fifth year with the Pirates, Wilson, taking advantage of the cavernous dimensions of Forbes Field, began to establish a hitting mark that is nearing a century old, the longest standing hitting record in baseball. In 1912 Owen Chief Wilson hit 36 triples, a record that has never been challenged, either in the major leagues or the minors.

The irony is that during the 1912 season, no one realized that he was setting a record. Even as the season ended, there was no mention of a triples record. The Bible of baseball, the Spalding Record book of 1912, credited Larry Lajoie with 43 triples in 1903, which made him to appear to be the all time leader in three base hits. As Wilson drilled triple after triple, he was still going to be short of the 43 mark. The problem was that Lajoie had hit only thirteen 3-baggers in '03. The "43" was obviously a typographical error. Lajoie did not come forth to set the record straight. His lack of integrity was harshly criticized when it was finally determined that Wilson, not Lajoie, held the triple's record.

As the 1912 season ended, Wilson did not know that he had set the gold standard for triples. It was not until the following year that Ernest J. Lanigan challenged the Spalding Record Book. He looked at the 1903 season game-by-game to determine that Larry Lajoie of the Naps had in fact hit only 13 triples! In 1913 Owen Wilson was finally recognized as the triples champ of all-time.

ERNEST J. LANIGAN was the first man to recognize Owen *Chief* Wilson had set the major league record for triples in 1912 as a member of the Pittsburgh Pirates.

Owen Wilson played his home games in **Forbes Field** where the outfield dimensions were asymmetrical and deep: Left Field: 360 ft. Left-Center 406ft, Left of straight away Center field: 462 ft, Center Field: 442 ft. Right Center:416, Right Field 376 ft.

Also Note that of Wilson's 59 home runs, 31 were inside the park homers.

The Sporting News

VOLUME 154   ST. LOUIS, OCTOBER 13, 1962   NUMBER 12

Triples Mark Stands After 50-Year Assault

Chief Wilson Belted 36 for Bues in 1912

No Other Hitter Has Rapped Over 26 Three-Baggers Since Campaign of 1900

By L. ROBERTS DAVIDS
WASHINGTON, D. C.

Forbes Field Ideally Suited for Triples, Ex-Bucs Assert

WASHINGTON, D. C.

Still the Champ

Owen (Chief) Wilson

Chief Was Expert Rapper of Liners Against Fences

WASHINGTON, D. C.

Moderns Fall Far Short of Record Total

Annual Leader Averages 1: Now; Clemente Sets Pac With a 5-Year Haul of 4:

Fifty years after John Owen *Chief* Wilson hit 36 triples, the record had stood the test of time. Now nearing the 100th anniversary of that feat, Wilson's record seems even more safe and enduring. He used one bat for the entire 1912 season, and even though he did not realize that he had set the record, he whittled "36" on the bat and brought it back to his home near Austin. Finally in 1913 the 1912 record was recognized and today remains a baseball milestone.

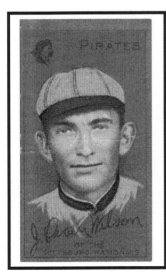

Thanks to Honus Wagner, Owen Wilson became "Chief" Wilson.

This faded newspaper picture was taken in Haines Park in Fort Worth.

137

Record Time
A DOUBLE HEADER
August 26th, 1906

The summer of 1906 was an exception to the normal Texas weather pattern. Only twice since records have been kept has the temperature failed to reach 100° in north central Texas, with 1906 being one those years. In addition, rain showers came more frequently that summer, interrupting and threatening many of the scheduled Texas League games.

August 26th, 1906 was a Sunday, and a day in which larger crowds normally showed up for Panthers' games. The general rule was that Sunday accounted for about a third of a season's total attendance.

Sunday double headers in Fort Worth were scheduled for 3pm, allowing plenty of time for the fans to attend church, eat lunch, then take the trolley to Haines Park. On this August day a nice size crowd headed toward the ball park despite the fact that the skies were heavy with clouds.

Bill Ward, the Panthers' owner surveyed the sky, worried that rain might cost him a nice payday. With the smell of rain heavy in the air, Umpire Mackey yelled *Play Ball!* at the appointed time of 3pm.

The Waco Navigators were in town, and indeed from the looks of the clouds, a boat captain seemed fitting for this day.

Games meant money, and the players well understood that, and so both teams hustled, with the intent of getting the double header into the record books. Eight hits, one walk, and two runs later, Fort Worth emerged victorious in game one that concluded at 4:13pm, one hour and thirteen minutes after the first pitch. Nine innings in 1:13!

The teams took only a very short break before game two was underway. No rain had yet fallen, but everyone knew at any moment the sky would start falling. Then a light mist filled the air. The Panthers doubled their first game scoring output, while Waco finally got a runner across the plate. The second game ended, again with the Panthers on top, 4-1. The extra runs had slowed down the game. Game two took one hour and eighteen minutes: 1:18!

Two games, 18 innings, all played within 2 ½ hours!

Earlier in the year, the Dallas Morning News writer complained about any game that lasted more than two hours. He would have been pleased that afternoon in Fort Worth.

In 1949 Fort Worth celebrated its centennial. The Fort Worth Press and The Fort Worth Star-Telegram sought out as many citizens as possible to help recall as much of the city's history that could be gleaned from their collective memories. One man recalled that forty years ago the Panther's baseball park was *where the bus company now sits.* The picture of the old bus facilities was taken by my father, Red Whitten.

...No one knew at the time...
RAILROADERS LAST HOME GAME AT GORMAN PARK

Monday, August 27, 1906

Two weary teams arrived in Cleburne on the early morning train from Dallas. It was Monday, August 27th. The Giants and the Railroaders had just completed four games in two days, and again were facing a double bill scheduled at Gorman Park that afternoon. Rain had played havoc with the 1906 schedule, and now with the sun out, makeup games were coming fast and furious.

Saturday the teams had split the pair, then again on Sunday the teams again played two, and also split those games. And now as they arrived in Cleburne the teams faced the prospect of playing games five and six in three days. It was just too much baseball in a short space of time.

Captain Ben Shelton looked at his lineup in hopes of finding two pitchers able to go that afternoon. The previous Saturday he had called upon Walter Dickson to pitch both games of the twin bill. Sunday Rick Adams and Dode Criss each pitched a game. Dickson was in no shape to go again this soon. Adams claimed fatigue and so it was up to Dode Criss, but he too begged off.

Ben Shelton approached his brother-in-law and captain of the Dallas Giants about doing away with one of the games, and he found the Curly Malone receptive to the idea. Thus a single game would be played that afternoon beginning at 4pm.

This was not the last game scheduled at Gorman Park. In fact the last game was scheduled for the following Saturday, September 1st against the Panthers.

As the fans arrived at Gorman Park, they had no way of realizing that this was the last Texas League ever to be played in their city. Perhaps had everyone known, there might have been a special ceremony, but as it were, it was just another game in the schedule, and it would not be a pretty game for the local fans. Criss was, as promised, arm weary, and his defense was no better. Dallas jumped on Cleburne for three quick runs, coasting to a 5-2 victory.

The fatigue showed on both sides as they combined for an embarrassing total of ten errors, with Cleburne committing six, Dallas four. Bobby Wright committed three of Cleburne's six errors. Hastily signed George Reed, subbing for injured Mickey Coyle, made one error.

A few minutes before six that afternoon, Monday, August 27th 1906, Ben Shelton hit a lazy fly ball into left field. Curly Maloney squeezed his mitt around the ball, ending the game, and ending Cleburne's brief interlude into Texas League history. The Dallas players made their way back to the Cleburne Hotel hoping for some rest in preparation of the last week of the season.

Anticipating a hard run at the second half flag, the Cleburne fans were expecting an exciting game schedule next Saturday with Fort Worth scheduled at Gorman Park.

On August 26th, Mickey Coyle's season ended in Dallas when Dick Clark hit a line drive that broke his finger, *"the bone protruding out of the skin when he had the finger bandaged. He is probably out for the season."*
The Cleburne Enterprise, August 27, 1906

IX
TEXAS LEAGUE 'SECOND HALF' CHAMPIONS
THE CLEBURNE RAILROADS

WALTER RALEIGH DICKSON
THE MAN WHO WON THE PENNANT

Overview of the 1906 Race
Two Halves: *First Half*: Fort Worth, *Second Half*: Cleburne
Full Season Champion: Cleburne Railroaders

The 1906 Texas League schedule mapped out a 120 game season, with each team playing the other 24 times. As so often happened in the first two decades of the league, the schedule created in the spring had to undergo severe modification when teams folded during the middle of the season due to economic hardships.

In 1905 the league began with six teams on the schedule, but soon financial troubles arrived. Two teams were dropped; the decision was to continue on, minus the two clubs, who were dropped from the daily standings of the Texas League, giving the standings a bizarre look: all four of the remaining teams were above .500, and all four of the teams ended the season with more wins than losses. As the season concluded, Fort Worth won eleven games in a row to take the pennant on the last day of the season, but the decision not to split the season left no possibility for a playoff.

As the plans for the 1906 were developed, the owners wished to find a way to prevent the repeat of the problems of 1905. Stricter guidelines were developed to assure the financial well being of all teams, especially the small city teams, namely Cleburne, Temple and Greenville.

The Cleburne the Athletic Association guaranteed the financial well being of that franchise. In Greenville Joe Gardner, who owned the Dallas club, secretly bankrolled the Hunt County team. If the city gave the team any measure of support, then Gardner would be out only a small amount of funding, with a benefit to him of using Greenville as a feeder team for his well-healed Dallas Giants club. Temple began the season owned by Doak Roberts' good friend, Ewing Edens, who later sold his interest to a group of businessmen in that city.

The 1906 season looked locked, financially safe and set for completion of the schedule, but that was not be: there was hint of trouble as early as June 6th, when the Hunters forfeited a game to Cleburne in protest of not being paid. Three weeks later Greenville was scheduled to play two with Temple, but the Greenville players were angry, seemed more intent on making a mockery of the game than playing it. The first game ended with a Temple victory 16-15! By the sixth inning of the second game they were trailing 24-2, and at that point refused to continue to play. The following day, there was a pause from the bad news in Greenville, when the game scheduled for the 25th was rained out. With the rain gone, the papers reported that the Hunters failed to show for the June 26th game because of a dispute over the splitting of the gate receipts, resulting in a forfeit to Temple, signaling that once again there was trouble brewing in the Texas League.

Clearly the Hunters were embarrassing the league. Joe Gardner stepped in to guarantee the players' salaries. That temporarily put an end to precarious situation, and once again Greenville could concentrate on baseball. On the 27th, they not only showed up, but defeated the Waco Navigators.

The peace was short lived: Gardner pulled his support from the team, and no other individual or business group was willing to step to the plate to pay the expenses for continued play in Greenville. The Texas League was back to its usual form of scrambling to find a way to complete the season.

With one team gone, league officials would have to drop one other team to keep the schedule even, and so the choice was between Cleburne and Temple. Doak Roberts, the President of the league, also owned the Railroaders, the conflict of interest that Joe Gardner had warned back in December was now reality.

Temple had the burden of being the southernmost city, and hence incurred greater travel cost than Cleburne, snuggly located near Fort Worth. As a results Temple was informed that they had drawn the short straw and would no longer be on the league schedule for 1906.

Greenville left quietly, but the Temple owners and players were furious, and caused a great deal of consternation for the owners. Players out of a job showed up at the parks where they had been scheduled to play, demanding to be allowed onto the field. Of course, they were denied, but the Temple business owners threatened a lawsuit. The league ignored the Boll Weevil players' demands, published a new scheduled and continued play.

With the strong possibility of legal intervention, league official had to find a way to resolve the pesky dispute with Temple. In an unannounced deal, they were promised a slot in the 1907 league configuration.

After solving the Temple issue, there was the matter of the 1906 season schedule. The owners had not been satisfied with the 1905 arrangement, in which the whole season schedule was completed, creating a close race, but not a playoff scheme. Their decision in 1906 was to split the season, with the first half winner meeting the second half winner in a saw-off series.

Fort Worth had won the first half, and a good Dallas team seemed a good choice to win the second half. And so it was agreed to end the first half schedule on June 30 and restart a new season on July 1.

The decision to split the season looked to be fortuitous for Cleburne. At the beginning of the first half season, the Railroaders had dug themselves a deep hole beginning on the very first day of the season with the preseason pick, Dallas. Cleburne promptly lost all three games, making the Giants look like champions they were picked to be.

Their next series was with the defending champs, Fort Worth. Again the Railroaders went 0-3. Six days out from the beginning of the 1906 season, Cleburne was 0-6, and apparently heading nowhere. During the next six games, Cleburne split, but still at 3-9 the team was in last place in the Texas League.

The Railroaders began to turn things around, but on May 30 the Railroaders were still at a mediocre 17-18. Doak Roberts continually looked for new talent in order to strengthen his club. It worked. One of his new rookies was 18 year old Tris Speaker.

The team found its talent, winning 21 of its last 27 games of the first half season. It gave Cleburne a respectable record of 38-24 by the end of the first half race, June 30[th.]

Respectable only gave them 3rd place, four games behind the Fort Worth Panthers, who won the pennant in a spectacular fashion on the last day of the first-half season.

Now as the new second season began, based on their fast finish in June, Cleburne seemed likely to be in the thick of the second half race. That was not to be. The Railroaders started out the first half with a 1-6 record, then repeated that record at the start of the second half with the exact same record, 1-6. The pennant fight, it now appeared, would again continue to be between Fort Worth and Dallas, with Waco and Cleburne battling for third place.

Just as in they had done in the first half, Cleburne started a slow comeback, yet on July 30th the Railroaders were only 14-14. This was the exact record the team recorded after 28 games of the first half. The difference, however, was at 14-14 the team was only 2 games behind Dallas in July. Last May their 14-14 record put them seven behind the leader.

It didn't feel like to the fans, but Cleburne was in the race. They would win 25 of their last 36 games, which catapulted them into first place on the last day of the season, giving them the second half flag.

Cleburne won the pennant, but strangely the fans of Cleburne were largely deprived of pennant fever. The slow start in the first half kept the team so far back, that by the time they made their push, the Giants and the Panthers had garnered all the glory. There was no ongoing sense that Cleburne was joining the pennant party.

Again, the same scenario played out in the second half. The Railroaders' slow start left them behind the same two cities that had been dominating the Texas League. Pennant fever escaped Gorman Park for most of the season. It was not until the season was nearly over that it appeared Cleburne might have a chance, but even then it seemed more likely that Fort Worth was slacking off a bit to give the Giants a better shot of winning the second half flag, ensuring a playoff series between the two large cities.

Cleburne messed up the Fort Worth versus Dallas post season party.

LABOR DAY: It was dark, dreary and rainy on Labor Day of 1906, the holiday that is traditionally last day of the regularly scheduled season. The games in Fort Worth and Dallas were rained out. Bill Ward and Joe Gardner both lost big gates.

As a matter of fact, every team in 1906 reported losing money. Waco, with its dismal record, was not drawing fans. The small towns were never able to put enough people in the stands, but the biggest surprise were loses reported in Dallas and Fort Worth. Gardner blamed fan apathy to their loss to Fort Worth in the series that determined the first half championship. Ward pointed to the numerous rainouts in 1906.

Bill Ward met with his players that rainy day, proclaiming to the newspaper reporters that gloom and doom had set in. He blamed the rain, but more likely it could be laid to the feet of the Cleburne Railroaders who had swept the double header on Sunday, and had made any games on Labor Day meaningless.

Ward announced that he could not hold the team together. There would be no saw-off games with Cleburne. He ceded any claim to the trophy to Cleburne.

A beautiful trophy had been designed by a Fort Worth silversmith, no doubt in anticipation of his hometown boys winning the 1906 Texas League Pennant.

The trophy was given instead to Doak Roberts.

There was never any mention of it every being displayed in Cleburne. Winners without a team, without a trophy or pennant. Lost to history, that great team of 1906.

The Champions of Naught Six: The Cleburne Railroaders!

The Silver Cup designed for the 1906 Texas League Champion had been forged by a Fort Worth silversmith no doubt in anticipation of his hometown team winning the pennant. When Bill Ward withdrew his team from post season play, the cup was awarded to the Cleburne Railroaders.

and now for the Details...
THE 1906 TEXAS LEAGUE SEASON
WRAPS UP AN EXCITING SECOND HALF RACE

.....UGLY RUMORS

There were ugly rumors during the last days of the 1906 Texas League race: the Panthers, in first place, might slack off a bit, giving the Dallas Giants an opportunity to slip into first and claim the second half flag. Thus by losing, the Fort Worth players would give themselves a chance to earn a little extra cash thanks to a playoff series with, presumably Dallas. Winning both halves of the season would give them the flag, but no *saw-off games.* Might it serve them best to win only the first half, then to win the season flag after a post season series with the Giants?

If this were ever the plan, that little team from Cleburne was a problem. There was no guarantee that it would be Dallas that would be sitting on top at the end of the second half schedule. As a matter of fact, Ben Shelton's boys were hanging ever so close to the Panthers in the chase. Many of the Cleburne players were on the 1905 Temple club that lost the championship to Fort Worth by mere percentage points. They were determined to turn that around in 1906.

Reality......

As the road to the championship wound down, Fort Worth, with seven days left in the season, held a 2 game lead over Cleburne, and 4 games over Dallas.

On Sunday, August 26th the standings looked like this:

	Won	Lost	GB
Fort Worth Panthers	35	23	--
Cleburne Railroaders	32	24	2
Dallas Giants	30	26	4
Waco Navigators	17	41	18

The following day, Dallas defeated Cleburne, while Fort Worth and Waco were idle. The Panthers lead had increased to 2 ½ games over the Railroaders. It more and more seemed likely that within 6 days, Fort Worth would be crowned the champion of 1906. Things looked especially bad for the Railroaders. Not only had they lost a crucial game to Dallas, in that game Dick Clark hit a line drive that struck Mickey Coyle, breaking his finger, ending the feisty second baseman's season, but then suddenly things changed.

Red Jarvis was in the box for the Panthers opposing Dallas pitcher Dick Clark, who stepped out of left field onto the mound. In Waco the Navigators were playing their home games in front of empty seats at Katy Park, and continued their dreadful ways, losing 9-3 to Cleburne. Walter Dickson won the game, thanks in part to Tris Speaker's three doubles. In Fort Worth, star pitcher Jarvis lost to the Giants. The combination of a Cleburne win and the Panthers loss shrunk their lead to 1½ games: Fort Worth at 35-24, Cleburne 33-25, with Dallas 32-26 still in the hunt.

Doak Roberts reached out to Lillian, Texas for one of its native sons, Wingo Charlie Anderson, to give some relief to his exhausted pitching staff. While Criss, Dickson, and Adams rested, Anderson pitched Cleburne to a disputed win over Waco. Dallas shut out the Panthers two straight times. The Railroaders were steadily gaining on Fort Worth, with a little help from Umpire Ed Mackey, as detailed below: a game protested:

Special to the News:

Waco, Tex., Aug.29- Cleburne won today's game in a contest marked by much wrangling and hard fighting by both sides for the victory. Umpire (Ed) Mackey having a hard time of it from both teams, especially the locals who had good grounds for their contentions, and would have won but for adverse decisions by the arbitrator in two instances. As it was, the game stands protested by Manager Hickey, the argument being over the two runs scored in the 5th inning on a hit by Arbogast, the Cleburne catcher failing to touch first base. He was put out at second trying to stretch his hit, but two men had already scored. The umpire saw the player miss first base, but decided the ball should have been thrown to the first baseman which was not done, the Waco players claiming Arbogast being touched by Welch as second base was all that was necessary. The game will come up before the league directors for final hearing.

Standings the Morning of Thursday, August 30th

	Won	Lost	GB
Fort Worth	35	25	----
Cleburne	34	25	½
Dallas	33	26	1 ½
Waco	17	43	18 ½

That Thursday morning Doak Roberts declared that Dode Criss had been sold to the St. Louis Browns. His tall, lanky lefty would finish the season with Cleburne before moving onto the majors. Roberts also announced two additional changes to his team. With Coyle out, Roberts signed veteran George M. Reed to play second base. Reed's career stretched back to 1896 when he played the first of several seasons with Houston.

Although the Giants were in third place, they still had a shot at the flag. Then it all came unhinged. Later that Thursday afternoon Fort Worth behind the pitching of Merkel bested Clark, 8-3, dropping Dallas back to 2 ½ games out, while Dode Criss kept Cleburne in the hunt with their 7-1 victory over Waco. At the end of the day Fort Worth was now 36-25, Cleburne 35-25, Dallas falling to 33-27.

Friday

The season was quickly coming to an end. On this last Friday of the season, Fort Worth and Dallas battled for 11 innings before darkness ended the contest, with the score still knotted at 3-3. No decision. The Cleburne game, originally scheduled for Waco, was switched to Corsicana with the hopes of attracting a larger crowd.

Wingo Anderson, who had pitched on Wednesday, was brought back into the box with only one day's rest. Ben Shelton was anxious to save his star pitching staff for the crucial weekend series with Fort Worth. Anderson was just good enough. The Railroaders won, 5-4. There were no notes in the paper to indicate the size of the crowd at the Corsicana ball park. Wingo's season with the Railroaders was over. Two games in three days, and a winner in both contest.

The Railroaders were in desperate straits as the season entered its last week. Their three star pitchers had worn down through the long hot summer days.

One of the better known pitchers on the local sandlots was a Lillian man, Wingo Charlie Anderson. Roberts made a call to the 20 year old youngster and he reported immediately for duty.

Twice in a space of three days he pitched the Railroaders to crucial victories. Not great, but good enough, allowing Cleburne to gain ground on the Panthers. Without his temporary help, Cleburne may not have taken the second half flag, and with that the 1906 Texas League Pennant.

WINGO CHARLIE ANDERSON

In 1910 he became another of Roberts' many signees, who made a major league roster, playing with the Cincinnati Reds in the National League. Anderson is probably the only major league player born in Lillian, Texas. (note, some sources list his birthplace as Alvarado, just up the road from Lillian.)

FINAL THREE DAYS of the 1906 Season

And so it was, the final three days of the 1906 season, scheduled to end on Labor Day, Monday, September 3rd.

At the end of the day, Friday August 31, 1906:

	Won	Lost	GB
Fort Worth	36	25	---
Cleburne	36	25	---
Dallas	33	27	2 ½
Waco	17	45	19 1/2

The league announced that because of the impact of the Dallas-Fort Worth game, Friday's tie would be rescheduled as a part of a double header on Labor Day, with the Giants taking on the Panthers in a morning game at Haines Park, while the regularly scheduled game between Cleburne and Fort Worth to be played at 4pm in the same park. Dallas would take the Interurban back to Dallas to play Waco that afternoon. (This bizarre arrangement of playing one game in Fort Worth and one in Dallas would be revised in the early 1960s when Dallas and Fort Worth shared a team. Sunday afternoon the team would play at LaGrave Field, then they would take the bus to Dallas to play the night game in Burnett Field).

Labor Day, 1906, shaped up to be one of the most exciting days in the history of Fort Worth baseball.

Built It and They Will Come... well, not so much in Cleburne:
Saturday, September 1st

There was *that* problem with Cleburne. Cleburne's final home game of 1906 was scheduled for Saturday, September 1st at Gorman Park. However, lagging attendance made playing the game in Johnson County unattractive to Fort Worth. With so much on the line, Haines Park would likely be filled, provided that the game was switched. The winner of Saturday's game between Fort Worth and Cleburne would be in first place with two days to go. A home game in Fort Worth would likely draw over 1,000 fans, a far greater payday for the Panthers and the Texas League.

Bill Ward announced that Doak Roberts had agreed to play Saturday's contest in Fort Worth. From all appearances, Roberts had been coerced to make the concession of giving up a home game in Cleburne.

The fans in Cleburne were furious, and again antagonized by the sheer brute force of the Fort Worth ownership. They had fought hard to gain recognition and equality with those larger cities, and now, with so much on the line, the team was yanked from them, without a chance as so much a chance to enjoy the season's end.

To the few Cleburne fans it was now apparent that Monday's game on the 27th had been the last game of the season at Gorman Park. It was now too late to plan for any season ending celebrations in Cleburne. There would be no more home games in the city unless the team made the post season championship series.

The Cleburne newspapers, the businessmen, and fans all reacted with anger towards the owner. Roberts, more concerned about the Cleburne Athletic Association, attempted to do some damage control by issuing the following public announcement, which was published Saturday morning:

> We have notified Manager Ward that he must come to Cleburne or there will be no game. We think it likely that he will reconsider the matter and will come to Cleburne on the early train. We will arrive in Cleburne from Corsicana on the first train. We expect Rick Adams to pitch Saturday's game in Cleburne. Of course, if Fort Worth does not come, I do not know what steps will be taken, but we expect to send the banner about the city announcing the game, so everybody will be prepared to attend. This being the last game in Cleburne, a very large crowd should attend, as good sport will be given…. J. Doak Roberts

Doak Roberts, who was suffering large monetary losses, probably had in fact agreed, as Bill Ward claimed, to play the Saturday game in Fort Worth. In his bravado statement, he had given himself an "out" when he stated, *if Fort Worth does not come….* Roberts was tied to the Cleburne Athletic Association for financial support, and realized that if he angered that group of businessmen, he would jeopardize his chances of receiving cash from the consortium. It was Roberts' obligation to play the ends against the middle. And in reality, he had little leverage thanks to the poor attendance at Gorman Park. Moving the game to Haines Park was just plain good business sense, but the Cleburne fans did not see it that way.

Captain Ben Shelton Disagrees….

If indeed Roberts had made such an agreement with Ward, it became obvious that Captain Ben Shelton was not part of the deal. Shelton openly stated that if Fort Worth failed to arrive in Cleburne, he would not go to Haines Park. That Saturday morning he watched the 9:30 train arrived at the Santa Fe Station. He was incensed when indeed the train was devoid of the Fort Worth club. Shelton announced that the Railroaders would not be going to Fort Worth.

Roberts stepped in and took charge of his team, directing them to Tarrant County on the early morning train, sans the presence of Shelton, still holding to his word not to go to Fort Worth. In Fort Worth the game banners announced the game would begin at 4 pm in Haines Park.

An angry Railroader club had lost the first battle. And now without their leader and first baseman Ben Shelton, as well without their peppery Mickey Coyle, the real battle would be played between the lines. Utility man Charlie Moran replaced the replacement, George Reed at second base, and pitcher Dode Criss would be given Ben Shelton's first base mitt. Thus, short two stars, the Railroaders would take to the field that Saturday afternoon to play the most important game in their short history.

Rick Adams, as previously announced, took the mound. Roberts had told the Cleburne papers that his star pitcher would be in the box at Gorman Park. Adams took the field, not in Cleburne as Roberts has promised, but not in Cleburne, but in Fort Worth, knowing that he would soon be going to St. Paul for the handsome sum of $200 a month. Stepping onto the mound for the Fort Worth Panthers was Red Jarvis.

A loud boisterous crowd greeted the two teams that afternoon. Bets were heavy. The Fort Worth fans bet with their heart, which soon would be broken.

Umpire Problem

Doak Roberts, wearing two hats, as President of the League, and owner of the Cleburne organization, was confronted with a severe problem in this most important of games. An explanation was lacking in the local papers as to why, but the regularly scheduled umpire failed to show up for the game. Was he sick or still in Cleburne? Roberts had to find a man to put into the arbiter's role. Cleburne pitching ace Walter Hickory Dickson was selected for this important game. It was a salute to his integrity that the Fort Worth team accepted him in this position without any public protest.

That Saturday the score was close, but in reality the Railroaders dominated Fort Worth, as they pounded Jarvis for 16 hits and 6 runs. Six of the Railroaders had 2 or more hits, with Akin, Moran, and pitcher Rick Adams getting three each. Ironically, the hard-hitting Tris Speaker was held hitless.

The Railroaders had won 6-5. Dallas defeated Waco in, what was now, a meaningless game. There were two days left in the 1906 Texas League season, and for the first time, there was a new team in first place. As the day ended that Saturday, September1st, there was joy in Cleburne, Texas. A look at the standings published in Sunday's papers explained it all. Cleburne was, as promised last spring, in first place, and indeed, they were *not a piking team.....* winners instead they were:

That Sunday Morning: September 2, 1906

The Texas League Standings:

	Won	Lost	GB
Cleburne	37	25	----
Fort Worth	36	26	1
Dallas	34	27	2 ½
Waco	17	46	20 ½

Sunday, September 2: Two Double Headers: Fort Worth vs Cleburne, Dallas vs Waco

As the 3pm time approached for the opening pitch for games that Sunday afternoon, Dallas hosting Waco, and Fort Worth against visiting Cleburne, no one suspected that these would be the final games of the 1906 season. The expectation was that the two double headers wound set the stage for an exciting Labor Day.

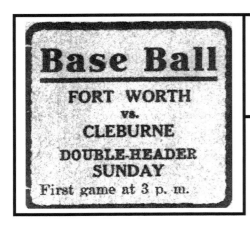

The League expected Dallas and Fort Worth would be in the championship playoffs, but the Cleburne Railroaders shocked everyone by suddenly sweeping passed the Panthers.

CHARLES MERKEL
1906 Ft. Worth Panthers

Leo Walsh

THE SCORE CARD PICTURE OF THE 1906 PANTHERS

150

Iron Man
Walter Dickson Pitches Both Ends of Double Header

Walter Hickory Dickson took to the mound 42 times during the 1906 season, winning 26, losing 11, with 3 games ending in a tie. One of the tie games was the July 23rd 19 inning 0-0 game played at Haines Park, with Dickson pitching the entirety of the game. On June 5, Dickson went the entire 15 innings in a 4-4 tie with Waco, a combined 34 innings with no decision!

As the season entered its final month, Ben Shelton, with his small roster, more and more had to deal with an exhausted and sometime hurt pitching staff. On August 7th Dickson took to the mound two times in one day, the first of what eventually would be three double headers in which he pitched both games, defeating Dallas twice, 4-3 and 2-0. On August 25th Walter was again asked to pitch two games in one day, and again against the Giants, this time recording a split decision, winning 2-1, before losing 4-3.

September 2: what would become the third Dickson double header was not a planned event. He was to take the mound for game one, with Dode Criss on tap for game two. Criss warmed up for the second game, but was not able to go. Dickson found himself called on to pitch the second game as well, and he proved up to the task. *Ole Hickory* was in total command. Twice the Panthers got 6 harmless hits, and not a single run in either game. Cleburne scored twice in each game. Each game lasted well under two hours, and when the day was over, the Cleburne Railroaders had swept the important series. In Dallas the Giants won twice over the undermanned Waco Navigators.

The sweep clinched the second half championship for Cleburne. Monday's game were now meaningless.

Sunday, September 2, 1906

Texas League

	Won	Lost	Pct.	GB
Cleburne Railroaders	39	25	.609	---
Dallas Giants	36	27	.571	2 ½
Fort Worth Panthers	36	28	.563	3
Waco Navigators	17	48	.262	22 ½

Texas League Schedule, Labor Day, 1906
Dallas at Fort Worth 10 a.m.
Waco at Dallas 4 pm
Cleburne at Fort Worth 4 pm

X

THE 1906 TEXAS LEAGUE SILVER TROPHY AWARDED TO THE CLEBURNE RAILROADERS THE CHAMPIONS OF NAUGHT SIX

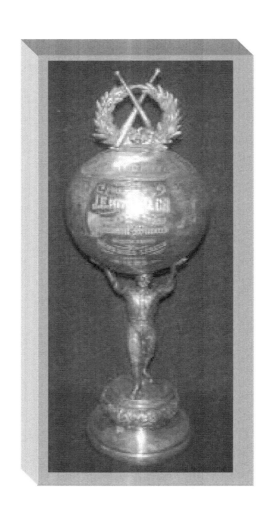

LABOR DAY, Monday, 1906
It rained today and this gave everybody the glooms....

The Fort Worth fans had looked forward to Labor Day, 1906. The last games of the season were scheduled to end on this holiday, and as good luck would have it, Cleburne's sudden success meant that likely the championship would be determined on this season ending game at Haines Park. Anticipating a barn-burner ending, the league had scheduled an exciting day of baseball:

LABOR DAY'S STRANGE SCHEDULE

First, Dallas would travel to Haines Park for a morning make-up game with the Panthers. The previous Friday the two teams battled to a tie when the game was called because of darkness. Since the game appeared to have an impact on the final standings, it would be replayed. Dallas would be in Fort Worth for a 10am game, then the Giants would catch the train back to Dallas, where later in the afternoon they would play their regularly scheduled game with Waco. Fort Worth would complete the unusual double with an afternoon game with the Railroaders. Not only would the two game sets bring one of the most exciting finishes ever to the Texas League, the unusual arrangement would bring out three large crowds, two in Fort Worth and one in Dallas, a nice paycheck for both Bill Ward and Joe Gardner.

But it didn't happen that way.

First, Walter Dickson had taken the steam out of Fort Worth. Pitching both ends of Sunday's double header, Hickory crushed the Panthers, with 18 innings of shut-out ball. By the end of the day, everyone realized that Cleburne had become the dominating team in the league, thanks to their incredible pitching staff of Criss, Adams, and Dickson. With the sweep, the Railroaders had an insurmountable lead. They were the champions, no matter the outcomes of Monday's games.

What about the double header scheduled for Monday at Haines Park?

It didn't matter. The city awakened to heavy thunderstorms. Mother Nature had no respect for the league's schedule. *It rained and this gave everybody the glooms.*

In one day it all went to pieces. Cleburne, sitting atop the league, was anticipating a series of saw-off games, if not with Fort Worth, at least the champions of the South Texas League, the Austin Senators. Perhaps had it not rained, or if Fort Worth had been able to win one of the games played on Sunday, it would have been different.

Gloomy Monday. The season was long. Players had reported for play last March, and many had been away from home for months. They were tired, and perhaps dispirited, especially in Fort Worth and Dallas.

The owners looked at their ledgers and were discouraged by the monetary losses. Cleburne had won, but their meager fan base would hardly make extending the season financially worthwhile. There had been some talk that if post season games were to be played, they would be divided between Dallas and Fort Worth, but the question was whether or not the Dallas fans would be willing to watch a Cleburne-Fort Worth series at Gaston Park. And such an arrangement would further inflame the Cleburne Athletic Association, and at this point, Roberts was still hoping to recoup money from that organization. The last thing he wished to do was to give the Cleburne group even more ammunition for refusing to ante-up the money owed to the team.

Then confirmation came that the Texas League season was over. *Neither of the managers has announced the personnel of the team which they hope to win the pennant.* The papers in Fort

Worth were more direct: *It is stated that both teams will be disbanded at once, and several of the Panthers will leave the city tonight and tomorrow for their homes.*

Bill Ward, owner, was more direct about the conclusion of the season: *there will be no saw-off series between the Panthers and the Railroaders, the matter having been decided today.*

We Are the Champions of ……..

On September 3rd the Texas League pennant was awarded to Cleburne. Bill Ward stated he was not able to hold his players together *as several were called home on account of business reasons and one on account of a serious illness in the family. The Cleburne Railroaders are the champions of 1906.*

Doak Roberts returned to Cleburne (no mention was made of the Silver Cup) to meet with Mayor Phil Allin to go over expenses of operating the team. In discussing the awarding of the pennant to Cleburne, Roberts explained:

They (the Panthers) had been up against Cleburne and down deep inside they believed that they could not do anything with the Cleburnites and hence suddenly developed homesickness that caused Bill Ward to pay them off and let them go. Then he acted the manly part and yielded the pennant to Cleburne. It was not the ending we looked for, and not the ending that the fans expected. Many thought Dallas would get the pennant, because the saw-off games would be played between Dallas and Fort Worth. Fort Worth had won the first pennant by Cleburne's help over the Giants, and all hands agreed to let it go at that.

The players were dazed when they found that there was nothing to contest for. The Fort Worth players began to scatter. The Cleburne players took the train back to Cleburne. The Railroaders arrived back to an empty station, devoid of fans or excitement normally associated with winning a pennant.

Where's the Celebration?

The end of the season had been so sudden and unexpected that the city had no time to prepare for the champion team. The team got off the train. No fans greeted them. No bands played. All at once it was over. From March until just last Sunday the players hustled. There was tension and excitement, but now nothing.

The Baseball Season of 1906 is now a Thing of the Past:

The boys had conducted themselves well and they had brought the name of Cleburne to the world. Then with the sudden demise, no one in Cleburne seemed capable of pulling together a celebration in such a short time. *A winner with no celebration, and fans without a place to celebrate.*

The players themselves had to deal with their own lives. Their small monthly checks from Roberts would not keep them in money for long. Each had to find employment in the off season, and most were anxious to get back home. Few were willing to stick around Cleburne until a proper celebration could be planned. Within a day the most of the players were gone.

Charley Moran headed back to Nashville to be with his wife, to finish the season with the city's local team in the Southern League. Ben Shelton went back to Ennis to sell cotton. Roy Akin and Dee Poindexter were off to Waxahachie. George Whiteman was headed to his home in Peoria, Illinois.

154

Dode Criss had plans to join the St. Louis Browns for the remainder of the 1906 season, while Rick Adams headed back to Paris, Texas for a short visit before going on to St. Paul.

The players did not leave empty handed. One article noted that *Dode Criss was seen with a large number of new ties and socks given to him by the local fans.*

Speaker, the young star….

In talking to one of the Review reporters, Doak Roberts stated *that something should have been given to Speaker. He had played hard, and was paid less money than any other man on the team. Had it been a flush year with me, I would I would have made a little private contribution to him, but I have not collected up and am behind in some things.*

Doak Roberts was lavish in his praise for his 18 year old star: *He is young and yet his work with the Cleburne team this year will bring him to the front during the coming year. He may be one of the stars in the coming year. He is quiet and unassuming, but the way in which he is wielding the stick is sure to put money in his pockets. It may be true that he did not make much money this year, but he has his day coming.*

Tris left Cleburne, reportedly planned to go to Rosebud, 40 miles south of Waco, to work in a cotton gin.

Four years after leaving Cleburne, fans were reading reports of the success of "our little Speaker" way up in Boston. Just a year after signing with Cleburne, Speaker saw action in the American League with the Red Sox. His 1907 statistics were hardly the stuff of a future Hall of Fame player. He batted 19 times in '07, with three hits. A year later, the 21 year old Hubbard boy saw action in only 31 games, raising his average from .158 in 1907 to .220 in 1908.

Then came his breakout year of 1909. He was 22 years old when he batted .309.

When this picture appeared in the 1910 newspapers, Tris Speaker had become a hitting force. Hitting for a hefty .340 average that year, there was no doubt that Speaker had become a super star long before that phrase had been coined.

Fans all across the Texas League were recalling the days when young Tris was developing his talents in the league.

A Stillness at Gorman Park

The ball season is now over. Gorman Park will not resound with the yells of the rooters for months to come, in fact it may never resound again with the yells for as fine playing as now has been done this year.

The fans have had their fun. Manager Roberts at times has appeared a little exacting, but none can say but that he felt that he held together one of the best baseball teams that ever won a baseball pennant. Capt. Ben Shelton is a favorite here, and whenever he gets tired of living anywhere, he can come here and live, and he will be heartily welcomed. Here is a kind farewell to all the boys and a wish for a safe "home run" to which ever direction, or in whatever contest they may enter.

The boys of the Cleburne team gathered for the final talk. Charlie Moran grasped Captain Ben Shelton by the hand and said: "Ben, Old Man, you have made a better man out of me, and I am glad I came to Texas. I will bid you farewell; we may never be gathered together again." This said, and there was some crying and the big utility man for the Cleburne team was off to Nashville. **The Cleburne Morning Review, September 5, 1906**

Benefit Game: September 5

Doak Roberts was embarrassed at not being able to help out some of his more needy players. His cash reserves were being used to pay pressing bills. The few players remaining in Cleburne got together to do what they could to raise some extra cash: they played an exhibition game that they hoped would draw fans to Gorman Park. The players were divided into two teams, with amateurs filling in the gaps. Parker Arbogast pitched for one side, while Doak Roberts was in the box for the other team. Charles Thacker got to play umpire. The game was played under miserable conditions, as the rainy weather continued. After 7 innings, the players gave in to the mud and rain. There was no mention about the amount of cash raised in the charity game, nor exactly how many of the Railroaders were still in town to participate in the game. It was an attempt at nobility in an ignoble season.

THE REAL POWER RESIDED IN FORT WORTH AT THE END OF 1906

The real power of the Texas League resided in Fort Worth and Dallas. When Dallas failed to capture the second half flag, the authority shifted entirely to Bill Ward. Even as President of the league, Doak Roberts understood that the post season belonged to the team that brought money to the plate. Cleburne's attendance struggles relegated her as spectator, powerless, at this point of the season.

For most players, baseball was only a part time occupation. When the season ended, the men went back to their career jobs. Many of the players were involved with cotton, one of the biggest industries 1906. In late summer, the cotton crop began coming in, being baled and readied for market. Post season play was only attractive if the boys could make more money between the lines that with their off-season jobs. It did not appear that would be the case in 1906.

As Bill Ward sat around that rainy Labor Day, everyone, including the players and management, were exhausted. The season actually began in March, and for six months the daily grind had taken its toll. The long hot summers in Texas slowly wore the players down.

Many of the players traveled long distances for a chance to play, and were getting homesick. The dreary clouds that day added to the exhaustion and melancholia of the players.

156

Talking amongst themselves, the relayed the message to Bill Ward that their preference was to end it all, give the trophy to Cleburne, and go home and back to their regular jobs.

There had been talks that perhaps the playoff games might be divided between Dallas and Fort Worth, with Cleburne home games moved to Dallas. Many of the league officials doubted that the Dallas fans would attend in very large numbers to see a Cleburne-Fort Worth series. Earlier in the year some had suggested that the Texas League champ would take on the South Texas League winner. But now on this rainy September day no one mentioned an all-state series.

All the talk for continuing the season disappeared under a blanket of water. Blame it on the dark, damp weather. At least that is what Bill Ward did. More likely it was the gloomy weather that matched his glum mood at not having a Fort Worth-Dallas saw-off series.

Doak Roberts was a beat down man by the end of the 1906 campaign. He had obligated himself to the Cleburne Athletic Association, and their continual threats, both financially as well as legally left him with little room to maneuver. As the rain pelted the empty ball parks in Fort Worth and Cleburne, Roberts was content to let the Fort Worth owner make the decision.

Ward called the owners together and announced that he was relinquishing any claim to the cup, and it would be awarded to the Cleburne Railroaders. There apparently was no one willing to put up a fuss otherwise, and so it was in that anticlimactic fashion that Ben Shelton and his boys would have their picture featured in the Official Spalding Guide for 1907 with the title of *1906 Texas League Champions*.

The trophy, forged by a Fort Worth silversmith, who expected the trophy to reside in his city, was instead given to Doak Roberts. The Cleburne papers were silent about the actual trophy, and it is likely that no one in the Johnson County city ever saw the cup publicly displayed.

Doak Roberts was locked in a battle with the Association to claim at least some of the money he lost in his venture into Cleburne. When the figures were eventually made public, he reported losses amounting to $1200-$1400. The Association refused to pay, citing his refusal to bring the team to Cleburne that last Saturday of the season, as well as a three game set that was moved to Corsicana during May.

Thacker, at least publicly, was silent about the split between Roberts and the businessmen. Had he had the means, likely he would have paid Roberts in order to keep the team in his home town. He simply did not have the money to save grace.

Little was done in Cleburne to celebrate the city's championship. The players returned to Cleburne, gathered together for one last time, then said goodbye, leaving Gorman Park empty.

Left out of the 1907 season…..
November 10, 1906

On November 10, 1906 officials of both the Texas League and the South Texas league met to discuss the future of professional baseball in Texas. Unofficial talks had started long before this meeting. A merger of the two leagues offered the only chance of long-term stability for the new league.

From 1902 until 1906, the Texas League never consisted of the same collection of cities from year to year. The South Texas League had a somewhat better track record, but beginning in 1903 until 1905 there were only four teams in the league. In 1906, the southern league expanded to six teams, but like the Texas League, there were too many financially shaky franchises. The ticket to success was a merger into one state-wide league, consisting of the largest and most financially stable franchises.

The November meeting was attended by Morris Block of San Antonio, Moritz Kopperl of Galveston, Claude Rielly of Houston, Wilber Allen of Austin, Bill Ward of Fort Worth, Joe Gardner of Dallas, and surprisingly, Charles Thacker of Cleburne.

Eight invitations were extended to various cities, including one to Cleburne, Texas. Baseball would be back in Gorman Park, despite the fact that Doak Roberts reported losses of $1200-$1400 related to his 1906 Railroaders' club, promises made by the Cleburne Athletic Association never fulfilled.

GRANDSTAND TO CHICKEN COUPS:

Thacker left the meeting pleased about the league's decision, but soon after returning to Cleburne he realized that there was no enthusiasm amongst his fellow businessmen to put up any more money to support professional baseball. Disgusted by his city's lack of support from both fans and the business community, Thacker returned the invitation to the Texas League. He told the local Cleburne writer's that *as for as he was concerned, they could take the wood out of Gorman Park and turn it into chicken coups.* The 1907 Texas League season began without a Cleburne team. The history of the Texas League in Cleburne was completed after only one season: a championship club that would never defend its title.

A FAREWELL TO THE GAME OF BASEBALL:
DOAK ROBERTS RETURNED TO CORSICANA:
"out of the game"

Doak Roberts returned to Corsicana. He was out of the game. Too many years of losing money, all capped off by his bitter fight in Cleburne. He had several players under personal contract, excellent players. He could recoup some of his money, if anyone was willing to pay him for those contracts. But he did not have a team, and hence the players were no longer obligated to him under those circumstances.

His good friend in Houston, Claud Rielly was anxious to bring several of the players to Houston. It looked like a good deal for the Buffaloes. However, things did not start well in Houston in the new all Texas league. Soon Claud was on the phone to Corsicana. He knew a good baseball man when he saw one. Doak rushed to Houston. At last he could use his talents without suffering financial loss. The two men forged a long lasting relationship in Houston, and during the next decade they produced a series of winning teams. Eventually Roberts returned to the Texas League as its president during the halcyon days of the 1920's.

Lola Roberts was not particularly pleased that once again her husband was chasing after his expensive baseball dreams, but she suffered in frugal silence.

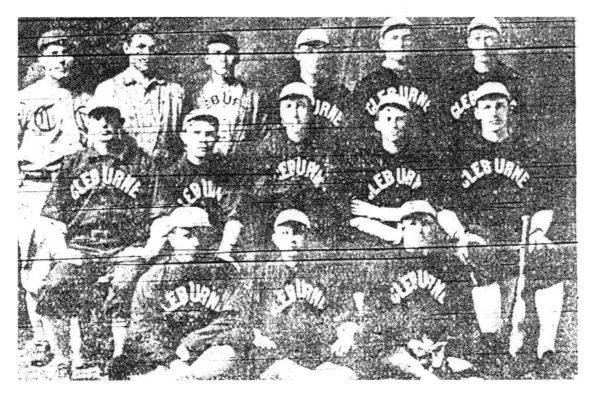

CLEBURNE'S SECOND PROFESSIONAL TEAM PLAYED IN 1911

Below: THE 1912 SANTA FE APPRENTICE CLEBURNE BALL CLUB

TEXAS LEAGUE NO- HITTERS 1906

The 1906 Texas League was a pitcher's league, with low batting averages and an incredible seven no-hitters. The batting title was won by George Whiteman with a .281 average. Only Dode Criss, himself a pitcher, found a way to consistently hit the ball hard. With 57 hits in his 143 at bats, Criss nearly hit .400. Unfortunately he did not have enough at-bats to win the title. The stars of the Texas League were the pitchers: Charley Pruiett, Dode Criss, Walter Dickson, and Alex Dupree.

April 28:   Waco vs Temple Henry **Hiett** no-hits Temple, 2-0
May 8   Greenville vs Cleburne: **Frank Farmer Moore** no hits Railroaders, 1-0
May 28:   Fort Worth vs Greenville: **Alex Dupree** pitches the third no hitter of '06 5-1
June 26:   Fort Worth vs Waco: **Alex Dupree** pitches his second no hitter of the year 1-0
              Dupree only faced 27 men. He walked one hitter that was out on a double play
  Two no hitters same day!
              Dallas vs Cleburne: **Eddie Rodebaugh** no-hits Railroaders, 3-1. It is the second time that Cleburne is no-hit.
June 30:   Cleburne vs Temple: **Walter Dickson** pitches first no hitter for Railroaders, 5-1
August 23:   Cleburne vs Waco: **Rick Adams** becomes the sixth pitcher to no-hit, and this was the only no-hitter in the second half of the season

Cleburne was involved in 4 of the 7 no-hitters, winning two and losing two.

Weather in 1906...
Cooler Wetter Than Normal
GAME POSTPONED: WET GROUNDS

In the more than 100 years that the weather conditions have been tracked in the north central Texas area, only twice has the temperature failed to reach 100° at least once during the year. One of those two was 1906. It was still a hot summer, but by Texas standards, a little less so.

However, more significantly, it was a summer of rain. Normally in this part of Texas the rains come in April and May, then are scarce until the fall. Such was not the case in '06. It must have pleased the farmers and ranchers, but it played havoc with the Texas League baseball schedule.

Rain plagued the Cleburne Railroaders all season long. Their May 3 and 6th games were rained out, then five times in June the club was idle. The trend continued into July with four rainouts, and then August was a repeat, with postponed games on the 5th, 11th, 20th, and 21st. The final coup-de-ta was Labor Day, 1906, when rain ruined the holiday, turning away hundreds of fans from the ballpark, ending the season on a dark, dreary note.

Sixteen times in 1906 the Cleburne Railroaders set idle watching the sky instead of fly balls. The loss of games was especially hard on Doak Roberts, whose team was already struggling financially. While double headers made up the scheduled games, it did not make up for the revenue lost. There was little other revenue stream for owners, and every game was needed to make payroll, train fare, and the other numerous cost of running a team.

Perhaps had 1906 been a normal hot and dry Texas summer, the Cleburne franchise might have survived another season. With so much lost to the weather in an already tight financial situation, the future of the franchise was doomed. It's difficult to say precisely how much revenue was lost, but it was likely close to $4,000, in an era when many on the team made between $50 and $200 a month. Those few thousands of dollars would have paid a lot of salaries.

The farmers and ranchers had a great season. The Railroaders did not. Rain and baseball do not mix.

WATCHING THE FLOOD FROM MAIN STREET BRIDGE—FORT WORTH, TEXAS

HOSTING: 3 Non-League Cities hosted League Games
Corsicana, Clarksville, and Gatesville

Over the years spring training has been a time for teams to roam, playing in a variety of cities away from home. In 1906 three cities played host to Texas League games despite the fact that they did not have a franchise in the league.

Four Cleburne "home games" (a fifth was rained out) were played in Corsicana. Doak Roberts's battle with the Cleburne Athletic Association forced him to bring his club back to his home town for three games at the beginning of May. Two were played, with the game of May 3rd rained out. For a while it seemed that the Railroaders might end up playing out the season in Corsicana, but facing the potential of a law suit and promises made by the association persuaded Roberts to honor his commitment to Cleburne. And besides Corsicana was not much of an improvement over his situation at Cleburne. Neither city was large enough to ensure crowds significant enough to pay the bills.

Two other cities were able to snag league games to their ball parks. On July 26th Gatesville played host to the Dallas-Waco game in conjunction with a local carnival and summer holiday events. Two games had been scheduled but the previous day's game was called because of rain.

On August 8th and 9th two more Waco games were switched away from home, this time to Clarksville. Clarksville had lured the clubs to play by a guaranteed gate. Again the games were played in conjunction with a carnival and local revelry.

The final home game away from home came near the end of the season, when Waco moved its final two home games to Corsicana. With an abysmal season record, fans were staying away from Katy Park. Corsicana promised to be a more lucrative draw at the gate for the Waco owners.

Attendance figures were seldom announced, and seldom mentioned in the story line, and so it is not possible to know how well attended the games were. In the case of Gatesville and Clarksville it is likely the games drew capacity crowds, since they were in conjunction with city celebrations.

BEATON STREET, LOOKING NORTH, CORSICANA, TEXAS.

CORSICANA, TEXAS 1906

Clarksville, Texas. Home of Long Staple Cotton.

Clarksville, Texas

Extra Inning Games In 1906

Eighteen times during the season, teams went into extra innings to settle the score. Despite going beyond nine innings, several games were left on the line, due at times to darkness while the rain finally put an end to the others.

In early June Dallas took 18 innings to put Greenville away, but that was not to be the longest game of the season. That honor was shared by the Panthers and Railroaders, who battled 19 scoreless innings before the setting sun put an end to the scoring futility, as the fans walked away in amazement, having watched 19 inning 0-0 game, and of course both pitchers stayed the course. There was honor won that day, but no win for either Alex Dupree or Walter Dickson. July 23, 1906, a date that both men remembered until their dying day.

The most extraordinary day was June 3 when all six teams were extended into extra innings. Dallas and Greenville went 18, Cleburne and Waco went 14, while Fort Worth and Temple stopped at 10 when the game was called because of darkness, which was second game of a double header.

Extra Inning and Tie Games

April	29th	Fort Worth 4	Cleburne 3	12 innings
May	8th	Fort Worth 3	Waco 2	11 innings
	11th	Greenville 7	Temple 6	12 innings
	23rd	Dallas 4	Greenville 4	10 innings, called, rain TIE
June	3	Fort Worth 1	Temple 1	10 innings, darkness (game 2, doubleheader) TIE
		Dallas 2	Greenville 1	18 innings
		Cleburne 5	Waco 0	14 innings
June	5th	Waco 4	Cleburne 4	15 innings darkness TIE
June	10th	Temple 3	Greenville 3	13 innings darkness TIE
	13th	Temple 5	Cleburne 4	13 innings
	20th	Cleburne 5	Greenville 5	5 innings rain TIE
July	17th	Fort Worth 1	Dallas 1	10 innings darkness TIE
	18th	Dallas 2	Fort Worth 1	10 innings
		Waco 3	Cleburne 1	13 innings
	21st	Cleburne 2	Fort Worth 1	10 innings
	23th	Fort Worth 0	Cleburne 0	19 innings darkness TIE
	28th	Fort Worth 2	Cleburne 0	7 innings, called for train schedule
August	7th	Cleburne 4	Dallas 3	11 innings
	10th	Fort Worth 3	Cleburne 2	10 innings
	18th	Dallas 4	Cleburne 3	11 innings

Team Records in Extra Inning Games:

	Won	Lost	Tied
Dallas	3	1	2
Fort Worth	3	2	3
Cleburne	3	5	2
Greenville	1	1	1
Temple	1	1	3
Waco	1	2	1

WHAT WAS THE VALUE OF A PLAYER'S CONTRACT?

PLAYER CONTRACTS:

For most of early years of the Texas League, income to the team was largely limited to ticket sales. There was some minor income from advertisement signs, especially those in the outfield. Scorecards provided additional sources, but without fans in the stands, teams suffered financially. However, owners who scouted good talent had the advantage of selling contracts to clubs in higher classification baseball. In 1906 the Texas League attempted to have its classification raised from Class D to Class C. The change was more than just cosmetic. Rules in place determined the value of a player based upon the classification of the team selling the player: the formula was simple:

Class D = $200 - Class C =$300 - Class B $500 Class A $750

Had the Texas League been successful, each player's value would have increased by $100.

Player Backs Into Engine, Intent on Getting Foul

PITTSBURGH, Pa., July 25. ---

B.F. Hicks, employed at the roundhouse of the Pennsylvania railroad at Pitcairn, was instantly killed during a game of ball there between two teams composed of employees.

He was playing right field for one of the teams and went after a high foul fly, which went over the railroad tracks. So intent was he in his efforts to catch the ball that he failed to notice the approach of a freight train.

His companions shouted to him, but the warning came too late. The locomotive struck him just a second after he caught the ball. He was instantly killed and his body badly mutilated.

In his hand he still clutched the ball. He was 23 years of age and single.

Sport Stories and Pictures 1906

Kosse, Texas Ball Club of 1906

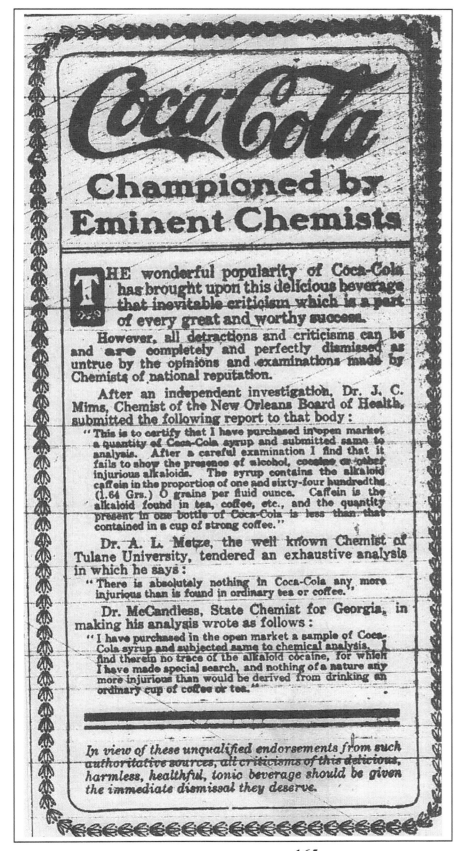

Cocaine and Coke:

In 1906 Coca-Cola used ads to fight the rumors that the drink contained cocaine

...no traces of alkaloid cocaine

IN THE FIFTH INNING

LOUDEN AT BAT INTERFERES WITH THROW TO ERWIN AND UMPIRE ALLOWS RUN

PANTHERS LEAVE FIELD

Refuses to Continue Play After Unfair Decision — Cavender Gets Home Run

Dallas 9   Fort Worth 0

Dallas, July 20--(Special.) --The final game in the Dallas and Fort Worth series ended most unsatisfactorily to all concerned and with much uproar among the players of the two clubs. The score stood 2 to 1 in favor of Fort Worth when Dallas went to bat in the last half of the fifth inning. Meyer was on third base and started for home. The ball was fielded to Erwin at the plate to catch Meyer. Louden was at the bat for Dallas and as the ball came home to Erwin, the Dallas batter made some kind of a movement and Erwin dropped the ball. The Fort Worth players insisted that Louden had interfered with Erwin and made him drop the ball. Umpire Bailey could not see the play in that light and declared Meyer safe and the run was counted, making the score a tie, 2 to 2. Captain Cavender refused to permit his men to continue play unless the decision were recalled and Umpire Bailey declared the fame forfeited. While the teams were wrangling, Maloney came home from second base, but as the game was forfeited on the decision in favor of Meyer, the last score could not count. There was much division of opinion on Umpire Bailey's decision. Many of the spectators supported it, while many others declared that Louden interfered with Erwin and that Meyer should have been declared out.

..The Fort Worth Record July 20, 1906

FORFEITS WERE FAR MORE COMMON IN BASEBALL IN THE EARLY DAYS OF THE TWENTIETH CENTURY.

Texas League forfeits and protested games 1906

May 31 Cleburne 4 Temple 2
   Game played on scheduled off day..Temple played then later refused to acknowledge game
June 6 Cleburne 9 Greenville 0
   Greenville team missed train
   Failed to arrive at Cleburne
   Game forfeited to Cleburne
June 24 Temple 9 vs Greenville 0
   Refused to take field
June 26 Temple 9 Greenville 0
   Refused to take field dispute over gate
July 20 Dallas 9 Ft.Worth 0
   ←see inset to left
July 22 Cleburne 2 Ft.Worth 1 protested
August 29: Cleburne 5 Waco 3 protested

MAJOR LEAGUES: four times in the major leagues in 1906 games were forfeited:

Pittsburgh vs Philadelphia June 9
New York vs Philadelphia A's July 2
Chicago Cubs vs New York Aug 7
New York vs Philadelphia A's Sept 3

XI

BIOGRAPHIES
THE CLEBURNE RAILROADERS

THE OLD MEN OF CLEBURNE, INDEED OLD MEN OF THE TEXAS LEAGUE REMEMBERED THAT WONDERFUL YEAR OF 1906, WHEN GIANTS WERE AMONGST THEM

As the years passed and separated 1906 from the present, the men around Cleburne more and more realized that once they indeed had a unique privilege afforded to few, a chance to see greatness in its early stages, to see boys who became men amongst great baseball players. The marquee player was of course Tris Speaker, the Hubbard lad, 18 years old that summer of 1906, but soon to become a national sensation. Speaker never forgot his roots, and after a long career returned to live around Hubbard, working as a volunteer fireman, hunting and fishing until his death in 1958 at Lake Whitney.

Speaker was not alone in going on to *faster company*. All three of Railroader pitchers saw major league action, two of its three outfielders. The utility player, Uncle Charley Moran had an incredible life, as a major leaguer, a major league umpire, and a football coach, still remembered for the greatest upset of the first 70 years of the 20th century. Early in the season the fans could have seen Roy Mitchell, while another Roy, Roy Akin, was given a serious look by the Boston Red Sox. Wingo Anderson, a late season hero, made it to the Cincinnati roster. The list of Railroaders in the major league book of books: Adams, Anderson, Dickson, Mitchell, Moran, Speaker, and Whiteman. Not bad for a little class D team. And not to forget Doak Roberts, who was president of the Texas League for over ten years.

THE 1906 CLEBURNE RAILROADERS ROSTER

The Texas League rosters were severely limited in 1906, 12 men plus the captain. Because of the limited number of players available at any one time, the rules were relaxed and bent as far as movement of players was concerned. An injury to even one player was devastating to a team. There simply was not a long bench, and so the managers and captains had a list of players always anxious to have an opportunity to play. During the 1906 season, 31 different players wore a Railroader uniform.

Player	Birth	Place	Death	Place
Adams, Rueben "Rick"	12-24-1878	Paris, Tx	03-10-1955	Paris, Tx
Akin, Roy B.	06-15-1882	Murray Co, Te	11-09-1933	Teague, Tx
Anderson, Wingo Charlie	08-13-1886	Lillian, Tx	12-19-1950	Fort Worth,Tx
Arbogast,Carl Charles Parker	01-01-1884	Paris, Tx	1955	Corpus Christi,Tx
Bates, "Red" "Windy"	U	U	U	U
Clayten, Zena	U	Corsicana, Tx	U	U
Coyle, Frank "Mickey"	U	U	1944	U
Criss, Dode	03-12-1885	Sherman, Ms	09-08-1955	Sherman, Ms
Dickson, Walter Raleigh	12-03-1879	Summerfield, Tx	12-09-1918	Ardmore, Ok
Earthman, Cal C.	U	U	U	U
Fisher, Gus	U	U	U	U
Jones, W.C."Doc"	U	U	U	U
Kellog, Bill William Dearstyne	05-25-1884	Albany, NY	12-12-1971	Baltimore, Md.
Lewis, Cal	U	U	U	U
Moore, W.P.	U	U	U	U
Moran, Charles B.	02-22-1878	Nashville, Tn	06-14-1949	Horse Cave, Ky
Pease, Walter	U	U	U	U
Pennell, Arthur L.	U	U	1941	U
Poindexter, Dee	8-16-1876	Ellis Co, Tx	12-09-1954	Corsicana, Tx
Powell, "Bill" Willliam F.	U	U	U	U
Ransom, Julian "Dude"	12-24-1886	Corsicana,Tx	01-07-1963	Corsicana,Tx
Reed, George M	U	U	U	U
Shelton, Ben	U	Terrell, Tx	1945	U
Speaker, Tristam Tris	04-04-1888	Hubbard,Tx	12-08-1958	Lake Whitney,Tx
Whiteman, George	12-23-1882	Peoria, Ill	02-10-1947	Houston, Tx
White, Robert "Bobby"	U	U	U	U
Wicker, Francis	U	U	U	U
Womack, Harry	U	U	U	U
Wright, Robert "Bobby"	U	U	U	Dallas,Tx
Yeager, Robert	U	U	U	U

U=Unknown

Thinking of the Cleburne Bunch....December 31, 1908

On December 31, 1908 Charles Thacker received a letter from his old comrade, J. Doak Roberts. The two men had exchanged letters for over twenty years, but this one had a ring sadness, regret, and yet a sense of pride realizing that once there was a team of men worth knowing, men who had achieved, men that became great players and good friends. For a quiet few sentences Roberts shared not so much the agony of dealing with a day now no more, but with the satisfaction that they had been there, that they were responsible in bringing such talent to one spot in that magical year of 1906. And there was still good times to come. Who was the next star?

Dec. 27, 1908

To: Charles H. Thacker:

I was thinking of the Cleburne bunch, and can tell you that nearly all of whom have gone to faster company. I think Cleburne holds the record for promotion. These are the players that were on that team and where they are today:

> *Dode Criss – St. Louis Browns*
> *Tris Speaker – Boston Americans*
> *George Whiteman – Boston Americans*
> *Roy Akin – Boston Americans*
> *Charles Moran – St. Louis Cardinals*
> *Rick Adams – Denver of the Western League*
> *Parker Arbogast – Vancouver of the Pacific Coast League*
> *Walter Dickson – Atlanta of the Southern League*
> *Bobby Wright – Charleston, South Atlantic League*
> *Dee Poindexter – Married, out of the game*

Advise me of the address of Fred Colquitt. I have written two letters to him at Rio Vista, but have not received a reply.

What do you think of Louis Drucke as a pitcher?
Regards to all the Gang

Sincerely,
   J. Doak Roberts

Post Note:
Thacker's response to Roberts is unknown, but we know that Louis Drucke was 14-4 with the 1909 Dallas Giants. Drucke was a star at TCU while that school was still located in Waco. He went on to pitch four seasons with the New York Giants, 1909-1912.

CLEBURNE RAILROADERS IN THE MAJOR LEAGUES:

RUEBEN "RICK" ADAMS   Washington

WINGO CHARLEY ANDERSON   Cincinnati

DODE CRISS   St. Louis Browns

WALTER R. DICKSON   New York Giants
                                          Boston Braves
                                          Pittsburgh (Federal)

WILLIAM "BILL" KELLOGG
                                          Cincinnati

ROY MITCHELL   St. Louis Browns
                                          Chicago White Sox
                                          Cincinnati

CHARLES BETHAL "Uncle Charley" MORAN
                                          St. Louis Cardinals

TRIS SPEAKER HoF   Boston Red Sox
                                          Cleveland
                                          Washington
                                          Philadelphia Athletics

GEORGE WHITEMAN   New York Yankees
                                          Boston Red Sox

WINGO CHARLIE ANDERSON
Pitcher

Born: August 13, 1886   Died: December 19, 1950
Lillian, Texas   Fort Worth, Texas
                                Burial: Dallas, Texas

MAJOR LEAGUE: 1910 Reds National League
    Pitching: Won 0 Lost 0 GS: 2 used in relief
                     Appeared in 7 games, total of 17.1 innings ERA 4.67
    Batting: AB 5 R 1 H 1

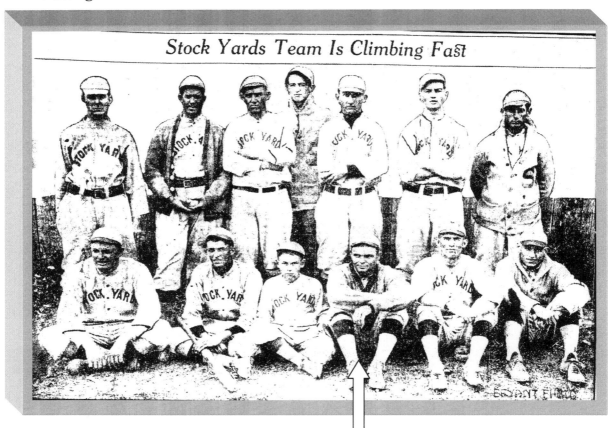

Stock Yards Team Is Climbing Fast

WINGO CHARLIE ANDERSON
(Front Row, 4th from Left)

An unlikely as well as an unsung hero of Cleburne's championship season was a local boy, born in Johnson County in the nearby town of Lillian. Earlier in the season he had a shot at making the Railroader roster, but was dropped after his only appearance, losing to Fort Worth on April 30. Anderson actually pitched well, giving up only five hits to the Panthers, but the defense behind him was spotty, with Cleburne committing 4 errors in the 6-4 loss. Wingo was only 19 years old that day in April, but it would not be his only appearance that year.

Wingo Anderson continued to sharpen his skills with various semi-pro teams, including the one in Venus, Texas, just down the road from Lillian. Roberts kept an eye on the youngster. Rotating three pitchers was a perilous proposition, with injuries and fatigue always a possibility. Earlier in the year, Dode Criss was injured, suffered with an illness that briefly sent him home to Paris. As the year waned towards the finish line, Rick Adams, Walter Dickson, and Dode all battled sore arms and tired bodies.

It was drawing to the last week of the season when Roberts re-signed Wingo, sending the young man to Corsicana to join the Railroaders. Waco had transferred their final home games to that city in hopes of drawing larger crowds, based in part on the fact that they club's miserable record had dramatically affect attendance. Besides, Corsicana was Doak Roberts' hometown.

The weekend series with Fort Worth loomed big, and Roberts needed his aces rested and refreshed. On Wednesday, August 29th, Wingo pitched the Railroaders past the Navigators in a game marred by protest. After one day's rest, Anderson was back on the mound the following Friday. Again, he pitched well enough. Two wins in three days, and more importantly bought time for Cleburne's tired arms.

Wingo finished the season with 2 wins and 1 loss. All three games were on the road, ironically, in Corsicana, a city that was not even in the Texas League. He never pitched in Cleburne.

In 1910 he had a short moment in the major leagues, appearing in 7 games for the Cincinnati Reds. On June 22, 1910 he was demoted to the team in Dayton, Ohio. However, his journey through the minor leagues is sketchy. From various newspaper reports, he apparently played in El Paso, later for the Shreveport Pirates, in 1912 was with the Tyler Ebertas, as well as the Longview Cannibals. In 1913 he worked out with the Panthers, but an injury kept him from returning to the Texas League.

Wingo Anderson died in Fort Worth on December 19, 1950 and was taken to Dallas for burial. His obituary was sketchy about other details of his life.

Information about Wingo Anderson's professional career is very sketchy. We know about his brief stint with Cleburne in 1906, and that he was with Cincinnati in 1910, and the following year with Nashville of the Southern Association, when he was only 24. In 1908 Wingo was with a semi-professional team in Venus, Texas. He advanced in the minors, finally showing up in Cincinnati for a brief stint. Wingo started the 1913 season with Fort Worth, but was injured early on, released then went to the Stock Yards team in North Fort Worth, where he played in the North Texas League that included Cleburne as a league member.

CECIL "DEE" POINDEXTER
Left Field

Born: August 16, 1876   Died: December 9, 1954
Lone Oak Community   Oakwood Cemetery
Ellis Co, Texas   Corsicana, Texas

The long time historian of the Texas League, William Ruggles, engaged in conversation with one of baseball's icons, J. Doak Roberts, who spent most of the 1920's as the President of the Texas League. Roberts' memory of baseball in Texas stretched back into the 1880's. From 1902 until 1906 he either owned or ran some of the best clubs in the Texas League. By the late 1920's he had seen hundreds of players, some average, some good, and a handful that were great. During one session with Ruggles he described his 1906 Cleburne outfield as the best that he ever saw.

In centerfield was a man who played 1,432 Texas League games, along with five seasons in the major leagues, including his last in 1918. Playing left field for the Boston Red Sox, Whiteman was a star of the 1918 World Series, but Boston had a new left fielder ready for the 1919 season. Babe Ruth was giving up his duties on the mound for a fielder's glove. George Whiteman would finish his baseball career as a Texas League star.

In left field for the 1906 Cleburne Railroaders was Dee Poindexter, the old man of the group: Speaker was 18, Whiteman 23, Dee was 30.

Cecil Dee Poindexter was born in Ellis County in the community of Lone Oak, near Waxahachie, on August 16, 1876, the year of America's first centennial as a nation. Dee was a star athlete in school, before moving onto the sandlots and semi-pro teams around Ellis County.

When the Texas League gained new life in 1902, Dee Poindexter was there as an umpire. What is not known is any professional experience he might have had before the '02 season. He was 26 years old that year, so it seems likely that he must have gained some type of professional experience prior to his Texas League days. He was too talented to spend his time as an arbiter, and was soon playing the outfield, playing first for Waco, then Dallas. From 1902 until 1905 he was a mainstay with the Fort Worth Panthers. Roberts was delighted to grab the veteran after his release by Bill Ward. The Panthers had a chance to sign Owen Wilson off of the Austin club, and Poindexter was released. He was 30 years old when Roberts signed him up to play left field for the Cleburne Railroaders.

He played in Temple and Corsicana in 1907, before moving on to Waco for the 1908 season.

Then in 1909 he moved on to Ellsworth, Kansas (Central Kansas League), where he won the silver trophy as the league's leading hitter at age 33, hitting .324 in this era of the dead ball.

In 1911 Cleburne once again hosted professional baseball, this time in the Texas-Oklahoma League. As a 35 year old outfielder, he was referred to as "the Old Man".

Dee Poindexter was the only member of the famed Cleburne outfielder not to play in the major leagues. Dee declined invitations to the major leagues. He preferred staying close to his family, and he had firm connections in the cotton industry. In Texas cotton came to market about the end of the baseball season, making a transition from baseball to cotton convenient.

1902: Waco, Ft.Worth, Dallas, Corsicana
1903: Ft. Worth
1904: Ft. Worth
1905: Ft. Worth, Temple
1906: Cleburne
1907: Temple   1908: Did Not Play
1909-1910: Ellsworth, Kansas
MANAGED: 1912 Tyler, Texarkana
         1913: Texarkana
         1914: Kaufman , Waxahachie   1915: Waxahachie

CAL C. EARTHMAN
Centerfield

Cal Earthman lost his starting position to George Whiteman, and his roster spot to Tris Speaker.

He was a teammate with Dee Poindexter in Ellsworth, Kansas, 1909

1906: Cleburne, Texas League
1907: Unknown
1908: Newport Pearl Diggers, Arkansas State League
1908: Waco Navigators, Shreveport Pirates, Texas League
1909: Great Bend Millers, Kansas State League
1909: Ellsworth Worthies, Central Kansas League
1910: Unknown
1911: Corpus Christi, Southwest Texas League

Cleburne began the 1906 season with Cal Earthman in centerfield. He might have well become a part of the immortal Cleburne outfield, playing alongside of future Hall of Famer Tris Speaker had the Fort Worth Panthers not have elected to release George Whiteman. Roberts recognized the great talent of Whiteman, and quickly signed him to a contract. Despite the fact that Cal had started the season, going 7 for 20 (a .350 batting average), he was put on the bench in favor of Whiteman. With Speaker and Criss on the roster, both heavy hitting pitchers, Earthman was unnecessary extra weight. Cut from the Railroaders, Cal floated around the minor leagues for a few years, finishing in 1909 with Ellsworth, Kansas, playing with his old friend Dee Poindexter. That year he saw limited action in Kansas, batting only 34 times.

Cal Earthman played in Waco and Shreveport, then became a forgotten ball player, ending his career in the Southwest Texas League team of Corpus Christi.

JULIAN 'DUDE' RANSOM
Right Field

When Doak Roberts died in 1929, the memorial service in Corsicana was held in the home of his long time friend, and Corsicana neighbor, Julian Ransom, more familiarly known as *Dude*. He is little more than a footnote in the history of baseball. On May 23, 1906 he strolled to the plate to oppose a tall, thin Lindy Hiett. The right handed twirler let go a high, fast, inside pitch. The 19 year old Ransom was slow to react, taking the ball to the right side of his head. In the small ball park the sound of the ball hitting Ransom was sickening. He immediately dropped to the ground, unconscious. The game came to an immediate stop. Waco's pitcher was visibly shaken by the sight of Ransom on the ground. A hack was summoned to take him to the local infirmary. A young, brash pitcher by the name of Speaker quickly lobbied to take his spot in right field. His enthusiasm at that moment was offense to many of the Railroaders, but Speaker got his way, and on that day played for the first time as a professional in the outfield.

175

Ransom was only turned 19 when his professional career ended in one pitch. His replacement was one year younger than Dude. Tris Speaker would play for the next 22 years.

Dude Ransom may have quit playing baseball because of his injury in May of 1906, but he did not leave the game entirely. When Corsicana returned to professional baseball, Ransom became the President and Stockholder of the city's Texas-Oklahoma League club. Later he operated teams in the Texas Association as well as in the Lone Star League.

Mr. Ransom inherited a grocery store on South Beaton Street in Corsicana. He would live for 74 years, dying in 1963.

TRAGEDY REPEATS

Tris Speaker's first chance to play in the outfield came about as the results of a horrible injury. In 1920 Speaker once again was touched by a tragedy in baseball. As the playing Manager for the Cleveland Indians, Speaker was certain that his club could get to the 1920 World Series. He was correct. They won the Series that year, but it came at a great cost. Ray Chapman had been an outstanding shortstop for Cleveland since 1912, and had planned to retire at the end of the 1919 season. He was one of the few ball players financially independent of baseball. Tris Speaker begged him to stay on. Chapman agreed to play one more year. On August 16, 1920 submarine thrower Carl Mays threw a high and tight pitch. Chapman had the reputation of crowding the plate, and the combination was deadly that day.

The legend has it that Ray Chapman was cursed by the number "2". He was number two, came to bat in the second inning with two men on base and two men out. Mays hated seeing players crowding the plate, and with the count at 2-2, threw Ray Chapman a tight high fast ball. Chapman hesitated. Some felt that a soiled ball was difficult for him to see, and he failed to get out of the way of the deadly throw. He was at first dazed, helped to his feet, then collapsed and never regain consciousness. Ray was taken to a local hospital, where a piece of his skull was removed. He lived 12 hours before becoming the only man to ever be killed during a baseball game. Speaker was devastated. For the second time he witnessed a teammate laying helpless on the ground after taking a ball to the head.

Back in Corsicana, Dude Ransom must have seen the news reports of the death of Chapman. His reaction to the horrific incident has been lost to time, but surely he must have recalled that day fourteen years earlier when he was the one laying on the ground.

Carl Mays, the pitcher who threw the fatal ball, always considered Chapman's death the shortstop's fault for being too close to the plate. He blamed the public's reaction to the incident for keeping him out of the Hall of Fame. The public judged Mays harshly, in part because he never appeared apologetic about the death of Ray Chapman. Ironically, Speaker blamed himself for his friend's death. He kept a small bust of Chapman in his home as a reminder.

Tris Speaker watched in shock as Dude Ransom's career ended when he was hit in the head in May of 1906. In 1920 he watched in horror when his good friend Ray Chapman died after being hit by Carl Mays.

FRANK B. "MICKIE" COYLE, 2B

1902: Dallas
1903: Corsicana, Paris
1904: Corsicana, Beaumont
1905: Temple
1906: Cleburne
1907: Temple

Mickey Coyle's most notable action during the 1906 season was the morning he met Doak Roberts at the Waco train depot to strongly object to the hiring of Tris Speaker. Later, Speaker, tired of dealing with the pugnacious Coyle, the stereotypical *fighting Irishmen,* took the matter to fist when he reached out from the Pullman car, slugging Coyle as he walked by. Speaker stayed. Mickey stayed, and ironically a few months later, when a the team spent their wild night in Hell's Half Acre, the two young men shared in the fun, too much alike not to be friends.

Coyle's career in the Texas League started in Dallas in '02. He split his time in 1903 between Corsicana and Paris. In 1904 he went to Beaumont in the South Texas League, then returned to the Texas League to umpire for a while before joining Roberts' team in Corsicana. He remained with Roberts for the '05 season in Temple, the '06 season in Cleburne, then back to Temple the following year. In 1911 he came back to Texas as a league umpire. According to the Texas League baseball historian William Ruggles, Coyle was one of the most picturesque players in the early part of the century, *a peppery, wiry Irishman who went after every fielding chance.* For a while Mickey worked in Texarkana, where he managed a pool hall owned by Ben Shelton. Mickey died in 1944.

ROBERT "BOBBY" WRIGHT
Shortstop

Doak Roberts thought his infield was set when the Railroaders took to the field for their opening game April 25. Roy Akin was at short and Zena Clayton was in the hot box at third base. Clayton had left Houston because of a contract dispute. The Buffaloes management was not keen on losing Clayton and demanded that he return to Houston. Zena and Roberts resisted, but when the South Texas League team threatened to take the matter to court, Roberts was not interested in incurring a legal battle. That left him with a big hole at an essential part of the infield. Akin was a talented fielder, and so Captain Ben Shelton moved him to third, then acquired Bobby Wright, who was put in at shortstop.

Bobby was steady and dependable at his position, giving the Railroaders one of the best defensive units in the league, Akin, Wright, Coyle, and Shelton. The modern fan may look at the defensive stats and wonder just how good the old players were, but in doing so it must be remembered that these men played with small, thin gloves on infields that were rough and hard. In one picture of Ollie Gfroerer taken at Haines Park, one of the more interesting aspects is to look at his feet for a view of the playing surface. It was little better than grounds of some of the local amateur parks. Weird bounces and sudden direction changes were common in balls hit on the ground.

Bobby followed many of his teammates to Houston in '07, then finished the season at Temple. His final season in the Texas League was as a member of the Dallas Giants.

Ollie Gfroerer, Fort Worth Outfielder, 1906

Bobby Wright, Shortstop

1906: Cleburne
1907: Temple, Houston
1908: Dallas

This photo was taken at Haines Park in 1906. Look carefully at the ground. This area is albeit in foul territory, but likely the entire playing surface was given minimal care, unlike today's fields, which are as flat as a billiard table. Also visible is the small gloves worn in 1906, all combined to make fielding averages much lower than today's standards.

ROY B. AKIN
Third Base

Born: June 15, 1882
Murray Co., Tennessee
Mother: Ida Akin
Married: Carrie Barber 1903 until her death 1917
Children: Roy Akin, Jr., Lee Akin

Died: November 9, 1933
Teague, Limestone Co.,Texas
Burial: Mexia, Texas

Roy Akin's simple four letter last name was spelled perhaps more inconsistently than any other player in the league, often as *Aiken*, sometimes *Aken*. His Texas league career started with the Paris Reds in 1902, moving to the South Texas League with Galveston in 1903 and 1904. In 1905 he left Galveston to join Doak Roberts in Temple. He stayed with Roberts when the team moved to Cleburne, then onto Houston when Roberts moved his players to that organization. He moved around, back to Waco in 1912 and 1914. Took time off in 1915 to become an umpire, returning to play with Fort Worth and Houston in 1919. The last time his name was seen in a lineup was at Mexia in 1922, when he was 40 years old.

That famous unassisted triple play: May 9, 1912
In 1911 Akin was playing in the Pacific Coast League. He received the kind of notoriety that he preferred not to have gotten: he hit into an unassisted triple play. But he had karma on his side. On May 9, 1912, his Waco team had gone to Houston for an early season game. In the first inning, Houston threatened to score with John Fillman on third, and Gilbert Britton at second base, no outs. Red Davis stepped into the batter's box. The captain flashed the bunt sign. Akin anticipated the bunt, which was lined toward the Waco third baseman. Fillman and Britton started running when they saw Davis square up. Akin grabbed the line drive, stepped on third for the second out, then reached out to tag Britton, producing the first unassisted triple play in the history of the Texas League.

An abandoned baby boy....
In 1908 Houston was scheduled for its first trip north to Dallas and Fort Worth. The players were settling in, when the word came that someone had spotted a smiling baby boy, but a thorough search failed to locate the mother. The team decided to make his welfare a club responsibility. Several times during the year baseball audiences contributed to the small endowment fund set up for the youngster. At the end of the season, Roy and his wife Carrie opted to adopt the child to raise him as their own.

A failed tryout..but a move up....
Roy was given a tryout with the Boston Red Sox, but failed to make the big league roster. He moved on to the North West League.

AKIN. SEATTLE N.W.L.

ROY B. AKIN, COTTON BUYER AND BASEBALL MAN DIES AT TEAGUE FUNERAL AT METHODIST CHURCH

Roy B. Akin, 50, widely known cotton buyer and baseball man, died Thursday afternoon in a hospital at Teague, where he was taken last week for an appendix operation. The operation showed the appendix had bursted and fear for the life of this widely known man was felt since this time. He was reported near death Wednesday night and relatives were advised that death was near.

Akin has served as umpire in a number of baseball leagues, has managed baseball clubs and coached baseball at Trinity University a number of years and was a scout for the Galveston team two years, his last baseball connection.

Apparently in fine health, Akin was suddenly attacked a week ago and rush to the Teague hospital from his home on Milam Street.

MEXIA, TEXAS November 11, 1933

Roy Akin was 40 years old, playing shortstop for the Mexia Gushers of the Texas-Oklahoma League when this box score was published on August 7, 1922. The 1922 Mexia team had two future major leaguers on its roster, Firpo Marberry, and Fred Johnson.

Roy was expected to be Cleburne's shortstop in 1906, but early in the season was put in the hot box at third, where he remained for the rest of the season.

Teams:

1902: Paris
1903: Galveston
1904: Galveston, Kansas City
1905: Galveston, Temple
1906: Cleburne
1907-1908: Houston
1909-1910: Seattle
1911: Los Angeles
1912: Waco
1913: Houston, Ft.Worth
1914: Waco
1917: Mexia (Mngr)
1922: Mexia (Mngr/IF)

Lifetime Minor League
Batting Average: .255

Prince Ben Shelton
Captain, First Baseman

Ben Shelton may have been the only player ever to have pinch-hit for Tris Speaker. In 1906 he was the captain of the Cleburne Railroaders, in charge of the day-to-day game details. The title of Manager belonged to the business leader of the team, a bit confusing for today's fan.

Shelton began his Texas League career in the 19th century when he played first and was captain in Galveston, then later in Houston. He moved around, but was always in demand, and as a result had fans and friends all over the state. He played in Galveston, Houston, Corsicana, Paris, Denison, Sherman, Temple, and Cleburne, earning respect in each city.

"Prince" Ben Shelton in his 1910 Dallas Giants uniform

Captain Ben Shelton

1899: Houston
1899: Galveston
1900: Great Falls
1901: Tacoma, Spokane
1902: Rock Island
1903: Pine Bluff, Corsicana
1904: Corsicana, Galveston
1905: Temple
1906: Cleburne
1907: Temple
1908: Houston
1909: Waco

MANAGED:
1904: Galveston
1906: Cleburne
1908: Houston
1909: Waco

At Temple in 1905 Shelton led the league in hits, doubles, runs and total bases. When he moved to Cleburne he again led the league in fielding. He was one of the best liked teammates in the first decade of the century. At the end of the 1906 season, Charley Moran put his arms around Shelton, and said, "You've made a better man of me…" Ben died in 1945

On August 17, 1906 Ben Shelton hit the only "Over the Fence" Home Run at Gorman Park, which was described as the park with the deepest outfield walls. On that day Tris Speaker hit 2 triples.

DODE CRISS
Pitcher, Hitting Star

Born: March 12, 1885   Died: September 5, 1955
Sherman, Mississippi   Buried: Sherman, Mississippi

Dode's family moved to Waxahachie, Texas when he was a small child, then later resettled in Lamar County. The Criss family lived on a farm, but by the time Dode reached his teenage years, he was playing in local amateur games, and as he grew into his 6'2" frame, his talent at ball impressed those around Paris, Texas. When he was 19 one of the state's better semi-pro teams, the Wichita Falls Cremos, sponsored by the Cremo Cigar Company, signed him to play on their squad.

Those paying attention could see that he was developing into an outstanding player, both as a pitcher as well as a hitter, a great combination. Doak Roberts was indeed taking note of the

Ex-Mississippi youngster, and soon signed him to a contract with his Cleburne team for the 1906 season. After a year in the Texas League, he was sold to the St. Paul Saints of the American Association in 1907. In 1908 he was in the major leagues with the St. Louis Browns, where he struggled as a pitcher, but starred as a hitter. He remained with the Browns until 1911. In 1912 the New York Americans brought him to spring training but he failed to make the team, returning to the minors, first to Louisville, before returning to his adopted native state. He signed once again with his old friend, Doak Roberts, who was now with Houston.

Dode stayed with Houston for six years, finally retiring from baseball in 1917. His return to the minor leagues took him back to the mound, where he was one of the outstanding pitchers during that time.

Criss' most significant injury came in 1915. The Buffaloes were in Shreveport for a series of games when Dode was hit by a *jitney bus,* which cut a deep gash in his left leg.

Dode Criss is a baseball freak. When he was 10 years old, a good fairy came to Dode and after examining the size of his feet, said: "Son, you are going to be a great man. Ask me what you will and you may have your wish. Dode took a week off and thought then he said "Please Mr. Fairy, I'd like to get a hit every time I come to bat!" "You are a greedy boy", said the fairy, "but to show you I am on the level, I'll let you get a hit every third time you come to bat." However, Dode forgot to ask for a new pair of feet. In consequence his extremities grew large and heavy and he has never been able to run. He is one of the awkwardest men who ever disgraced the national pastime. As a result, Dode never has been anything but a pinch hitter. In the National League, the Southern Association, and even in the Texas League, Dode has Been chiefly valuable because of his pinch hitting proclivities. ED REMLEY, 1912

Dode Criss claimed to have never signed a contract with a reserve clause in any of his baseball stops, preferring to keep his options open. Dode was signed in 1906 by Doak Roberts, then returned to play for Roberts in 1912 in Houston. He respected Mr. Roberts to the extent, that he named his son Doak in honor of the team owner.

St. Louis, July 19

Locals are taking the greatest interest in the wonderful pinch hitting of Dode Criss, the big pitcher who is being used chiefly as an emergency batter by the Browns. Criss is leading the American League in hitting with an average of .371. He has not pitched a full game this year, having started one and finished a couple of others. But he has been sent into nearly every game in which the Browns were behind in the 9th inning simply to bat and he has made good more than one-third of the time.

Ten days ago he was hitting at the tremendous pace of .410, but has dropped off 80 points. He has appeared in twenty-seven games, and has been at bat 27 times with 10 hits and five runs scored. Manager McAleer intends to carry him all season, even if he never uses him in the box. Criss is a big fellow, standing six foot two inches, and the most powerful of physique.

He began his professional career in 1906 at Cleburne, Texas in the Texas League where he hit .396. Last year he was at St. Paul, batting .281. Manager Armour of Toledo said of him at the close of last season:"Our batters used to hate to see him go to bat..."

Criss is a right handed pitcher and a left-handed batter. He is only 23 years old, and Jimmy McAleer considers him to be one of the finds this year.

The Cleburne Daily Enterprise, July 20, 1908

Much had changed from the days of 1906 when this picture was taken in 1914. Charles Thacker was dead, Tris Speaker was a huge star in the American League, Doak Roberts had finally found financial success with his association with the Houston club. However, what had not changed was Roberts' ability to find and sign talented ball players as the flags in this picture verify.

DODE CRISS PLAYED FOR:

1906: Cleburne
1907: St. Paul
1908: St. Louis Browns
1909: St. Louis Browns
1910: St. Louis Browns
1911: St. Louis Browns
1912: Houston
1913: Louisville
1914: Houston
1915: Houston
1916: Houston
1917: Houston

Dode Criss Won-Lost Record

Month	Date	(W)on/ (L)ost	Opponent	Score	Concurrent Won-Lost Record	
May	1	W	Waco	7-1	1-0	
	25	L	Temple	2-0	1-1	
	27	L	Dallas	3-1	1-2	
	30	W	Temple	4-2	2-2	
Jun	4	W	Waco	5-2	3-2	
	8	W	Greenville	2-1	4-2	
	11	L	Fort Worth	11-1	4-3	
	14	W	Temple	9-7	5-3	
	21	W	Greenville	6-3	6-3	
	24	W	Dallas	2-0	7-3	
	26	L	Dallas	3-1	7-4	
	28	W	Temple	2-0	8-4	

END OF FIRST HALF

Month	Date	(W)on/ (L)ost	Opponent	Score	Concurrent Won-Lost Record	
Jul	1	L	Fort Worth	3-0	8-5	
	5	L	Dallas	6-3	8-6	
	8	W	Waco	3-0	9-6	
	13	W	Dallas	8-3	10-6	
	18	L	Waco	3-1	10-7	13 innings
	21	W	Fort Worth	2-1	11-7	
	28	W	Fort Worth	4-2	12-7	
	31	W	Waco	12-3	13-7	
Aug	3	W	Waco	6-4	14-7	
	10	L	Fort Worth	3-2	14-8	10 innings
	13	L	Fort Worth	5-2	14-9	
	16	W	Fort Worth	9-6	15-9	
	19	W	Dallas	1-0	16-9	12 innings
	24	W	Waco	5-0	17-9	
	26	W	Dallas	5-3	18-9	
	27	L	Dallas	5-2	18-10	
	30	W	Waco	7-1	19-10	

Summary of Pitching Record: Texas League 1906

vs. Dallas	Won 3	Lost 4
vs. Greenville	Won 2	Lost 0
vs. Fort Worth	Won 3	Lost 4
vs. Temple	Won 3	Lost 1
vs. Waco	Won 8	Lost 1
TOTALS	**WON 19**	**LOST 10**

Pitched: 5 Shutouts, including one 12 inning

Major League Record: St. Louis Browns											Pitching Record St. Louis Browns
Year	Games	AB	R	H	2b	3b	HR	RBI	BB	Ave.	
1908	64	82	15	28	6	0	0	14	9	.341	1908 Won 0 Lost 1
1909	35	48	2	14	6	1	0	7	0	.292	1909 Won 1 Lost 5
1910	70	91	11	21	4	2	1	11	11	.231	1910 Won 2 Lost 1
1911	58	83	10	21	3	1	2	15	11	.253	1911 Won 0 Lost 2
Total 227		**304**	**38**	**84**	**19**	**4**	**3**	**47**	**31**	**.276**	**TOTAL 3 Lost 9 ERA:4.42**

Dode Criss in middle

WALTER HICKORY DICKSON
Pitcher
1878-1918

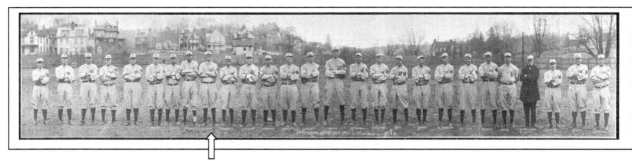

THE 1914 PITTSBURGH REBELS OF THE FEDERAL LEAGUE
Walter Hickory Dickson is 9th player from left

Walter Dickson was 25 or 26 years old when he made his Texas League debut with the Temple Boll Weevils in 1905. His official date of birth is 1878, but his son Frank Dickson listed the date as 1879*. Walter died in 1918, only a couple of years after a flood in Ardmore, Oklahoma destroyed his baseball scrapbook. The unfortunate combination left some holes in the history of Dickson's baseball career.

Given his age when Roberts signed him to his first Texas League contract it seems likely that Dickson had gain his skills in some type of league ball, either professional or semi-pro. Roberts was known to scout sandlots and semi-professional teams for new talent. Although he was born in Cherokee County, Texas, by 1905 it appears that he was living in Greenville, east of Dallas when he was signed by Roberts. .

In 1906 Dickson figured largely in Roberts plans when the club was placed in Cleburne. Along with Rick Adams and rookie Dode Criss, Cleburne had the top trio of pitchers in the Texas League.

Roberts' decision to keep Dickson proved fortuitous, with his star pitcher ending up with a 26-12 record, and more impressively, he was 15-6 against Dallas and Fort Worth, the powerhouses of the '06 league. His record might have been better except for a several tie games. On June 5 he pitched 15 innings before darkness ended the game in a tie. On July 11 he had held the Dallas Giants scoreless through five when rain ended the game 0-0. Then came that extraordinary game on July 23rd, when he pitched 19 innings of scoreless ball only to see the game end in a tie 0-0.

Three times during 1906 Walter Dickson pitched both ends of a double header, including the pennant clincher in September when he shut out the Panthers twice in one day.

Walter was given the nickname *Hickory* when a broken bone healed much faster than normally would be expected.

Walter eventually made it to the major leagues, first with the New York Giants, eventually going to Boston's National League team for the 1912 and 1913 seasons. We can only speculate if he and cross town star Tris Speaker might have met to discuss their Cleburne days. Speaker was gaining immortality with the Red Sox, while Dickson struggled with the Braves.

When the "third" major league came into existence, the Federal League, Dickson was able to find a spot on the Pittsburgh Rebel squad. His final game with Pittsburgh came on

October 2, 1915. The following year Walter returned to Texas to once again pitch with Doak Roberts' Houston team. He finished his Texas League career with a 49-20 record.

Shockingly, he died in 1918 during the horrific Spanish flu epidemic.

WALTER DICKSON – HIT IN THE HEAD-GIVES UP 17 HITS 8 RUNS- WINS

After an illustrious Texas League career and stints in the major leagues, Walter Hickory Dickson proved himself to have been an outstanding pitcher. However, he could not have looked back at June 9th, 1906 with much pride. The Fort Worth Panthers pounded him for 17 hits and 8 runs. In the sixth inning a wild Red Jarvis pitch struck him in the head. *It was a hard jolt, but he pluckily finished out the game.* **The Cleburne Morning News June 10, 1906**

June 9, 1906 Line Score:
>   Fort Worth   201 300 002 – 8 -17 – 3
>   Cleburne   010 710 000 – 9- 12 - 4

My father was born December 3, 1879 in New Summerfield, Cherokee, County, Texas. Actually, he was born in the Lone Star Community, which is no more in existence, so New Summerfield is correct. He died December 9, 1918 in Ardmore, Oklahoma during the terrible flu epidemic. I was 2 years old at the time of his death. Frank P. Dickson, Sr. Note: The official baseball stat's list Dickson's birth year as 1878.

Frank P. Dickson, in a letter 1991

Walter R. Dickson, one of the most promising youngsters on the pitching staff of the Boston Braves, left the club in a huff. He was fined $50 by Manager Kling for alleged carelessness, and promptly ducked for his home in Greenville, Texas.

Baseball Gossip, June 28, 1912

Four years after leading the Cleburne Railroaders to the 1906 Texas League pennant, Walter Dickson was picked up by the New York Giants. This was the first of three years he would spend in the National League. In 1912 he was a work horse for Boston's National League team, appearing in 36 games, losing an astounding 19 times. Note that of the 123 runs he allowed, 42 were unearned! One in three of the runs scored off of him that year was the results of shoddy fielding work by his Boston teammates. Little wonder that he lost 19 games of the 101 that Boston lost in 1912. He returned in 1913, compiling a much better 6-7 record, but again 1/3 of the runs he gave up were unearned. Lured by an increase in salary, he jumped leagues to join the outlaw "third" major league, the Federal League. Again he lost 19 times despite having a 3.23 earned run average. In 1915 Walter finally had a winning record, 7-5, on a team that finished ½ game out of first place. Three years later he died during the great flu epidemic.*

* Story of the Great Flu Epidemic of 1918 that killed Walter Dickson
100 million worldwide, greater than the Black Plague

In March of 1918 soldiers at Fort Riley, Kansas were becoming suddenly sick, and despite being young and healthy, died in large numbers. It was the beginning of the devastating Spanish Flu Epidemic. By the summer of 1920 over 675,000 Americans had died of the disease, only a small percentage of the estimated 100 million who died of the flu during this short span of time. The 1918-1919 Flu Epidemic is the greatest medical holocaust in the history of mankind, surpassing the more infamous Black Death. Like so many of its victims, Walter Dickson was still a young, healthy 39 year old man. It puzzled many that healthy young men fell victim to the flu in such large numbers.

WITH FAST COMPANY....Walter Dickson in the Major Leagues

In 1910 Cleburne's Walter Dickson became a New York Giant, playing under legendary John McGraw, who piloted the Giants from 1902 until 1932. The ace of the staff was himself a legend, Christy Mathewson, who compiled a record of 27-9 in 1910. His ERA that season was a sparkling 1.89. There were other names on the roster that still garner admiration almost a century later: Doc Crandel, who was 17-4 in1910, the bizarre Rube Marguard, and of course the man who bore the unluckiest name of all-time Fred "Bonehead" Merkle, who despite a great career, could never escape his 1909 blunder.

THE NEW GIANTS 1910 PITCHING STAFF:
Walter Dickson's Teammates

Christy Matthewson	27-9
Doc Crandell	17-4
Hooks Wiltse	14-12
Louis Drucke	12-10
Red Ames	12-11
Bugs Raymond	4-11
Rube Marguard	4-4
Walt Dickson	1-0

Walter Dickson made his major league debut on April 26, 1910 at the most famous ballpark of its time, the Polo Grounds in New York City. Walter gave up 3 hits in his four innings, and due to his excited state of mind, threw two wild pitches.

Catching for Brooklyn that day was Tex Erwin. Four years earlier, while injured, Erwin was called on to umpire the famous 19 inning game between Ft. Worth and Cleburne, in which Dickson pitched all 19 innings.

Polo Grounds April 26, 1910

On May 19, 1910 Dickson made headlines in the New York Times sports section

188

Ames, Marguard, Crandell, and Dickson Fail to Defeat Cincinnati.

On the Cincinnati roster was Wingo Charlie Anderson. Only four years earlier they were pitching for Cleburne. Anderson's career in the majors was brief, only lasting for a short span during the 1910 season.

Souvenirs: The Sunday April 17, 1910 edition of the New York Times published a picture of the New York Giants, including the image of Walter Dickson. Likely the picture made its way into Walter's scrapbook. Unfortunately, around 1917 a flood destroyed the home of Walter Dickson, and along with it went his souvenir book of his days in baseball.

Being a member of the prestigious New York Giants was important when it came time to create the tobacco cards. Despite the fact that Dickson was with the Giants for only a part of the 1910 season, he was still included in the set of cards issued that season.

On December 27, 1908 Doak Roberts wrote a letter to Charles Thacker reminiscing about the 1906 Cleburne team. At the end, he asked Thacker his opinion of *Louis Drucke.* In 1910 Drucke was a teammate of Walter Dickson, winning 12 games for the Giants that year.

Walter played in the Texas League for three seasons, '5,'06, and finally in 1916, compiling an outstanding won-lost record of 49-20. He was 38 when he decided to end his pitching career.

Summary 1906 Season:

Vs. Dallas	Won 8	Lost 3
Vs. Waco	Won 6	Lost 3
Vs. Ft.Worth	Won 7	Lost 3
Vs. Temple	Won 3	Lost 1
Vs. Greenville	Won 2	Lost 2

Walter Raleigh Hickory Dickson
Pitching Profile: Cleburne Railroaders 1906

Date	Won/ Lost	Team	Score	Cumulative Won-Lost	Notes of Game
April					
25	L	Dallas	4-0	0-1	Season Opener, WP Pruiett
29	ND	Fort Worth	4-3	0-1	13 Innings, Criss (L) Relief 3 inn.
May					
2	W	Waco	8-3	1-1	
5	W	Dallas	6-3	2-1	Pitch Last 5 Inn. Relieved Criss
8	L	Greenville	1-0	2-2	Farmer Moore pitches no-hitter
10	W	Ft.Worth	4-3	3-2	Gives up 7 Hits
13	L	Temple	7-5	3-3	Gives up 11 hits
16	L	Greenville	4-2	3-4	Loses again to Farmer Moore
19	W	Greenville	9-0	4-4	Pitches 4 hitter
22	W	Waco	4-1	5-4	5K, 4 Hits
27	L	Dallas	6-2	5-5	
31	W	Temple	4-2	6-5	
June					
5	Tie	Waco	4-4	6-5	15 innings, called darkness
9	W	Ft.Worth	9-8	7-5	Gives up 17 hits, but wins
12	W	Temple	8-4	8-5	Hit hard again, 13 hits
15	W	Ft.Worth	3-0	9-5	10K
18	W	Greenville	5-2	10-5	Gives up 2 hits
21	ND	Greenville			Hit on Arm 2 inning leaves game
26	W	Dallas	6-0	11-5	Pitches 3rd shutout of Year
30	W	Temple	5-1	12-5	No Hitter, 7th Straight Win
July					
3	L	Fort Worth	11-5	12-6	2 innings, relieved by Speaker
4	W	Dallas	2-1	13-6	Gives Up 7 hits
7	L	Waco	4-1	13-7	Pitched 7 inn, relieved by Speaker
11	Tie	Dallas	0-0		Called 5th, Gives up only 1 hit
12	W	Dallas	5-1	14-7	
15	W	Dallas	2-1	15-7	Pitches 1 hitter
19	L	Waco	5-4	15-8	
20	L	Waco	6-5	15-9	
23	Tie	Ft.Worth	0-0		19 innings vs Alex Dupree
27	W	Ft.Worth	4-1	16-9	
30	W	Waco	7-5	17-9	Railroaders get 16 hits
Aug					
2	W	Waco	4-1	18-9	
7	W	Dallas	4-3	19-9	
	W	Dallas	2-0	20-9	Wins Both Ends Double Header
12	L	Ft.Worth	2-1	20-10	
14	L	Ft.Worth	3-0	20-11	Cleburne commits 10 errors
17	W	Ft.Worth	6-2	21-11	Holds Panthers to 4 hits
22	W	Waco	10-1	22-11	
25	W	Dallas	2-1	23-11	
	L	Dallas	4-3	23-12	Again Pitches both games
28	W	Waco	9-3	24-12	Cleburne Scores 8 runs in 9th
Sept					
2	W	Ft.Worth	2-0	25-12	Wins both games of double header
	W	Ft.Worth	2-0	26-12	Pitches Pennant Clinching Games

SPECIAL NOTES: Pitched Both Ends of 3 Double Headers (5-1) /Pitches two ties, 15 innings, 19 innings

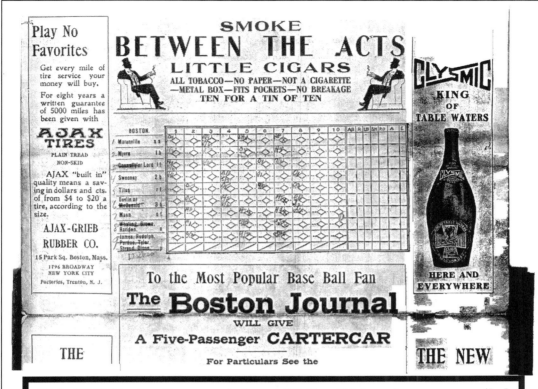

This 1912 Boston Scorecard shows Walter Dickson's name penciled into the lineup following a pitcher change. The starting players were pre-printed onto the card, which was a common practice for many years. Lineups were seldom altered, including the batting order. Some unknown fan from long ago preserved a moment in baseball history. Still a common practice today, baseball fans, unlike any other sport, buy scorecards, make entries play by play. Few fans are capable of scoring a football or basketball game, much less hockey. The baseball score card has largely remained unchanged since the nineteenth century.

Walter "Hickory" Dickson Played for:

1905: Temple
1906: Cleburne
1907: Grand Rapids Central League
1908: Grand Rapids
1909: Birmingham, Southern Association
1910: New York Giants
1911: Memphis, Southern Association
1912: Boston Braves
1913: Boston Braves
1914: Pittsburgh Rebels, Federal League, Major League
1915: Pittsburgh Rebels
1916: Houston, Texas League

CHARLES BARTHELL MORAN "Uncle Charley"

The Gentleman from Kentucky
Umpire Charley Moran leaves his position behind home plate to cover the play at third. The ball has eluded the third baseman

I Did Not Come Here to Lose!

He was not quite the star that Tris Speaker became, but Charley Moran was easily the most interesting man on the 1906 Cleburne roster. Doak Roberts extended him a generous offer to join the team that March. Unfortunately, very soon after arriving in Texas, he received word that his wife was seriously ill. He rushed back to Nashville, where upon arriving wired Roberts to let him know that she had been taken to out of their home to a Nashville infirmary. Things were grave. This was an era in which people were generally taken to the hospital to die.

Doak had serious doubts that the prized utility man would return to Cleburne. Without him on the roster, the Railroaders would be severely short of the kind of talent that Moran would bring to the team. With small rosters, a man of versatile talents was invaluable to the team, and certainly Moran fit the bill. He could catch, pitch, as well as play any position in the field. If something happened to Ben Shelton, he could even manage the team. He had been the captain of the Dallas Giants for two seasons, had seen major league action, and was the kind of affable man every team needs to keep the team unified and ready for battle.

And when absolutely necessary, Charley Moran could step in and umpire a game. He had the stature and respect of the players to keep a game in control.

Fortunately, after a few days, Roberts received the word that Moran was about to board the train back to Cleburne. The Railroaders would be a much better team as results.

Charley Moran's resume is unbelievably diverse. He played in the major leagues, both as a pitcher (1903) and a catcher (1908)! He managed in the minor leagues (Dallas, 1903-04), compiled an outstanding won-loss record at Texas A&M as their football coach for six seasons (38-8-4). In 1916 he went to the National League as an umpire, and remained in that capacity for 23 years. He was the coach of Centre College in Kentucky, and in five seasons his teams were 42-6-1. Moran was an NFL coach for the Frankford Yellow Jackets. As the Bucknell University coach he was 20-9-2.

When Charley and his wife left the A&M campus in December of 1914, the 875 members of the Corp of Cadets gave them a full-dressed parade in honor of his outstanding achievements while serving Texas A&M from 1909 until 1914.

Moran made winners out of the Texas A&M football team during his tenure that lasted from 1909 until 1914. However, there was a dark side to A&M's success on the gridiron. Rules governing the team were rather slack. Players were required to attend class only once in a week to be eligible to play on Saturday. The University of Texas viewed their cross-state rival with contempt, accusing A&M of running a rogue football program.

When Moran's teams became successful against arch rival Texas, especially following the 1909 season when A&M defeated Texas twice, 23-0, and 5-0, the situation came to a head. The University of Texas cited the lax attendance rules in College Station, announced after their 1910 game, they would no longer play a Charley Moran coached team. In 1911, 1912, 1913 and 1914, there was no Texas A&M-Texas match.

Out of the Texas standoff came one of Moran's great quotes. A member of the Texas A&M faculty asked Moran how he went about teaching his players to be *good losers*. Charley looked at the man with a puzzled look, and responded: *I didn't come here to lose!*

Despite his .821 winning percentage, Moran resigned his coaching position in December of 1914. Without Texas on its schedule, Texas A&M was losing about $15,000 a year, in effect forcing a coaching change. With Moran gone, Texas returned to the A&M schedule in 1915.

Moran's A&M Record:							
1909: vs Austin College	W 17-0	1911 vs Southwestern	W 22-0	1913 vs Trinity	W 7-0
TCU	T 0-0	Austin College	W 33-0	Austin College	W 6-0
Haskell Inst	W 15-0	Auburn	W 16-0	Polytechnic	W 19-6
Baylor	W 9-6	Mississippi	W 17-0	Mississippi St	L 0-6
Texas	W 23-0	Texas	L 0-6	Kansas St	L 0-12
Trinity	W 47-0	Baylor	W 22-11	Oklahoma A&M	L 0-12
Oklahoma	W 14-8	Dallas U	W 24-0	Haskell Inst	L 0-28
Texas	W 5-0	*Record (6-1) pts 134-17*		Baylor	T 14-14
Record (7-0-1) 130-14				LSU	T 7-7
				Record (3-4-2) 53-76	
1910 vs Marshall	W 48-0	1912 vs Daniel Baker	W 50-0	1914 vs Austin College	W 32-0
Austin College	W 27-5	Trinity	W 59-0	Trinity	T 0-0
TCU	W 35-0	Arkansas	W 27-0	TCU	W 40-0
Transylvania Ky	W 33-0	Austin College	W 57-0	Haskell Inst	L 0-10
Arkansas	L 0-5	Oklahoma	W 28-6	LSU	W 63-9
TCU	W 23-6	Mississippi St	W 41-7	Rice	W 32-7
Texas	W 14-8	Tulane	W 41-0	Okla A&M	W 24-0
Southwestern	W 6-0	Kansas St	L 10-13	Mississippi	W 14-7
Tulane	W 17-0	Baylor	W 53-0	*Record(6-1-1) 205-33*	
Record 8-1 203-24		*Record (8-1) Pts. 366-26*			

CENTRE COLLEGE SHOCKS HARVARD 6-0!

On October 29, 1921 Coach "Uncle" Charley Moran brought his Centre College team out of Danville, Kentucky to the epicenter of college football, The Stadium on the Harvard campus. The Crimson had not tasted defeat since their 1916 season. While the Harvard team strutted about in the glow of the national spotlight, Charley Moran operated his club on a shoestring budget. He personally cobbled the player's shoes, while mending their torn jerseys. Charley was referred to by the eastern press as *home-spun,* but while there was a certain snicker to their assessment of the little college out of Kentucky, there was still admiration for a team which consisted of 16 players, noting that with the small squad, Moran's team had gone undefeated in 1919.

With an undefeated Harvard looking for glamour games, Harvard invited the overachieving bucolic team to their schedule for 1920 and 1921. In 1920 Centre was only one of two teams that scored on Harvard, as they lost 31-14. Harvard threw 7 shut outs in 1920. In 1921 Harvard held their first four opponents scoreless.

Then came the last game of October, 1921. The Praying Colonels of Centre College returned to Boston to take on the Eastern powerhouse. Centre proved tough that day, shutting down the Crimson 6-0, shocking the football nation, and even today, the game is considered the greatest upset of the 20th century.

A closer look at the Praying Colonels and the subsequent accomplishment of this small squad, the upset might not have been all that great. It began with Chief Myers, a graduate of Centre College, who ended up in Fort Worth, Texas coaching at North Side High School.

Mythology always plays an important part in recounting the exploits of young men who accomplish great things. The 1921 Centre College quarterback was Bo McMillan, a Texan who played for Myers at North Side. Bo, a poor boy who loved sports, attempted to sneak into Panther Park to see Fort Worth's Texas League team. The police were always on the lookout for teenage boys attempting to get into the park without paying, and spying the young Bo crawling into the park, began chasing the elusive future quarterback. Myers was there that day, and was impressed by the speed and agility of the young man, intervened, and soon invited him to the school to join his team. Part of the story may be true, but what is known is that by the 9th grade Bo earned the spot as the school's quarterback.

Chief Myers never lost his love for his native Kentucky, and eventually three North Side players were off to Somerset where they would play their last year of high school. Bo McMillan, Red Weaver, and Thad McDonald joined other Texans, Bill James, Mattie Bell, and Sully Montgomery.

Chief Myers recruited Charley Moran to coach the Centre Team. Moran had a reputation for toughness when he compiled a great record with Texas A&M, and had coached at Carlisle when the immortal Jim Thorpe played there. Moran was umpiring in the National League at the time, and had stopped off to see his son Tom play at Centre. Uncle Charley was convinced by Chief Myers to get back into coaching, albeit, a team that hardly had a budget.

Legend has it that the Centre team's uniforms had become so shredded just before the Harvard game that Coach Moran found some plain white tops at a rummage sale. He recruited his wife and several of her friends to die the jerseys gold, and then to paint white stripes on them so that the kids could look respectable.

The Harvard fans were stunned at half-time. The little team had their boys shut out, although the score was 0-0. Then early in the third quarter, Harvard punted the ball to around midfield, then a 15 yard penalty took the ball to the 32 year line. It was called the "cut-in" play by Myers, as quarterback McMillan followed by blocks by Red Weaver, broke free, as he neared the sidelines, stopped, lost the two Harvard defenders, then broke for the goal line, his shoe strings loose almost doing what Harvard could not do, struggling to keep his balance as he stepped into the end zone. Centre missed what could have been an important extra point, but when Harvard failed to score, the one touchdown rocked the nation.

COACH CHARLEY MORAN AT CENTRE COLLEGE, KENTUCKY

Gregarious Charley Moran

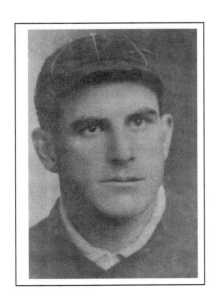

There are many stories about the great Uncle Charley. He was an affable, good natured man, driven to win. At the end of the 1906 season, it was Moran who took charge when the Cleburne Railroaders were left without a postseason playoff series. The team had been declared the champions on Monday, and now on Tuesday the boys shockingly realized there was no reason for them to remain together. They were the champs without a celebration. For the final two weeks a dozen men had pulled together for a frantic finish, winning the Texas League silver cup.

It was a rainy, dark Tuesday, no more games to be played. There was nothing left to do except tell one another *goodbye.* As the Railroaders gathered for one last time, it was Moran who grasped the moment's significance. He knew that there were teammates he might never again see, and others he would see only when they were in town playing various clubs. He was the one man not afraid to give a last hug to his boys, interjecting a few wistful words of farewell.

And now for a little humor…

Thanks to Ernie Harwell, the long time baseball announcer, who shared a couple of Charley Moran stories, we know the humorous and witty side of Uncle Charley.

In one game Fresco Thompson became disgusted at a strike call made by Umpire Moran. He stepped out of the batter's box, and without looking at Charley, he tried to insult Moran with a reference to his coaching days at Centre, whose team was called the Praying Colonels:

With you as their coach, no wonder your team prayed! Thompson was proud of his putdown of the Umpire.

Without blinking an eye, Charley Moran responded: *Young man, since you've turned this conversation into religious channels, suppose you to go the clubhouse and baptize yourself with an early shower!*

HUNTING DOGS:

Charley was a known hunter, who raised prized hunting dogs, which resulted in this exchange:

Hughie Critz of the New York Giants was at the plate. Critz was a Mississippi boy who also loved to hunt.

As Critz took his bat into the box, he said, *Charley, they tell me you some good dogs. What are you asking for a good one?*

Moran replied *A hundred and fifty dollars. BALL ONE*
That's a lot of money, said Critz
Best dog in America! STRIKE ONE
Is he fast?
Fast?! He can outrun a train! BALL TWO
What color?
Liver and white. Real handsome animal. STRIKE TWO
Can he retrieve?
Through Hell and High Water! BALL THREE
Okay, I'll take him
That's fine. BALL FOUR TAKE YOUR BASE

Uncle Charley extraordinary:
1. Major league Player
2. NFL coach
3. Legendary College coach Texas A&M Central Bucknell
4. National League Umpire

At that point Gabby Barnett, the Cubs' catcher whipped off his make, wheeled around and stuck his reddened face toward Umpire Moran

If it's the same to you, Charley, don't be selling no more bird dogs to .200 hitters while they're up here at the plate!!

Horse Cave, Kentucky

Charley's son Tom inherited his father's athletic ability. First signed by Tris Speaker in 1921 to a major league contract, he later showed up in the NFL, playing for the New York Giants. He died a young man, leaving his father to wonder about what he might have accomplished had he lived.

At the end of the 1939 season, Charley Moran, the Gentleman from Kentucky, Uncle Charley, retired as an umpire, spending the last ten years of his life in Horse Cave, Kentucky, before dying of heart disease in 1949.

CLEBURNE'S NFL CONNECTION

By the fall of 1927 Charley Moran's football career had given way to his National League umpiring profession. After successful stints at Texas A&M, Centre College, and the Citadel, Charley was out of football, when in the fall of 1927 he was offered an opportunity to become the head coach of the Frankford Yellow Jackets of the NFL. Frankford would be defending their 1926 crown, and so Uncle Charley Moran jumped at the chance of adding another layer of accomplishments to his impressive resume.

There was one small glitch in his plans to step into the NFL limelight: the National League invited him to be one of the four umpires to call the 1927 World Series, which would feature the immortal New York Yankees and the Pittsburgh Pirates. It was an honor that Moran could not pass up. With luck, the series would only take a week, and then the umpire could return to his new job in the NFL. In his interim, son Tom Moran would be put in charge. Tom had been a star at Centre College and had a brief stint as a player in the NFL.

As many had expected the World Series was short. The Yankees and Pirates played but four games, the Yanks winning 4-0. After this short absence, Charley was free to return to Frankford. However, his return found a team unhappy. The defending champions had not been pleased that the team had been sold, that a new coach had been hired, a coach who left them, even for a short time, and who had left his young, inexperienced son in charge. In a four game stretch, the club that had looked so good in 1926 could only score one touchdown during those four games, losing 13-0, 27-0, 20-7, and finally 14-0.

The team was infuriated; Philadelphia's neighborhood of Frankford was up in arms. For one of the very few times in his life, Charley Moran was caught up in a morass of failure. For a man who had always been a positive force and a leader, was now in a situation that he could not control. On November 4th, 1927, Charley Moran left the NFL, with a record of 5-5-1, with three of those wins against non-league opponents.

CHARLIE MORAN QUITS JACKETS

Uncle Charley Moran, coach of the Frankford Yellow Jackets, has resigned his berth as the results of an explosion over his continued losses of games by the champions in the dominion of national professional football. Moran's resignation was virtually forced by the uprising of folks in Frankford, long the citadel of football in this neck of the woods….. Philadelphia Record, November 4, 1927

The man from Horse Cave, Kentucky began his association with The Texas League early in his career. Moran played with the Dallas Giants beginning in 1902. This is a picture of the 1903 championship Dallas Team. Moran is in the middle of the middle row #7

Charley Moran returned to the Texas League in 1910, with his son Tom Moran serving as the team mascot. When the Spalding Guide and Reach Guides were published, this composite picture of the Dallas club was evident that the team had won the 1910 Texas League pennant. But in the riotous Texas League things are not always so simple. The league had thrown out games played during the season, Waco refused to play a makeup game in Houston on the last day of the season, Dallas defeated Fort Worth in a double header, the Buffalos scheduled a triple header (3 five inning games) in order to have a chance to catch Dallas. Houston lost the first game, and for all appearances, seemed to be the pennant winner. When the 1911 schedule was composed, the league decided to declare a tie for the 1910 season. Spalding sent both teams a pennant, but Houston refused to accept the official flag, creating one locally. The President of the Texas League did not attend the flag ceremony in Dallas. The season was a mess. That season Waco had its own problems, losing a 23 inning game, and worse, losing 35 one-run games, while compiling a 38-99 season.

Teams: CHARLEY MORAN	
1902: Dallas, Little Rock, Chattanooga	Major League Teams:
1903-1904: Dallas	St. Louis Cardinals 1903
1905: Dallas, Ft.Worth, Galveston	St. Louis Cardinals 1908
1906: Cleburne	Appeared as C, P, SS
1907: Grand Rapids	
1908: Savannah	
1909: Milwaukee	
1910: Dallas	
1911: Montgomery	
1914: Austin	

CHARLES H. THACKER
Businessman, Official Scorer, Superintendent

Born: 1858   *Died April 2, 1911*
Christian County, Kentucky   *Cleburne, Texas*
Wife: Kate Early (1869-1906)   *Daughter: Lois Thacker Parker (1892-1986)*

Census Records:

     1880: Christian County, Kentucky Occupation: Bookkeeper
     1890: Living in Waco, Texas: in 1886, 1887
         Occupation: Trains News Agent
     1910: Living in Cleburne, Texas Age 51, daughter Lois, age 17

CHARLES H. THACKER DIES
April 2, 1911

Charles H. Thacker died Sunday afternoon, April 2, at 45 minutes past 12 o'clock. He was stricken Tuesday morning, March 28 with pneumonia and in spite of the best medical attention, skilled nursing and kindly ministrations of many friends, he grew gradually worse until the end.

Friday it was realized that he had only a fighting chance to live and his daughter, Miss Lois, who is attending school at Sweet Briar, Virginia, was telegraphed for, and she is expected in Cleburne tonight at 10 o'clock on the Santa Fe from Dallas.

Mr. Thacker was 55 years of age, strong and vigorous, a man who had been sick very little in his life, and up to a few years ago, always went into training once a year, keeping his muscles supple and his energy undimmed.

In his younger years, he was very active in promoting clean sports, especially baseball, golf, and bicycling. He was an earnest advocate of good roads, he and Jink Lee doing practically all the work necessary to secure the funds to build the first good gravel road in Johnson County, the Blue Hole Road, now known as the Country Club Road.

He was one of the most active men in Cleburne in promoting the Cleburne Country Club.

He accumulated a quite nice bit of property, which together with his only life insurance, will go to his only child, Miss Lois, who is quite a lovable and talented young lady, with many friends, who will sympathize with her in her bereavement. Her father's death leaves her an orphan, her mother have died several years ago. (1906)

Mr. Thacker leaves a father, a mother, two sisters, and a brother to mourn his departure. His father and mother are both quite old, both past 80.

His sister, Mrs. Booher, and his mother live in Cleburne, on North Main Street, where the remains are now, awaiting the funeral hour. His other sister, Mrs. Willie Marshall, lives in Shreveport, Louisiana. There is also another brother in Portland, Oregon.

His brother, Ed, and his father live in Fort Worth. His brother-in-law, Walter Earley, who lives in Brownwood came in yesterday morning and was the last person Mr. Thacker recognized, before he passed into the slumber from which he never awoke.

All the immediate relatives came in response to telegrams and will attend the funeral.

Mrs. R.J. Corson and Mrs. William Fonash went to Dallas today to meet Miss Lois, and will accompany her home tonight.

The funeral will be some time tomorrow, presumably at 3pm from 812 North Main Street, but the time has not yet been definitely set. The services will be under the auspices of the W.O.W and B.P.O.E. Mr. Thacker was a member of the Fort Worth Lodge, B.P.O.E, and also a member of the Woodman of the World.

He had his faults, just as you and I have. Unfortunately for him, he always put his worst side forward to the public, and hid in his heart for his close friends, those jewels of kindness and charity than more than atoned for the follies and frailties that beset him as well as all other human kind. He did not belong to any church, nor was he bound by any creed, but yet he felt the need of Christian hope, and knew the power of human sympathy. He had confidence in the mercy of an Alwise God, knowing all things, he believed, would be just and fair to all humanity.

THE CLEBURNE DAILY ENTERPRISE, April 4, 1911

Both Cleburne Papers Carried Story of Thacker's Death:

From the Morning Review: Charles H. Thacker

Cleburne's other newspaper also carried the death of Thacker on its front page. The story was basically the same as the one in the Enterprise with a few exceptions. First the Morning Review carried more details regarding his worldly goods, acknowledged his contribution to baseball, as well as adding a few additional names. Note that the Morning Review was not judgmental in describing him as a man with personality flaws.

...at one time a good baseball player. He knew all the old timer players in Texas and in the big leagues. ....

Owned a brick building on East Chambers Street, also a ranch northwest of the city and lots in Hillsboro. ..

he carried a $3,000 policy...

was interested in making baseball prove a success.

....Miss Lois was joined by two old schoolmates, Miss Isabel Garden of Dallas, and Miss Mary Harris of Comanche.

.......Reverend H. H. Johnston, rector of the Episcopal Church will conduct the funeral services and immediately afterwards the members of the Elks and Woodman of the World will take charge and officiate at the interment.

THE CLEBURNE MORNING REVIEW, APRIL 4, 1911

An embittered, disappointed Charles Thacker, seeing his dreams of baseball in Cleburne dying, told the Morning Review man: "as far as I am concerned, they can make chicken coups out of the wood from Gorman Park."...

Reuben Alexander "Rick" Adams

Born: December 23, 1879   **Died: March 10, 1955**
Paris, Texas   **Paris, Texas**

Rick Adams came to Cleburne as one of the few players with previous major league experience. Rick had compiled a 13-3 record with the Temple Boll Weevils in 1905, before being sold to the Washington Senators in July. Like so many players, Adams' jump to the major leagues proved to be overwhelming. He was unable to match his minor league proficiency, falling to 2-6 in his eleven games in the American League.

Cut by Washington, Doak Roberts was quick to offer him a contract with his 1906 club in Cleburne. Rick picked up right where he left off in 1905, joining Dickson and Criss in creating the strongest threesome in the league. Rick not only won 24 games for the Railroaders, he led the league in strike outs.

The earliest records of Adams professional career start in 1901 at Tacoma in the Pacific Coast League, where Rick played under the guidance of John McCloskey. He was sold to Cleveland, but never reported, instead went back home to Paris, where he played with his home town team during their 1902 venture in the Texas League.

In 1903 Rick played for the New Orleans Pelicans, then was sold to the New York Americans, then was sent to Montreal, finishing with the Baltimore Orioles, at that time a minor league team.

From 1907 until 1911 Rick played with the Denver Grislys, after which he bought the local Paris team and operated it for one season. Owning a team did not suit Rick, and he sold the team after one year.

He returned to the Texas League in 1912 as a coach.

Afterwards he dabbled in baseball, coming back to manage the semi-pro Paris Coca Cola Bottlers.

He died in Paris at the age of 75.

Rick Adams claimed to have been the man to have signed Tris Speaker. In an article written in 1947 by Orville Lee of the Paris newspaper, Rick was quoted: *I was in the hotel room, (I was rooming with Ben Shelton the manager of the Cleburne Club) but had not gone out to the park. In fact I was late. We were playing Waco and I was pretty well worn out, as I was playing the outfield everyday and taking my turn on the hill. Tris walked into the room, just a country ball player, and asked for the manager, saying he wanted a job playing ball I found out he was southpaw and then asked what he could do and he said 'I can do anything there is to do.' He didn't have any extra spikes, glove or any kind of equipment but it happened my spikes would fit him, do so I said, "here, you take my stuff and take my place today. I'm tired." Ben raised Cain when we got to the ball park and I was not suited up. I told him I had found him a man who could do anything needed and Ben was so mad he started him against Waco. They beat him 1-0. We just didn't get any runs.*

Next day Ben put Tris in the outfield and he collected a pair of knocks and made three fine catches. He never pitched another game. He and Tony Thebo were the greatest outfielders I ever saw. *

*(Rick was 68 years old when he gave this interview, over forty years having passed since that May day in 1906, obviously the passage of time obscuring his memory of what actually happened.)

He continued: *I never drew higher than $600 a month. That was the year I was with Washington.*

Cleburne 1906   **Denver Grislys**

TEAMS:

1901: Tacoma, Spokane	**Major Leagues:**
1902: Paris, New Orleans	Washington W 2 L 5
1903: New Orleans	
1904: Montreal	
1905: Temple	
1906: Cleburne	
1907-1910: Denver	
1911: Houston	
1913-1914: Denison	

RICK ADAMS
PITCHING PROFILE 1906

Date	Won/Lost	Team	Score	Cumulative Won-Lost Record	Comments
April					
27	L	Dallas	7-4	0-1	
29	L	Ft.Worth	4-3	0-2	Relieved Dickson 3 innings
May					
4	L	Dallas	3-2	0-3	
9	W	Greenville	3-1	1-3	
12	W	Ft.Worth	4-1	2-3	
15	W	Temple	16-3	3-3	
18	W	Greenville	8-4	4-3	
20	L	Waco	3-2	4-4	
23	W	Waco	8-1	5-4	
26	W	Temple	3-2	6-4	
June					
3	W	Waco	**5-0**	7-4	14 inning game, 2 hits
7	W	Greenville	**6-0**	8-4	Back-to-Back Shut-outs
10	L	Ft.Worth	5-4	8-5	
13	L	Temple	5-4	8-6	
16	W	Ft.Worth	4-1	9-6	
19	W	Greenville	13-3	10-6	
22	W	Greenville	11-1	11-6	
29	W	Temple	9-7	12-6	

END OF FIRST HALF Won 12-Lost 6

Date	Won/Lost	Team	Score	Cumulative Won-Lost Record	Comments
July					
2	L	Ft.Worth	4-0	12-7	
6	L	Dallas	3-0	12-8	Cleburne shut out in first two losses
10	W	Dallas	**5-0**	13-8	
14	W	Dallas	2-1	14-8	
19	W	Waco	7-4	15-8	
22	W	Ft.Worth	2-1	16-8	* Game Protested
25	L	Ft.Worth	2-0	16-9	
29	W	Waco	3-1	17-9	
August					
1	W	Waco	7-3	18-9	
6	W	Dallas	**2-0**	19-9	
8	L	Ft.Worth	3-2	19-10	
12	W	Ft.Worth	**3-0**	20-10	
15	W	Ft.Worth	**2-0**	21-10	
18	L	Dallas	4-3	21-11	
23	W	Waco	**6-0**	22-11	NO HITTER
23	W	Waco	3-1	23-11	Wins Both Ends Double header
26	L	Dallas	3-2	23-12	
September					
1	W	Ft.Worth	6-5	24-12	

Final Record 24-12, 7 Shut-outs, 1 No-Hitter
Led League in Strike Outs
Pitches a 14 Inning 2 Hitter vs Waco.

	Won-Lost	
Vs Fort Worth	6	5
Dallas	3	5
Greenville	5	0
Temple	3	1
Waco	7	1
Totals	**24**	**12**

"Carl" Charles Parker Arbogast
1884-1955
Catcher
1906, Temple, Cleburne

Parker Arbogast never made it to the major leagues. However, his career took him to the Pacific Coast League, where many players were well compensated, and where the league enjoyed a reputation for excellence; some believed that the west coast league was in fact at a major league level.

Arbogast had a short career in the Texas League, starting in 1904 with both Paris, and Fort Worth. In 1906 he started the season with Cleburne, went to Temple, returning to finish the year with the Railroaders. He was back in Texas to finish his Texas League career in Beaumont.

In 134 appearances at the plate, Parker got 33 hits, a .246 average. However his full season combined average was .224 (72 hits in 321 at bats.). By finishing his season with Cleburne, Parker was featured in Spalding's 1907 Guide pictured as a part of the championship team. Parker died in 1955 in Corpus Christi, Texas.

TEAMS:

1904: Paris, Ardmore, Ft. Worth	1913: Los Angeles	MAJOR LEAGUES: None
1905: Temple	1914: Oakland	Lifetime Batting Average .218
1906: Temple, Cleburne	1915: Oakland, Beaumont	
1907: Seattle		
1908: Vancouver		
1909: Hartford		
1910: Columbus		
1911-1912: Omaha		

George "Lucky" Whiteman
Centerfield

Born: December 23, 1882   Died: February 10, 1947
Peoria, Illinois   Houston, Texas

George Whiteman was the ironman of the Texas League, having played 1,432 games with the league. His career began in Waco in 1905, and continued until 1929. Doak Roberts picked him up in 1906 when the Panthers dropped his contract. He proved quite a find for Roberts, winning the league batting title while playing centerfield for the Railroaders.

Whiteman had three different stints in the major leagues, all in the American League. In 1907 he appeared in four games with the Boston Red Sox. In 1913 he got another cup of coffee with the New York Yankees. He would have been an easily forgotten player in the majors if not for his exceptional defense in the 1918 World Series.

He appeared in 71 games for the Red Sox during the '18 season, alternating left field with a man making the transition from the pitcher's mound to the outfield: Babe Ruth. Although he played a major part in Boston's 1918 series title, afterwards Whiteman returned to Texas where he resumed his star status in that league.

George was born in Peoria, and at the end of the 1906 season returned to Illinois, but after his lengthy Texas League career, he made the state of Texas his home, dying in Houston 41 years after being a part of the legendary Cleburne outfield. He played beside Tris Speaker and shared his position with Babe Ruth.

George Whiteman, 1906
Babe Ruth with Boston (below)

WHITEMAN GETS NEW BAT

This newspaper learns it on good authority that center fielder George Whiteman is happy again. A few days ago, when the Railroaders were giving a few fancy stunts in batting, some one in the grand stand yelled to Whiteman to knock the ball over the fence, that there was a suit of clothing coming. He went to bat and hit the ball so heavily the bat was broken in two. The ball didn't go over the fence, but the man who attempted to catch it was turned around in his tracks, and Whiteman was safe on first.

The bat was an old favorite and was greatly prized. While in Dallas last week, Whiteman searched all through the shops and wagons factories in that city and finally located an old ash wagon tongue. This was brought to Cleburne and was turned over to the Osborn Mill and a new bat has been turned out, which may yet get the ball over the fence for him. If it does, he still stands ready to take that suit of clothes. With only a few more games to play here it would be something unusual if Whiteman did win that suit of clothes, but he may do it. He may wait for that single game with Fort Worth before putting the finishing touches on the pellet.

.........The Cleburne Morning Review
August 22, 1906

George Whiteman, 1918
Boston Red Sox

1905: Waco	**1921-1922: Houston**
1906: Cleburne	**1923: Galveston, Wichita Falls**
1907-1908: Houston	**Oakland**
1909-1910: Montgomery	**1924: Galveston**
1911: Missoula	**1925: Ardmore**
1911-1913: Houston	**1926: Ardmore, Joplin**
1914-1915: Montreal	**1927: Salisbury-Spencer**
1916: Louisville	**1928: Salisbury-Spencer**
1917: Louisville	**1929: Winston-Salem**
1919-1920: Toronto	**Lifetime BA: .283**

Tris Speaker

Born April 4, 1888- Died: December 8, 1958

Playing Career:

Cleburne (1906)-Houston (1907)-Little Rock(1907)-Boston Red Sox(1907-1915)
Cleveland (1916-1926)* Player, Manager-Washington (1927)-Philadelphia (1928)

Games	*AB*	*R*	*H*	*2B*	*3B*	*HR*	*RBI*	*SB*	*BA*
2,789	10,207	1,881	3,514	793	223	117	1,528	433	.344

Tris speaker is best known for his lifetime batting average of .344, but his talent in the outfield is enough to have put him into the baseball Hall of Fame. He is second in lifetime putouts and total chances in the outfield, and first in assists. In 1909 he had an amazing 35 assists from his centerfield position.

He won only one batting title (thanks to the hitting domination of his peer Ty Cobb) but six times he hit over .375. He has 793 lifetime doubles, and 223 triples. He also added 433 stolen bases to his totals.

In 1920 he managed the Cleveland Indians to the World Series pennant, batting .388 that year.

Tris Speaker took his spot in Baseball's Hall of Fame in 1937.

There are many legendary stories about Tris Speaker and his time in Cleburne. Most have a seed of truth, but then they sometimes veer off into the absurd. Stories of him giving up 22 runs or 24 pointed to the fact that, had Tris relied upon his pitching arm, likely he would have never amounted to any more than a journeyman minor league pitcher. The young man was fortunate that very early on in his career Ben Shelton and Doak Roberts recognized his talents at the plate and in the outfield. As the 1906 season moved on, Tris was used less and less on the mound, and more and more in the outfield. Cleburne had a great centerfielder, George Whiteman, so Tris was relegated to right field, the position he had inherited from Dude Ransom. He would become a centerfielder in Boston.

Speaker signed on with Cleburne in May of 1906, and by the end of the 1907 he was on his way to Boston. Despite the objections of his mother to a baseball career and her wish that he would become a businessman, there was no keeping Tris indoors.

He was a simple country boy from a small town, who after his career was over returned to his roots in Hubbard, Texas. He died fishing at Lake Whitney.

Speaker's exploits are available in many sources, but within these pages are his daily activities from 1906, primarily gleaned from the pages of the various local papers. Given the exaggerations about his days in Cleburne from other sources, the items within this manuscript were taken from contemporary accounts.

Of special interest are the comments made by Doak Roberts at the season's end. The owner took extra efforts to point out to the reporters the special qualities of the youthful Tris Speaker. If he spoke so elegantly about any of the other players, he was not quoted in the local papers. Obviously the star quality of Tris Speaker was evident at his tender age of 18.

Tris Speaker's scrapbook contained an article from Cleveland, probably in 1920, showing a picture of the contract signed by himself and Doak Roberts. Obviously

Roberts was extremely proud of being the man who scooped Speaker up from the semi-pro ranks.

Speaker played for the 1906 Polytechnic Parrots, today known as Texas Wesleyan University. However, hardly any of their box scores were published in the Fort Worth papers. One of the few stories featuring a Poly game placed Tris Speaker at shortstop. A left hand shortstop!.. a testament to the athletic talent of the young man.

The day-by-day compilation Tris Speaker as a member of the Cleburne Railroaders was taken from published box scores. The results vary from the numbers published in the Reich Baseball Guide. The differences may have resulted from sloppy bookkeeping (which is doubtful, since they were compiled by Charles Thacker, a trained accountant). Data was collected from published newspaper accounts, which are subject to error. Another variable was tie games. Were they put into the totals? Rain shortened games, and games called because of darkness were left as ties, and not replayed. A more sinister reason might have been to inflate batting averages.

Owners relied upon the sale of player contracts for supplemental cash to the team operations. A .250 batter would certainly bring in more cash than a .224 hitter.

The 1906 Texas League was dominated by pitchers, "dead" balls, and huge distances to the outfield walls. George Whiteman's official batting average of .281 won him the batting cup. In that context, Tris Speaker's official Reich BA of .268, especially considering he was an 18 year old rookie, looked exceptional. The batting average gathered from contemporary news paper accounts at .237 is still not a bad average. There is a variance of one game played from the 1906 newspapers and the Reich totals. The former indicated Speaker appeared 85 times, while the official records indicated he played 84 games.

Those are numbers for the baseball purist, but in reality, it is the accomplishments on the field and in subsequent years that have meaning. Tris Speaker, not as well remembered as he should be, was and is a giant in the annals of baseball lore.

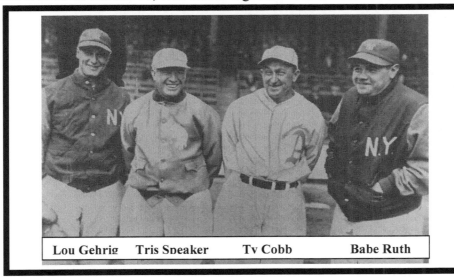

Lou Gehrig   Tris Speaker   Ty Cobb   Babe Ruth

During his days as a star of the American League Tris Speaker was held in the same high as regard as Lou Gehrig, Ty Cobb, and Babe Ruth

Speaker's boyhood home in Hubbard, Texas

Visitors to his grave side in Hubbard are often shocked at the simple marker that belies the super star status of this Hall of Fame ball player.

Robert Ripley began his newspaper career as a cartoonist before eventually creating his "Believe it Or Not" feature.

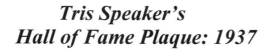

Tris Speaker's
Hall of Fame Plaque: 1937

On June 29th Tris Speaker hit his only home run in 1906 when a hard hit ball in the outfield hit a clump of grass and bounced over the outfield wall.

Tris Speaker: Ty Cobb- Scandal 1926

Two decades after signing his first professional contract with the Cleburne Railroaders, Speaker suddenly retired as the manager of the Cleveland Indians in December of 1926. His managerial record included one World Series flag (1920), and a combined won-lost record of 617-520 (.543). At the same time, Ty Cobb resigned as manager of the Detroit Tigers. The two "retirements" coming so close together aroused immediate suspicion by the press, who eventually discovered that American League President Ban Johnson had forced both men out of baseball.

Soon the public learned that the two megastars of baseball were accused of fixing a 1919 game between the Tigers and the Indians. Cleveland, by losing, enabled the Tigers to claim third place in the American League standings*, which meant that the Tigers would qualify for World Series money. * Detroit finished 4th, ½ behind third place New York.

The startling accusation came from one of the pitching stars of the American League, Dutch Leonard, who backed up his claim with two letters, one written by Ty Cobb and the other from Tris Speaker teammate, Smokey Joe Wood. The letters contained references that hinted at gambling and game fixing. Ban Johnson was put into a very difficult position. Cobb and Speaker were very popular stars of the game, and coming just a few years after the infamous 1919 World Series, another scandal might bring the major leagues crumbling. Confronted with the evidence, Johnson hoped to quietly take the men out of the game with minimum damage.

With both men resigning in such a short span of time invited too much suspicion to be ignored, and by January of 1927 the scandal hit the newspapers.

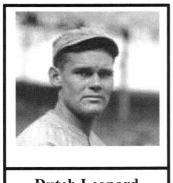

Dutch Leonard

Dutch Leonard was an embittered baseball player, basically forced out the game in the middle of the 1925 season. At the time he had a record of 11-4, but his long feud with Ty Cobb finally culminated in his release from the Tigers, and no team was willing to pick up his contract, which Leonard construed as a conspiracy between Ty Cobb and Tris Speaker. He vowed revenge to show the two super stars what it would feel like to be forced out of baseball.

On January 5, 1927 Judge Kenesaw Mountain Landis, the commissioner of baseball, called a formal hearing to settle the matter. Leonard failed to show up, and despite the two letters, the Commissioner, no doubt in deference to the potential devastating effect of having both Cobb and Speaker involved in another fixing scandal, declared the players cleared of the charges, and of no wrongdoing. Both players were reinstated to their original teams. Cleveland and Detroit both declined to sign them to another contract, and the two players were free agents.

Speaker signed with Washington in 1927, where he returned to centerfield, batting .327 with the third place Senators, who finished 25 games behind the immortal 1927 Yankees. Ty Cobb signed with the Philadelphia Athletics, batting .357. In 1928, Tris Speaker signed with the A's and the two great players were teammates, Cobb slowing down to .323, while Speaker dropped below .300 for the first time since 1908, batting .267.

Cobb had returned to baseball so that he could quit on his own terms. After the 1928 season, the two men were never again association with major league baseball. The true merits of the scandal remain unresolved.

HISTORICAL PLAQUE IN HUBBARD, TEXAS

HUBBARD CITY, TEXAS

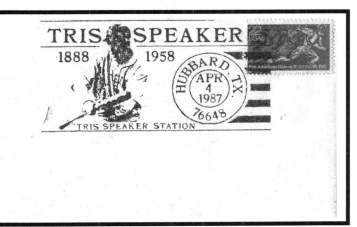

Tris Speaker (1888-1958), born in Hubbard City, Texas. He began his career as a pitcher in the minor leagues, but was an outfielder by the time the Boston Red Sox purchased him in 1907 for $400. From 1908 through 1928, he led the American League (AL) eight times in doubles, once in runs batted in and batting average, and twice in hits. In 1912, he was named the most valuable player in the league, with a .383 batting average and a league-leading 53 doubles. Speaker led the Red Sox to pennants in 1912 and 1915, the Cleveland Indians to a world championship as their player-coach in 1920. He retired with a lifetime batting average of .344, with 3515 hits, and AL records for doubles (793), putouts, and assists. Tris Speaker was named to the Baseball Hall of Fame in 1937.

Tris Speaker Honored by the US Post Office

THEY MADE A HIT, did the chorus girls of "Hit the Deck," at Philadelphia Athletics' ball park at Philadelphia. L. to r.: Tris Speaker, Helen La Vonne Eddie Collins, Polly Mara, Ty Cobb, Rita Nolan and Mickey Cochran.

(By Wide World)

HIT THE DECK: 1928
The 1928 Philadelphia Club was stacked with aging stars:
Tris Speaker- Eddie Collins- Ty Cobb- Mickey Cochran

Roy Mitchell
1885-1959

One of the great *might-have-been* players for Cleburne was Roy Albert Mitchell. In 1905 he won 20 games for the Temple Boll Weevils. Why he opted to stay in Temple in 1906, and why Roberts did not bring him to Cleburne is not clear. Most of the players who followed Roberts in 1906 had personal service contracts that tied them to the owner. Apparently Mitchell was not obligated by such an agreement. Had Roberts been able to add him to his 1906 team, considering the level of talent that was already on the team, the Railroaders would have been the overwhelming choice to take the pennant. However, had Roy Mitchell joined the Railroaders, it would have made signing Tris Speaker very unlikely, and the history of baseball might have been changed.

Teams:

1905: Temple (TL)

1906 – 1907: Unknown

1908: San Antonio (TL)

1909: Ft. Worth (TL)

1910: Houston (TL)

1910-1914: St. Louis Brown (AL)

1915-1918: Vernon (PCL)

1918: Chicago White Sox (AL)

1919: Cincinnati (NL)

1920: Oklahoma City (WL)

1921-1924: Dallas (TL)

1925: Unknown

1926: Temple (Age 41)

7 Seasons Major Leagues: W 32 L 37
14 Known Minor Leagues: W 177 L 158

Roy Mitchell won 20 games for Temple in 1905. He was one of the few players from the '05 team that did not follow Doak Roberts to Cleburne. In 1910 he made it to the major leagues as a pitcher for the St. Louis Browns, where he stayed through the 1914 season, compiling an overall record of 28-35 for a miserable team that finished out of the cellar only once. After the 1914 season, he did not see major league action until 1918, when he played with the Chicago White Sox. He was traded to Cincinnati in '18, coming back in 1919 for 7 games with the team that ironically would oppose Chicago in the great scandalized World Series of 1919. Roy's career in the major leagues ended with a record of 32 wins, 37 loses. However, like a lot of major leaguers with marginal records, did well in the minors. Roy appeared in 261 games in the Texas League, a 120-92 record, finishing his career in Dallas in 1924. After his playing career was over, Roy returned to Temple, Texas, living there until his death.

For the Briefest of Time:

William "Bill" Dearstyne Kellogg
Catcher
Born: May 25, 1884 Albany, NY
Died: December 12, 1971 Baltimore, Md.

On July 9th the Cleburne Railroaders were in Waco on a dreary rainy day. The state press release for the game was short:

> **Waco, Texas, July 9-(Special)—**
> The Indians (Waco Navigators) took the third game of the series with the Cleburne Railroaders in a slow game played in a rain which fell during most of the game. The rain served to make the ball hard to handle and numerous errors resulted, the Railroaders making a large majority of them which made victory possible for the locals.

Cleburne lost its mainstay catcher, Bill Powell. While Charley Moran could fill-in for a short period, he was not cut out to be an everyday backstop. Twenty-two year old Bill Kellogg was brought in, given the catcher's mitt on a wet, rainy day. His battery mate that day was Tris Speaker, who struggled mightily, being charged with 6 wild pitches, while Kellogg added another passed ball, creating one of the worst battery combos of the entire season. How many were truly wild pitches and how much of that was the fault of the novice catcher is difficult to know, but Ben Shelton grew impatient with Kellogg despite the fact that he had one hit in two at bats. Kellogg was taken out of the game, with Moran moved from first to catcher, Dode Criss taking over first base.

After those few disastrous innings, Kellogg was given his walking papers. The next day the Railroaders announced that they had signed Parker Arbogast, who was home in Canyon City after the disbanding of the Temple team. Arbogast took over the catcher's position and made a great contribution to Cleburne's championship run.

Kellogg had made his one and only appearance for Cleburne.

His career afterwards was a mystery until 1914, when he showed up in Cincinnati, opening up the season as an infielder, playing 71 games, batting a sad .175 on a team that finished in last place, with a 60-94 record. That was Bill Kellogg's only season as a major leaguer.

Baseball historians have identified Cleburne's Kellogg as the same man who showed up in Cincinnati eight years later, joining Wingo Charlie Anderson as a bit player from 1906 who later ended up in that Ohio city.

Bill Kellogg: Cleburne, 1906
Cincinnati 1914

William Ward, Former Baseball Magnate, Dies

Funeral to Be Held Today for Father of Texas League Activities Here.

William H. (Bill) Ward, 81, known as the father of Texas League baseball in Fort Worth and prominently identified with sporting and theatrical circles here for many years, died Friday at 4 a. m. in a hospital after an illness of a year.

Funeral services will be held Saturday at 11 a. m. at the Robertson-Mueller-Harper Funeral Temple. Mgr. Robert M. Nolan of St. Patrick's Catholic Church will officiate. Burial will be in Mount Olivet Cemetery.

Active until about three months ago, Ward was a staunch baseball fan until the last. In the victory of the St. Louis Cardinals he gained a wish he had expressed that "the Dean boys win" the World Series." He followed the first two games closely but was thereafter too weak either to listen to the radio broadcasts or read the sport pages.

One of the last links of the Texas League of the present with the Texas League of the nineties, Ward dated his baseball connection back to 1887, when he headed the Fort Worth semiprofessional club. When the Texas League was organized in the Fall of that year Ward was the logical man to take over the first franchise. His ownership of the club lasted through 1909, when he sold out to Frank Weaver and associate. He had owned the Fort Worth club in 1888, again from 1895 to 1898 and after the revival of the club in 1902 took over the team in 1903 from Ted Sullivan. His brother, John Ward, was associated with him until his death in 1903. From 1903 to 1909 D. C. Feegles of Fort Worth, Ward's brother-in-law, who lives at 3036 College Avenue, also was with the club as business manager and secretary.

After leaving baseball, Ward and Feegles were associated in the theatrical business here until 1928. They operated the old Imperial Theater, a vaudeville house. Their last venture was the old Rex Theater, a movie house. Ward retired from the theater business about the time the talkies appeared.

For 20 years Ward was owner of the old White Elephant Restaurant. He was active in politics also and for 15 years represented the First Ward as alderman. His love of sports was not confined to baseball. Prize

Late Sportsman

WILLIAM H. WARD.

fighting also held a large place in his affections. John L. Sullivan was his favorite fighter. He delighted in telling of the celebrated bare knuckle fight of Sullivan and Jake Kilrain in Mississippi, which he witnessed.

A native of Galena, Ill., Ward spent his boyhood in the vicinity of President U. S. Grant's old home and as a lad often played in the tannery operated by the Grants on the bank of Galena River.

Like his brother, Ward was a railroader in his younger days. He left a five-year connection with the Illinois Central to take a run as conductor for the Missouri-Kansas-Texas Railway out of Denison in 1874. He spent 10 years with the M.-K.-T. and then went into business in Fort Worth in 1884.

Ward was grieved over the apparent waning of public interest in baseball and only last year took an active part in the campaign to revive the Fort Worth Cats. He was one of the first to buy one of the $5 honor certificates in support of the team.

He is survived by his widow, Mrs. Pearl Rose Ward, and a niece in California. Ward resided at 424 South Ballinger Street.

TEXAS LEAGUE HALL OF FAME

MEN ASSOCIATED WITH THE 1906 CLEBURNE RAILROADERS NOW IN THE TEXAS LEAGUE HALL OF FAME:

J. DOAK ROBERTS

TRIS SPEAKER

DODE CRISS

GEORGE WHITEMAN

XII

THE NATIONAL GAME

Play Day at Gorman Park

THE MAJOR LEAGUE RECORDS OF 1906

The American League pennant winner of 1906 was the *Hitless Wonders,* **the Chicago White Sox**, a team that finished last in the league with a team batting average of .230. One starter, **Lee Tannehill** hit .183 after hitting a fat .200 in 1905. Did the manager keep him out of the last game of the 1905 season to keep him from falling below .200?

Chicago Cubs won the National League pennant with 116 victories

Victor "Vic" Willis was coming off a season in which he lost 29 games, barely missing his chance of becoming the only 30 game loser in modern baseball history. His record for Boston was 12-29. In 1906 he changed teams, going to the Pittsburgh Pirates, where his record vastly improved to 23-13.

Forfeits: there were four forfeited games in 1906: 3 in National, 1 in American League
> Pittsburgh vs Philadelphia June 9
> New York vs Philadelphia July 2
> Chicago Cubs vs August 7
> New York Americans vs Philadelphia A's September 3

Spring Training Sites: Three Teams trained in Texas in 1906:
> St. Louis Cards and St. Louis Browns in Dallas
> Cincinnati in Marlin

Streaks:
> Chicago White Sox won 19 in a row
> New York Highlanders (AL) lost 15 in a row
> Boston Red Sox lost 20 in a row
> Boston Braves lost 19 in a row

Hal Chase (NYA) had three triples in one games (August 30)
Harry McIntire (Brooklyn) lost a no-hitter to Pittsburgh (August 1, 1906)

George Mullin(Detroit) pitched two complete games in one day (September 22) vs. Washington

Oddities of the games:
> Both Chicago teams finished in first place
> Both New York teams finished in second place
> Both Philadelphia teams finished in fourth place
> Both Boston teams finished in last place
> Of the cities with two teams, only the two St. Louis teams failed to match their

cross town rivals in the final league standings: Cards finished in 5th, while the Browns were 7th

MAJOR LEAGUE HOMERUN RECORDS FOR 1906

1906 was the era of the **dead ball**, a time in which games were generally umpired by one man, who was given three balls at the beginning of the game. Every effort was made to retrieve balls hit into the stands, resulting in a rather mushy, soft baseball by the late innings, and in the era of no stadium lights, the ball would have become dark and difficult to see in the late innings as the sun set.

LEADING HOMERUN HITTERS FOR 1906:

AMERICAN LEAGUE			NATIONAL LEAGUE		
Davis –	Philadelphia	12	Jordan – Brooklyn		12
Hickman –	Washington	6	Lumley- Brooklyn		9
Stone -	St. Louis	6	Setmour – NY, Cinn		8
Seybold -	Philadelphia	5	Schulte – Chicago		7

TOTAL HOMERUNS BY TEAMS:1906

AMERICAN LEAGUE		NATIONAL LEAGUE	
Chicago White Sox	6	Chicago Cubs	20
New York Highlanders	17	New York Giants	15
Cleveland Indians	11	Pittsburgh	12
Philadelphia A's	31	Philadelphia	12
St. Louis Browns	20	Brooklyn	25
Detroit	10	Cincinnati	16
Washington	26	St. Louis Cards	10
Boston Red Sox	13	Boston Braves	16

The Chicago White Sox won the American League pennant while hitting only 6 home runs all season. The two Chicago teams combined for a total of 26 homers. The Philadelphia A's were the only team to hit over 30 home runs for the entire season.

An Epilogue to Self-Indulgence
The story of this manuscript

I have the good fortune to be a third generation fan of the Fort Worth Cats (nee☐ Panthers) and the Texas League. My mother's father escaped from Oklahoma around 1914, trading his Okie roots for Texas citizenship. Not long after settling in Texas, he was shipped off to France to fight in some war he knew nothing about. By the time he returned from the battlefields, he knew all the obscene songs about France, lyrics with which he agreed whole heartily.

Finally back in Texas he met and soon eloped with Eula. They had two daughters, then a third. That was my mother, whose birth ushered in the Great Depression. Three years later, Helen found herself relegated to an even lower status in the family with the birth of her brother. His entrance into the world deprived her of the status as the baby of the family. He was now THE baby, and as the first son, was given his father's name. My mother was now trapped between two older sisters and a younger brother who bore her father's name. She was lost in the crowd. Helen Stafford would have to find a strategy in order to curry favor with her father.

Baseball. Tobe Stafford loved the game. And so my mother would as well.

Tobe had the good fortune of being in Fort Worth during its finest moment on the ball field. Panther Park was the home of Jack Atz's pennant winning Panthers. From 1919 until 1925 the Fort Worth club won the Texas League pennant. Seven straight years! That would make a baseball fan out of anyone. And Tobe was amongst those at Panther Park cheering for the Atz gang.

Jack Atz brought a little mystery to the game, his personal history being clouded by a man given to tales. He once claimed he was born John Jacob Zimmerman, but changed his name to Atz because, he learned early on, that ball players were paid alphabetically and by the time the owner got to the Z's, they were out of money. It's not likely a true story, but the legends are generally more fun than the facts.

Jack Atz was born in Washington, D.C. on July 1, 1879. There is some confusion about his legal name, be it John Jacob Atz or Jacob Henry Atz. It didn't seem to a problem with him, since he just used the name Jack. He had stints in the major leagues from 1902 until 1909. He became the manager of the Fort Worth Panthers in 1914. His first two seasons with the Texas team were mediocre, and then in 1916 a meddling owner, Frank Weaver, personally pulled a pitcher when Atz refused to do so. He was fired, but was rehired in 1917 when W.K. Stripling and Paul LaGrave bought out Weaver's portion of the team. Atz finished in 2nd place. The Texas League suspended operation in 1918 because of the War. Then starting in 1919 until 1925 the great Jack Atz's teams dominated the league as no team since has done. The games were lively and so was the ball. The liveliest of all was Clarence Big Boy Kraft, whose bat lit up the Panther Park Scoreboard. Large crowds were in regular attendance at Panther Park. In 1925 the Fort Worth Panthers moved to their new location, still occupied by the modern Fort

After the 1925 season, the Panthers (Cats) were never quite as good, but still it was baseball daily. In the 30's the games were on the radio, and with little money to buy tickets,

Tobe listened to the games, with his daughter Helen at his side. When she played baseball with the boys, she always got to be *Rabbit McDowell*, Fort Worth's speedy, all-star second baseman, who played at LaGrave Field from 1937-1942. Could it be possible that any other girl in her neighborhood had the least idea of who Rabbit (Clyde) McDowell was? Not likely. But what other girl was determined to be her father's favorite *son*?

As the years passed, Tobe always had trouble distinguishing the voices of his daughters over the telephone, but he always knew it was Helen, her conversation would soon turn to baseball.

In 1948 as the Cats fought their way to a championship under the leadership of Bobby Bragan, Helen was sharing a home with her mother-in-law, who did not know a baseball from a rock, but by late summer Pearl Whitten was rooting as hard for Fort Worth as her son's wife. It was the era of baseball on the radio. Television was in its experimental stages in Fort Worth. Radio was still king. Dramas, comedies, news, just a little music, and the Fort Worth Cats, on nightly.

My father was never much of a sports fan. Probably because he worked long hours for little pay, driving buses and trucks. My mother's devotion to the sport began to wane under the need to care for her family, and like a lot of people in the early 50's there was television that garnered the evening's free time. Minor league ball suffered.

Then there was the year of my tenth birthday. It was summer. School ended Memorial Day and would not start back until Labor Day. The first day of summer was grand, but soon boredom sat in, and I was the *king of bored*. By the end of the first week I actually anticipated with great enthusiasm the start of the new school year.

My mother likely despaired of keeping me entertained. One evening she sat me down in front of our old tube-type radio my Dad had bought at the Goodwill Store. She tuned the radio to KXOL, 1360 *on any dial!* Out of the speakers came the wonderful sounds created by the controlled excitement in the voice of Bill Hightower. He was at LaGrave Field in Fort Worth, home of the Cats. He spoke of grounders, curves, sliders, errors, pitch-outs, strikes, bull-pens, walks, doubles and triples. I might as well have been listening to a German announcer. I had no idea what he was saying or talking about. We played ball on the school grounds at R. Vickery elementary, but it wasn't like what I was hearing on the radio.

I was not particularly interested in listening to this mess of words, but my mother just smiled. I was bored and had nothing else to do. *Just listen. Keep listening. Soon you will know and understand.* She didn't say the words, but she was telling me to *watch the game on radio*.

It has been too many years for me to recall the exact moment it seemed to click. Suddenly it seemed, I knew the starting lineup, knew a little about the other seven teams in the Texas League. Mother subscribed to both Fort Worth papers, The Press and the Fort Worth Star-Telegram. I could read the next morning what I had seen on the radio the evening before.

Sometime that summer my older cousin "Bubba" got his driver's license, and in car nearly as old he was, took me to LaGrave Field. He had it on good authority that we could save our ticket money and sneak into the ball park. Beyond the short right field wall where was once the Knothole Gang Section, but those stands had long since been demolished, leaving a grassy area between the home run fence and the large advertising signs 50 feet beyond. It was the underneath the large advertising boards that the breach in baseball security was initiated.

There were several teenage boys crawling under the fence, and so Bubba decided that we should try this. I have always been a law-abiding citizen and it made my stomach turn to think about breaking into the stadium. And as I expected, once inside the park, an usher rushed over and demanded to see our ticket stubs. Of course, we had no such items. I was certain at this point there would be police intervention, but to my relief he only escorted us to the ticket window. My ticket was fifty cents.

I have collected baseball memorabilia for most of my life, but to my regret that ticket is not a part of my permanent collection. Neither did I buy a scorecard. I was too wild-eyed just seeing the park in person. That flat, green field. A stadium that held 12,000 fans. I hardly remember anything else of that night. Who were the Cats playing, or who won? It didn't matter. I was there.

As I grew older, my friends were obligated to be baseball fans. There was Pat and Walter. We lived on the Poly bus line, which first took us to downtown Fort Worth, where we then caught the shuttle to LaGrave Field. Even as the game ended, the shuttle waited for our return to the Poly connection. The hour would be late, but we exited the bus with no fear or worry. It was summer and we had been to a ball game. The nights were cool and breezy and all was right with the world.

Things changed. The Cats stopped playing. Dallas and Fort Worth, so long rivals, became hyphened, represented by a team playing in some distant park, non-descript and dull. The new team had no tradition, it was located far from the fan base of either city, and it turned out that the hyphen was in fact the city of Arlington. *The Dallas-Fort Worth Spurs.*

By this time Walter, Pat and I were no longer kids, but one night for one last time we tried to find the magic of those nights in our youth at LaGrave Field. It was an elusive commodity. This was not LaGrave Field, but an ugly park with an ugly name, *Turnpike Stadium.* After a few innings, Walter shook his head and turned to Pat and myself *this just isn't the same.* The three of us would never again attend a game as a threesome.

Our lives went separate ways. The Rangers came to town. They took the stadium that had hosted the Dallas-hyphen-Fort Worth Spurs and tried to convince us that we were seeing a major league team. A disinterested Ted Williams was there as window dressing, a diversion from a bad baseball team, *the Texas Rangers.*

I tried to love the Rangers. Arlington Stadium, no longer Turnpike Stadium, would never be LaGrave Field. There was no *Fort Worth* in the name of the team, just the generic *Texas....* we were to share the team with the entire state of Texas, the *Texas* Rangers. At least the hyphen was gone.

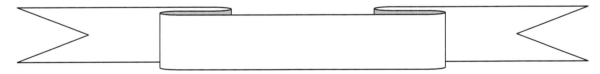

A STARTLING DISCOVERY

The seed for the research that led to this manuscript came sometime around 1990. It was a cold, rainy day when, taking an hour out of my day. I stepped into the Hurst Library, casually looking at the sports section, baseball, of course. I picked up a book about the history of minor league baseball. I opened the book, turned to the section on the Texas League. I was interested in how many times the Fort Worth club had won the league pennant.

The Texas League, in one form or another, claims a history that stretches back to 1888. As my fingers trailed down the page, there it was: an incredible entry that took me totally by surprise:: *1906. Cleburne, Texas, **League Champions**.* CLEBURNE!

I knew that city well. Maybe 20,000 people lived there. How could they have ever had a Texas League club! Certainly in 1906 the city must have been an even smaller burg.

There was nothing else in the book about that team: just that entry. I looked for more information about that Cleburne team in the library, but there was nothing to be found.

I wanted to learn what I could about the champions for the 1906 season. This was in the days before the internet. History was recorded mostly in books…although, as I was soon to find out, in the minds of those who lived through those days, and the stories passed down to our generation.

At first I looked for printed material, then began to search out the men who were the Cleburne Railroaders, a search that took me to many different places, a chance to visit with many fine people that I would never otherwise have met. I don't recall the exact length of time I spent on this labor of love. Perhaps five years.

It was a fun time. Searching and digging. In libraries, museums, and around old neighborhoods. Letters sent to places I had never seen, to people who were at first just a name, but soon to become living history.

The search was just a hobby, for my own benefit. I was curious and the chase was a pleasure. Eventually, having compiled several notebooks of pictures and various facts about the 1906 Cleburne team, and the Texas League, I decided to put together some of the stories into typed pages to be shared, and out of that came these few pages.

Where possible I have attempted to cite sources and dates, but for the most part, the data gathered here came from interviews in person, over the telephone or through correspondence. Since this is not necessarily an historical treatise, footnotes are not to be found. I have tried to be as factual as my information allowed for me to be, but this is, after all, the story of a minor league team long ago. A little mystery and obtuse facts are in order. This story is a mixture of memory and contemporary printed data as best I could locate.

There were trips to the Leland Museum in Cleburne, to the Special Collections Department at the University of Texas at Arlington, the Fort Worth Library, as well as those in Dallas, Waco, Greenville, Temple and Corsicana.

Invaluable are the old newspapers recorded on scratchy 35 mm films, scratched one time too many as they were drug across the lens of the old the microfilm readers. Cleburne had two excellent newspapers which have thankfully been saved for posterity. I did not have similar luck in Greenville or Temple. Corsicana's papers were destroyed long ago in a fire, tragic in its results, since so much of the details of the daily happenings were forever and irretrievably lost. Fort Worth and Dallas papers were excellent sources, but serving large cities, they tended to be a bit more stilted in their approach to the lives of the citizens they chronicled.

Of interest in the hundred year old newspapers are the traditions, attitudes, and customs of those who lived in that era. Stories of lynchings were common, and not necessarily without sympathy to the perpetrators. One such story illustrated the matching of age-old bigotry and modern technology. A young man had been captured, found immediately guilty by the gang, and was readied for his hanging. Someone took pity on the crying man, and so it was determined that he would be allowed to use the long-distance phone to tell his mother goodbye before his life would be taken from him at the end of a lynching rope. The story made the local papers, with praise for the mob's kindness towards its victim. It was not often that those to be lynched were given an opportunity to tell their mother *their final farewell.* A heartwarming tale of kindness.

1906 was a time of open gambling, of games attended almost exclusively by males, with exceptions for *Ladies Day*. The local Dallas paper might complain about gamblers openly plying their trade at Gaston Park, but it was an industry too important to the owners to enforce any type of prohibition. Gambling brought the crowds to the game. It was still over a decade away from the great Black Sox Scandal of 1919.

Of much more interest than the museums, newspapers, and libraries were the people I had the chance to meet. All of the players from the 1906 had long since been deceased, but several had children still living. They were most gracious when I contacted them.

The most amazing person was Louis Swartz, who at the time I interviewed him,(ca.1991) was 94 years old, still dressing dapperly each day he went to work at his cotton company in Corsicana. Astoundingly, as I talked with him, I discovered that as a child he attended games in Corsicana that featured the many of the players on the Cleburne squad. My interviews with him were casual, and to my regret I did not return for more in depth talks. However, from him I got a sense of the real men who played ball, not the stiff and flawed descriptions from the contemporary newspaper accounts.

Mr. Swartz laughed at remembering the insults hurled towards the players. Zena Clayton worked in a fish market, and so the fans called him the "Red Snapper Kid." Unfortunately, I did not make copious notes or record the interview with the elderly gentleman. I was perhaps a bit awe struck at finding someone still alive who had been where I was only in my mind.

There was a brief mention in a 1906 story of a one-armed Negro League ball player. Oscar Frame was in left field for the Cleburne *colored team*. I met one cold day with Clyde Head, who was in his early 80's, still a heavy smoker, under treatment for cancer. Mr. Head had written many years for the Morning Review in Cleburne, and was now doing a nostalgia column for the Cleburne Eagle, a monthly newspaper.

He did not have any information on Mr. Frame in his files, or better still in his long memory, but, with his old newspaperman's eye for research, he accompanied me as we conducted door to door search for information about Mr. Frame. We went to the east side of Cleburne, predominantly African-American, and went from door to door as if we were looking for a missing person. At last we were able to find a scant lead. Henry Slaton knew someone who might help us. Maynie Norton. From there, we got information that Janie Conner, who lived in Abilene, might be able to help us. Ms. Conner was kind enough to share further information. Senola Howard lived in the Stop Six area of Fort Worth, about a mile from Poly, where I had grown up.

Mr. and Mrs. Howard was an elderly retired couple in their modest home, and amongst their collection was the picture of Oscar Frame, who they said was called *Fudge* by his friends. From the Howards I learned about Oscar's sister, a principal in Cleburne and his burial site. From a single line in a paper long ago buried, I found an interesting life.

Dode Criss played for Cleburne, and since he also played in the major leagues, I was able to find his burial place, Sherman, Mississippi. I wrote a letter to the "history" department of the town's library. I had no idea if the letter might inspire a response, but I was delighted to learn that Dode Criss' daughter lived in the Fort Worth area. Ms. Mary Perry lived in the Euless area, and like so many others, invited me into her home, and shared with me items left from her father's time in the minor and major leagues. Apparently there was more, but someone long ago had borrowed a scrap book, which was in their home at the time the house was repossessed. All items in the home were confiscated, including Dode's scrap book. He was never able to get it back.

From Albuquerque, New Mexico came a response from Frank Dickson, son of Walter Dickson. He shared a few items with me, but since his father died when he was only two, he had no memories of his father. As it turned out, he was interested in the items I was able to uncover. We exchanged several letters. Finding baseball memorabilia was a little more difficult in that day before eBay and Amazon. As I recall, he was not aware of the tobacco card of Walter Dickson. He asked that I locate one for his grandson, which I was proud to do. We never met in person, but Mr. Dickson was a great addition to the people I met along the way to finding the Cleburne Railroader story.

Tris Speaker Cobb was the niece of Tris Speaker. She had inherited a great deal of his baseball collection. She had grown suspicious of those who would barge into her home to look at the wonderful Speaker collection, and was reluctant to open her doors to very many. She told me of the lawyer who sent a blank check for anything that might have belonged to her uncle. She never cashed the check. These items were souvenirs of her family and she had no interest in cashing in on their value.

Mrs. Rufus Shell in Corsicana was extremely proud of her father, Cecil Dee Poindexter, and hoped that eventually my information would end up published. She wanted her father's memory to be shared with as many people as possible. From her I learned of his season in Ellsworth, Kansas. She was a proud lady proud of her father. She proudly displayed the silver cup he had won in Ellsworth, a memento of his batting title in 1909.

Coleman Liggins lived in the east side of Cleburne, remembered the Negro League teams around Cleburne. The Cleburne paper had referred to the team only as *Cleburne's colored team.* Mr. Liggins strained to remember the real nickname of Cleburne's all black team. He suggested that they might have been called the *Oilers*, but he could not be certain. He had no pictures or written material, just his cloudy memories of those times decades earlier when the Negro League teams would play before mixed crowds of black and white fans. *And they were courteous. The white people were our guest and they acted such.* It had made a mark with him that the two races could find a common ground in an age that was often otherwise.

Ironically, another Euless family was descended from one of the old Cleburne bunch. Jodie Adams was the granddaughter of Rick Adams. She shared her scant information with me, and was proud to show pictures of her son, who was playing high school baseball at the time.

Owen Chief Wilson did not play for the Railroaders, but was an integral part of the 1906 Fort Worth Panthers before going on to star with the Pittsburgh Pirates. His son Owen Wilson, Jr. of Austin opened his home to me, allowing me to view many of the wonderful pictures and articles about his father. Mrs. Wilson was a gracious host who made the trip to Austin a wonderful experience. Martha Wilson Macken (Mrs. Joe P. Macken), daughter of Mr. Wilson, was equal gracious as I sought to find out about the life of her father. The two children of Owen Wilson were no doubt representative of the fine man that Chief Wilson was, modest and accomplished.

There were others along the way. Some whose names I failed to write down, and now are forgotten. All of the information was gathered in five large three ring binders, occasionally for my amusement, as I would flip through the pages to find something new, or something I had forgotten.

As a result of my research, I was more aware of errors in local history. One article I read gave credence to the story that Haines Park was named in honor of Al Hayne, the great hero of the Spring Palace Fire. That was not the case. Does anyone else know how Haines Park received its name? How many places have the Panthers/Cats played in? At last we know the answer to that mystery.

I have blown off the dust, gathered a bit of the information and struggled to lay out the story in these few pages.

There are without doubt factual errors, although I hope not. Some things will have to be trusted to me, since I had no original intent to put into a manuscript and thus will be without footnote.

It is all insignificant, except to those who love history, baseball, and the players who made it all possible. In a salute to their memory, I stood on the ground in Hulen Park in Cleburne, looked around for a shadow of those days past, thinking that once there was a ballpark, and what a grand time it was. ***Those Champions of Naught Six.***

When the Panthers left Haines Park, they moved to a modern structure first called Morris Park, then later Panther Park. The Park was located west of North Main Street, and remained the home of the Fort Worth Cats until 1925, when the team moved to the east side of North Main. The field was configured to accommodate football as well as baseball. High school and college games were played at this site. It was here the Clarence Big Boy Kraft hit 55 home runs in 1924. It was here that Tobe Stafford learned to love baseball.

View of downtown Fort Worth from La Grave Field taken in 1964, the last year the park was used before being torn town. The site would remain vacant until 2002 when the revised version of the Fort Worth Cats began playing at the new La Grave Field.

TOP
The park at the top of the page is where my Mother's father first attended games in Fort Worth. The other pictures are the LaGrave Field I first saw.

RIGHT:
LaGrave Field 1964

*The **Fort Worth Panthers/Cats** have played in 5 locations since 1888*

PANTHERS AT MORRIS PARK

STATISTICAL RECAP OF THE TEXAS LEAGUE 1906
Compiled from contemporary newspaper accounts

I.   Game by Game Recap: Date, Teams, Scores, Standings Game by Game Recap: Cleburne Railroaders
   a. Vs. Team
   b. Score
   c. Recap Batting Per Game
   d. Individual Player by Game

II.   Texas League Individual Extra Base Hits

III. Pitching Records *by Teams*
   Greenville Waco
   Temple Cleburne
   Dallas Fort Worth

IV. Texas League pitching records

V.   OFFICIAL TEXAS LEAGUE BATTING STATISTICS

VI. Cleburne Railroader Major League Statistics

VII. Minor Leagues of 1906 by Classification: AAA,A,B,C,D

Statistical Compilations: Texas League 1906

There was excellent print coverage of the Texas League in most of the cities with teams, including Cleburne, which had two competing papers, the morning paper and the evening paper. Fort Worth, Dallas, and Waco were also served by papers with extensive coverage of their league team. Only in Temple and Greenville were there limited published reports of professional sports.

The following statistical information about the 1906 Texas League season was gleaned from the pages of the various local papers, with the understanding that the box scores as printed were not the official summaries of the game. However, the stories and statistical compilations provided a highly accurate source for determining standings, pitching, and hitting data.

Note that there are discrepancies between the published records and the official stats, even to the level of won-lost records. According to the Texas League Greenville completed its only appearance in the circuit with a .500 record, 30-30. However, note that the contemporary newspapers published a different scenario, indicating that the Hunters left the Texas League with a 30-31 record.

Batting averages and pitching won-lost records determined from the newspapers in the six cities of the Texas League are often different than those listed in the Reach Guidebook of 1907, which published that year, listed the detailed records of the 1906 season. Without access to the details used to create the numbers in the national publication, it is impossible to reconcile the variants in the differing numbers, Reach versus the local press.

The numbers used in this publication are for all games, including ties and rain shortened games. The game-by-game layout of the Cleburne season is based on newspaper accounts.

Note that depending upon the local press exclusively has its limitations. Lured by the promised of a large gate guarantee, Waco moved a home game with Dallas to Clarksville. A short account of the game was provided to the newspapers, but within the story was a disclaimer that no box score had been kept of the game, and hence no statistical details were provided. There is a possibility that the league did obtain hitting and pitching details, but that is not known. That game went into the books, but was a wash as far as hitting and pitching records are concerned.

The greater story is the chronicle of the 1906 Texas League pennant race, and the men who were the league. The story is of great interest, but this is after all is a story about baseball, and baseball is a numbers sport. Most fans cannot help but to look at the statistics in order to gain the entirety of the narrative. Every player who appeared in a game in 1906 left a statistical footprint, no matter how briefly they played.

Before we leave the discussion of the baseball fan, and the obsession with numbers, note that in 1906 one very familiar stat did not exist. Shockingly there was no column for RBIs, with the emphasis on how often the player scored rather than how often he was able to advance a runner to the home plate.

The following statistical compilation is as seen through the eyes of the fans of 1906.

```
                    FIRST HALF 1906 TEXAS LEAGUE
      D=DALLAS C=CLEBURNE FW=FT.WORTH GV=GREENVILLE W=WACO T=TEMPLE


    DATE          SCORES          PITCHERS           STANDINGS WON-LOST

APRIL 25      GV 6   FW 5    W-DOYLE L-WALSH        GV  1 0    C  0   1
              D  4   C  0    W-PRUITT L-DICKSON     D   1 0    FW 0   1
              T  4   W  3    W-VANCE L-OEHME        T   1 0    W  0   1

APRIL 26      GV 6   FW 5    W-MOORE L-DUPREE       GV  2 0    C  0   2
              D  4   C  1    W-RODEBAUGH L-JONES    D   2 0    FW 0   2
              T  6   W  1    W-WOMACK L-HORNSBY     T   2 0    W  0   2

APRIL 27      GV 11  FW 2    W-MOORE L-WICKER       GV  3 0    W  1   2
              D  7   C  4    W-STOVALL L-ADAMS      D   3 0    FW 0   3
              W  18  T  8    W-BURNS L-GOEHBRIGG    T   2 1    C  0   3

APRIL 28      FW 4   C  2    W-WALSH L-YEAGER       D   4 0    W  2   2
              GV 4   D  3    W-DOYLE L-STOVALL      G   3 1    FW 1   3
              W  2   T  0*   W-HIATT L-VANCE        T   2 2    C  0   4
                    *No Hitter: Hiatt

APRIL 29      FW 4   C  3*   W-DUPREE L-ADAMS       D   4 1    T  2   3
              D  5   GV 0    W-PRUITT L-SPENCER     G   4 1    FW 2   3
              W  5   T  1    W-OEHME L-WOMACK       W   3 2    C  0   5
              *FW vs C 12 innings
APRIL 30      FW 6   C  4    W-WALSH  L-ANDERSON    D   5 1    W  3   3
              D  3   GV 0    W-RODEBAUGH L-MOORE    GV  4 2    FW 3   3
              T  2   W  0    W-WHITTENBERG L-COOK   T   3 3    C  0   6

MAY 1         T  2   GV 1    W-WHITTENBERG L-       D   5 1    FW 3   3
              D vs FW  Rain            JACKSON      GV  4 3    W  3   4
              C  7   W  1    W-CRISS L-BURNES       T   4 3    C  1   6
                    at Corsicana

MAY 2         GV 3   T  2    W-DOYLE L-WOMACK       D   5 1    FW 3   3
              D vs FW  Rain                         GV  5 3    W  3   5
              C  8   W  3    W-DICKSON L-HIATT      T   4 4    C  2   6
                    at Corsicana

MAY 3         D  4   FW 2    W-PRUITT L-JARVIS      D   6 1    FW 3   4
              T  5   GV 4    W-VANCE L-JACKSON      GV  5 4    W  3   5
              C vs W at Corsicana                   T   5 4    C  2   6
                          rain
MAY 4         GV 3   W  0    W-MOORE L-GEOHME       D   7 1    T  5   5
              D  3   C  2    W-RODEBAUGH L-ADAMS    GV  6 4    W  3   6
              FW 5   T  1    W-HUDDLESTON L-MERKEL  FW  4 4    C  2   7

MAY 5         C  6   D  3    W-DICKSON L-GARRET     D   7 2    T  5   6
              FW 3   T  2    W-HUDDLESN L-JONES     GV  7 4    W  3   7
              GV 6   W  3    W-SPENCER L-ZOOK       FW  5 4    C  3   7

MAY 6         ALL GAMES RAINED OUT
SUNDAY
```

229

```
                FIRST HALF 1906 TEXAS LEAGUE
    D=DALLAS C=CLEBURNE FW=FT.WORTH GV=GREENVILLE W=WACO T=TEMPLE


    DATE          SCORES      PITCHERS           STANDINGS: WON-LOST
MAY  7        D  5  T  0    W-LOWER  L-VANCE       D    8  2    T  5   7
              GV 17  C  4    W-DOYLE  L-WOMACK      GV   8  4    W  3   8
              FW  5  W  0    W-WALSH  L-BURNS       FW   6  4    C  3   8

MAY  8        GV  1  C  0*   W-MOORE  L-DICKSON     D    8  3    T  6   7
              FW  3  W  2**W-JARVIS  L-HIATT        GV   9  4    W  3   9
              T   2  D  0    W-MERKEL L-FARRIS      FW   7  4    C  3   9
                          * Moore: No Hitter
                         ** 11 Innings

MAY  9        C   3  GV  1    W-ADAMS  L-SPENCER     D    9  3    T  6   8
              D   2  T   1    W-PRUITT L-JONES       GV   9  5    C  4   9
              FW  4  W   0    W-HUDDLESTON L-OEHME   FW   8  4    W  3  10

MAY 10        C   4  FW  3    W-DICKSON L-CLARK      D   10  3    T  7   8
              T   7  GV  6    W-VANCE  L-JACKSON     GV   9  6    C  5   9
              D   4  W   3    W-RODEBAUGH L-HIATT    FW   8  5    W  3  11

MAY  11       C   3  FW  2    W-WOMACK L-WALSH       D   11  3    T  7   9
              D   7  W   1    W-GARRET L-ZOOK        GV  10  6    C  6   9
              GV  7  T   6*   W-DOYLE  L-MERKLE      FW   8  6    W  3  12
                          * 12 innnings
MAY 12        C   4  FW  1    W-ADAMS  L-JARVIS      D   12  3    T  7  10
              GV 10  T   2    W-MOORE  L-JONES       GV  11  6    C  7   9
              D   1  W   0    W-LOWER  L-BURNES      FW   8  7    W  3  13

MAY  13       FW 10  GV  5    W-DOYLE  L-SPENCER     D   13  3    T  8  10
              D   6  W   1    W-PRUITT L-ORT         GV  11  7    C  7  10
              T   7  C   5    W-VANCE  L-DICKSON     FW   9  7    W  3  14

MAY 14        FW  4  GV  1    W-DUPREE L-JACKSON     D   14  3    C  8  10
              D   5  W   4    W-FARRIS L-HIATT       FW  10  7    T  8  11
              C  11  T   6    W-WOMACK L-MERKEL      GV  11  8    W  3  15

MAY 15        D  10  W   3    W-RODEBAUGH L-BURNS    D   15  3    C  9  10
              C  16  T   3    W-ADAMS  L-JONES       FW  10  7    T  8  12
              FW vs GV Rain                         GV  11  8    W  3  16

MAY 16        W   6  FW  4    W-ZOOK   L-HUDDLESTON  D   16  3    C  9  11
              GV  4  C   2    W-MOORE  L-DICKSON     GV  12  8    T  8  13
              D  17  T   2    W-LOWER  L-VANCE       FW  10  8    W  4  16

MAY 17        W   4  FW  1    W-HIATT  L-WALSH       D   17  3    C  9  12
              GV 10  C   0    W-DOYLE  L-WOMACK      GV  13  8    T  8  14
              D   6  T   2    W-PRUITT L-MERKLE      FW  10  9    W  5  16

MAY 18        W   4  FW  0    W-DUNBAR L-CLARK       D   17  4    C 10  12
              T   4  D   3    W-VANCE  L-FARRIS      GV  13  9    T  9  14
              C   8  GV  4    W-ADAMS  L-SPENCER     FW  10 10    W  6  16
```

230

```
                    FIRST HALF 1906 TEXAS LEAGUE
        D=DALLAS C=CLEBURNE FW=FT.WORTH GV=GREENVILLE W=WACO T=TEMPLE

     DATE           SCORES          PITCHERS         STANDINGS: WON-LOST
   MAY 19      FW  9  W  1    W-DUPREE L-ZOOK        D   18  4     C  11  12
               D   7  T  3    W-RODEBAUGH L-JONES    GV  13 10     T   9  15
               C   9  GV 0    W-DICKSON L-JACKSON    FW  11 10     W   6  17

   MAY 20      FW  9  T  2    W-WALSH L-VANCE        D   18  5     C  11  13
               W   3  C  2    W-HIATT L-ADAMS        GV  14 10     T   9  16
               GV  8  D  1    W-MOORE L-LOWER        FW  12 10     W   7  17

   MAY 21      T   3  FW 2    W-SIMPSN L-HUDLSTN     D   19  5     C  11  14
               D   6  GV 2    W-PRUITT L-DOYLE       GV  14 11     T  10  16
               W   4  C  1    W-DUNBAR L-SPEAKER     FW  12 11     W   8  17

   MAY 22      T   5  FW 2    W-MERKLE L-CLARK       D   20  5     C  12  14
               D   5  GV 2    W-RODEB'GH L-JACK'N    GV  14 12     T  11  16
               C   3  W  1    W-DICKSON L-OHME       FW  12 12     W   8  18

   MAY 23      FW  6  T  2    W-DUPREE L-JONES       D   20  5     C  13  14
               D   4  GV 4*   D-GARRET GV-MOORE      GV  14 12     T  11  17
               C   8  W  1    W-ADAMS L-HIATT        FW  13 12     W   8  19
                            *10 innings rain
   MAY 24      FW  4  D  0    W-JARVIS L-PRUITT      D   20  6     C  14  14
               C   7  T  2    W-SPEAKER L-VANCE      GV  15 12     T  11  18
               GV  5  W  3    W-DOYLE L-DUNHAM       FW  14 12     W   8  20

   MAY 25      FW  2  D  1    W-CLARK L-FARRIS       D   20  7     C  14  15
               GV  9  W  1    W-SPENCER L-DUNHAM     GV  16 12     T  12  18
               T   2  C  0    W-MERKLE L-CRISS       FW  15 12     W   8  21

   MAY 26      FW  4  D  2    W-JARVIS L-LOWER       D   20  8     C  15  15
               GV 12  W 11    W-JACKSON L-DUNBAR     GV  17 12     T  12  19
               C   3  T  2    W-ADAMS L-WHITE        FW  16 12     W   8  22

   MAY 27      FW  9  GV 6    W-WALSH L-MOORE        D   22  8     C  15  17
               T   7  W  5    W-MERKLE L-HIATT       FW  17 12     T  13  19
               D   6  C  2    W-RODEB'H L-DICKSN     GV  17 13     W   8  23
               D   3  C  1    W-PRUITT L-CRISS

   MAY 28      FW  5  GV 1   *W-DUPREE L-DOYLE       D   23  8     C  15  18
               D  10  C  3    W-GARRET L-SPEAKER     FW  18 12     T  13  20
               W   7  T  5    W-DUNBAR L-MERKLE      GV  17 14     W   9  23
                          * Dupree: No Hitter

   MAY 29      FW  9  GV 7 W-CLARK L-HUDDLSN         D   23  9     C  16  18
               C  10  D  2 W-LEWIS L-FARRIS          FW  19 12     T  14  20
               T  16  W  4 W-SIMPSON L-DUNHAM        GV  17 15     W   9  24

   MAY 30      GV 15  FW 1 W-MOORE L-JARVIS          D   24  9     C  17 18
               D   4  W  0 W-FARRIS L-HIATT          FW  19 13     T  14 21
               C   4  T  2 W-CRISS L-WHITE           GV  18 15     W   9 25
```

231

```
                   FIRST HALF 1906 TEXAS LEAGUE
      D=DALLAS C=CLEBURNE FW=FT.WORTH GV=GREENVILLE W=WACO T=TEMPLE


      DATE         SCORES          PITCHERS          STANDINGS: WON-LOST
   MAY 31       GV  4  FW  1   W-DOYLE L-WALSH      D   24 10   C  18  18
                W   6   D  2   W-DUNBAR L-LOWER     FW  19 14   T  14  22
               *C   4   T  2   W-DICKSON L-VANCE    GV  19 15   W  10  25
               *Originally scheduled off day, but by agreement
                played/later Temple refusedto acknowledge game

   JUNE 1 AND 2 ALL GAMES RAINED OUT


   JUNE 3       FW 12   T  1 W-DUPREE L-MERKLE      D   25 10   C  19  18
                FW  1   T  1* FW-WALSH T-WHITE      FW  20 14   T  14  23
                D   2  GV  1**W-RODEBAUGH L-MOORE   GV  19 16   W  10  26
                C   5   W  0*xW-ADAMS L-BROWNING
                    * FW vs T 10 innings darkness
                   **D vs GV 18 innings/second game ppd dark
                   *xC vs W 14 innings/second game ppd dark
                     Adams allows 2 hits in 14 Innnings
                    Second games at Waco & Dallas Ppd dark

   JUNE 4       T   5  FW  3   W-VANCE L-WICKER     D   26 10   C  20  18
                D   6  GV  3   W-PRUITT L-HUDDLSTN  FW  20 15   T  15  23
                C   5   W  2   W-CRISS L-DANIELS    GV  19 17   W  10  27

   JUNE 5       W   4   C  4 * HIATT vs C-DICKSON   D   26 11   C  20  18
                FW 10   T  2   W-CLARK L-WHITE      FW  21 15   T  15  24
                GV  4   D  1   W-DOYLE L-GARRET     GV  20 17   W  10  27
                    * 15 innings called darkness

   JUNE 6       D   6   T  3   W-LOWER L-WICKER     D   27 11   GV 20  18
                FW  3   W  0   W-JARVIS L-DUNBAR    FW  22 15   T  15  25
               *C   9  GV  0                        C   21 18   W  10  28
               Greenville forfeits:failed to appear:missed train

   JUNE 7       D   7   T  2   W-FARRIS L-VANCE     D   28 11   GV 20  19
                FW  9   W  1   W-WALSH L-DANIELS    FW  23 15   T  15  26
                C   6  GV  0   W-ADAMS L-MOORE      C   22 18   W  10  29

   JUNE 8       FW 13   W  1   W-DUPREE L-ELLISON   D   29 11   GV 20  20
                C   2  GV  1   W-CRISS L-HUDDLSTON  FW  24 15   T  15  27
                D   7   T  6   W-ABLES L-MERKEL     C   23 18   W  10  30

   JUNE 9       C   9  FW  8   W-DICKSON L-JARVIS   D   29 12   GV 21  20
                GV  9   T  7   W-DOYLE L-MOORE      FW  24 16   T  15  28
                W   2   D  1   W-HIATT L-RODEBA'H   C   24 18   W  11  30

   JUNE 10      D   4   W  0   W-STOVAL L-BROWNING  D   31 12   GV 21  20
                D   1   W  0   W-GARRET L-DUNBAR    FW  25 16   T  15  28
                FW  5   C  4   W-WALSH L-ADAMS      C   24 19   W  11  32
                T   3  GV  3* WICKER VS MOORE
                    * 13 innings darkness
```

232

```
                    FIRST HALF 1906 TEXAS LEAGUE
         D=DALLAS C=CLEBURNE FW=FT.WORTH GV=GREENVILLE W=WACO T=TEMPLE


    DATE            SCORES         PITCHERS       STANDINGS: WON-LOST
  JUNE 11      FW 11 C   1   W-DUPREE L-CRISS      D   32 12    GV 22  20
               GV  3 T   0   W-HUDDLSTON L-VANCE  FW   26 16     T 15  29
                D  9 W   1   W-FARRIS L-DANIELS    C   24 20     W 11  33

  JUNE 12      FW  2 D   0   W-CLARK L-PRUITT      D   32 13    GV 23  20
               GV  4 W   0   W-DOYLE L-LOWER      FW   27 16     T 15  30
                C  8 T   4   W-DICKSON L-MERKLE    C   25 20     W 11  34

  JUNE 13      FW  2 D   1   W-WALSH L-RODEBA'GH   D   32 15    GV 24  20
               FW  5 D   1   W-DUPREE L-WARD      FW   29 16     T 16  30
               GV  4 W   2   W-MOORE L-BROWNING    C   25 21     W 11  35
                T  5 C   4  *W-NOWANCY L-ADAMS    *13 innings

  JUNE 14      FW  8 D   3   W-JARVIS L-PRUITT     D   32 16    GV 25  20
               GV  6 W   2   W-HUDDLSN L-DUNBAR   FW   30 16     T 16  31
                C  9 T   7   W-CRISS L-WICKER      C   26 21     W 11  36


  JUNE 15       W  4 T   2   W-LOWER L-WHITE       D   32 16    GV 25  20
                C  3 FW  0   W-DICKSON L-CLARK    FW   30 17     T 16  32
                D    GV  RAIN                      C   27 21     W 12  36

  JUNE 16       C  4 FW  1   W-ADAMS L-WALSH       D   33 17    GV 26  21
               GV  3 D   2   W-CURTIS L-STOVAL    FW   30 18     T 16  33
                D 10 GV  1   W-RODEBAUGH L-MOOR    C   28 21     W 13  36
                W  8 T   4   W-BROWNING L-BLUE

  JUNE 17       D  3 GV  0   W-PRUITT L-HUDLSN     D   35 17    GV 26  23
                D  3 GV  0   W-GARRET L-JACKSON   FW   31 18     T 17  33
               FW  3 C   1   W-DUPREE L-SPEAKER    C   28 22     W 13  37
                T 10 W   7   W-WICKER L-HIATT

  JUNE 18       D  5 W   3   W-RODEB'H L-LOWER     D   36 17    GV 26  24
               FW  6 T   4   W-JARVIS L-MERKEL    FW   32 18     T 17  34
                C  5 GV  2   W-DICKSON L-PHILP     C   29 22     W 13  38

  JUNE 19       D  3 W   1   W-FARRIS L-BROWN'G    D   37 17    GV 26  25
               FW 11 T   9   W-WALSH L-WHITE      FW   33 18     T 17  35
                C 13 GV  3   W-ADAMS L-STOVAL      C   30 22     W 13  39

  JUNE 20       D  6 W   0   W-GARRET L-SIMPSON    D   38 17    GV 26  25
               FW 10 T   9   W-CLARK L-WHITE      FW   34 18     T 17  36
                C  5 GV  5* MORAN vs JACKSON       C   30 22     W 13  40
                          *5 INNINGS RAIN

  JUNE 21       D  6 T   1   W-PRUITT L-VANCE      D   39 17    GV 26  26
               FW  6 W   2   W-DUPREE L-HIATT     FW   35 18     T 17  37
                C  6 GV  3   W-CRISS L-HUDLSTN     C   31 22     W 13  41


  JUNE 22       D  6 T   2  W-R'BAUGH L-WICKER  D  40 17 GV 26 27
                C 11 GV  1  W-ADAMS L-JACKSON  FW  36 18  T 17 38
               FW  4 W   0  W-WALSH L-DUNBAR    C  32 22  W 13 42
```

```
                    FIRST HALF 1906 TEXAS LEAGUE
        D=DALLAS C=CLEBURNE FW=FT.WORTH GV=GREENVILLE W=WACO T=TEMPLE


    DATE           SCORES        PITCHERS       STANDINGS: WON-LOST
  JUNE 23      D  6  T  2   W-GARRET L-WHITE    D   41 17   GV 27  27
               GV 5  C  1   W-PHILIPS L-GIBSON  FW  37 18   T  17  39
               FW 7  W  0   W-JARVIS L-LOWER    C   32 23   W  13  43

  JUNE 24      W  6  FW 0   W-BROWNING L-CLARK  D   41 18   GV 27  29
               C  2  D  0   W-CRISS L-PRUITT    FW  37 19   T  19  39
               T  16 GV 15  W-WICKER L-HUDLSTN  C   33 23   W  14  43
              *T  9  GV 0
              *Greenville forfeits game when they failed to take
               to the field in 1st half 6th trailing 24 to 2

  JUNE 25      D vs C Rain                      D   41 18   GV 27  29
               FW 2  W  1   W-WALSH L-HIATT     FW  38 19   T  19  39
               T vs GV Rain                     C   33 23   W  14  44

  JUNE 26      D  3  C  1  *W-RODEB'H L-CRISS   D   42 19   GV 27  30
               C  6  D  0   W-DICKSON L-WEBB    FW  39 19   T  20  39
               FW 1  W  0**W-DUPREE L-DUNBAR    C   34 24   W  14  45
              *T  9  GV 0***
                    ***Greenville forfeits failed to show for game
                       dispute over gate guarantee
                      * Rodebaugh Pitches No-Hitter
                      ** Dupree Pitches PERFECT GAME

  JUNE 27      D  3  FW 1   W-GARRET L-JARVIS   D   43 19   GV 28  30
               GV 7  W  2   W-DOUGHERTY L-LOWER FW  39 20   T  20  39
               C   vs T Rain                    C   34 24   W  14  46

  JUNE 28      FW 4  D  2   W-DUPREE L-PRUITT   D   43 20   GV 28  31
               C  2  T  0   W-CRISS L-VANCE     FW  40 20   T  20  40
               W  11 GV 6   W-BROWNING L-HUDLSN C   35 24   W  15  46

  JUNE 29      GV 9  W  7   W-DOYLE L-HIATT     D   43 21   GV 29  31
               FW 1  D  0   W-WALSH L-RODEB'H   FW  41 20   T  20  41
               C  9  T  7   W-ADAMS L-WICKER    C   36 24   W  15  47

  JUNE 30      C  5  T  1  *W-DICKSON L-VANCE   FW  42 20   GV 30  31
               C  10 T  2   W-SPEAKER L-WHITE   D   43 22   T  20  43
               GV 10 W  7   W-JACKSON L-DUNBAR  C   38 24   W  15  48
               FW 2  D  1   W-JARVIS L-GARRET
                      *Dickson:No Hitter
```

FIRST HALF STANDINGS
WHY THE DISCREPANCY?

The Official Texas League standings for the season of 1906
differs in two ways from the contemporary records gleaned from the
Dallas Morning News, the Fort Worth Record, and the Cleburne Morning
Review. First, the league records indicate that the Greenville
Hunters finished with a record of 30 wins and 30 loses. Newspaper
records of the era reflect one more loss, that is a 30-31 record for
the Hunters. Secondly, Temple is credited by the league with a
season of 20 wins and 44 loses. Again, newspaper records showed
that the Boll-Weevils lost only 43 games.
   Why the difference? William Ruggles, the official historian of
the Texas League for many years, compiled a composite league
standing, which gives some indication of the differences in the
official standings and in the contemporary record. In the case of
Greenville, Ruggles credits the Fort Worth Panthers with four wins
and five loses to the Hunters. Newspapers recorded five Panther
victories. Greenville and Fort Worth played ten times, the results
as follows:

```
Wednesday, April 25, 1906: Greenville 6 Fort Worth 5
Thursday,  April 26, 1906: Greenville 6 Fort Worth 5
Friday,    April 27, 1906: Greenville 11 Fort Worth 2
Sunday,      May 13, 1906: Fort Worth 10 Greenville 5
Monday,      May 14, 1906: Fort Worth  4 Greenville 1
Tuesday,     May 15, 1906: Game called Rain
Sunday,      May 27, 1906: Fort Worth  9 Greenville 6
Monday,      May 28, 1906: Fort Worth  5 Greenville 1
Tuesday,     May 29, 1906: Fort Worth  9 Greenville 7
Wednesday,   May 30, 1906: Greenville 15 Fort Worth 1
Thursday,    May 31, 1906: Greenville  4 Fort Worth 1
Fridy,Saturday June 1,2, : Both Games Rained Out
                 -------------------------------------
         Fort Worth won 5  Greenville won 5
```
==
Ruggles composite standings for Temple contends that the Boll-
Weevils lost ten times to the Fort Worth Panthers, when in fact
contemporary records mirror only nine loses:

```
Friday       May 4, 1906: Fort Worth  5  Temple 1
Saturday     May 5, 1906: Fort Worth  3  Temple 2
Sunday       May 6, 1906: Game Rained out
Sunday       May 20,1906: Fort Worth  9  Temple 2
Monday       May 21,1906: Temple 3  Fort Worth 2
Tuesday      May 22,1906: Temple 5  Fort Worth 2
Wednesday    May 23,1906: Fort Worth 6 Temple 2
Sunday       June 3,1906: Fort Worth 12 Temple 1
                          Fort Worth  1 Temple 1 Tie,10th,Dark
Monday       June 4,1906: Temple 5 Fort Worth 3
Tuesday      June 5,1906: Fort Worth 10 Temple 2
Monday       June 18,1906: Fort Worth  6 Temple 4
Tuesday      June 19,1906: Fort Worth 11 Temple 9
Wednesday    June 20,1906: Fort Worth 10 Temple 9
             ---------------------------------------
         Fort Worth won 9  Temple won 3
```
-----------------------------=========================

Apparently, William Ruggles' official records incorrectly listed one score incorrectly as having Fort Worth defeating Temple instead of Greenville. A comparison of the Texas League schedule for 1906 verifies the contemporary accounts and the final standings according to the newspapers of 1906.
****
Below is the composite standings according to William Ruggles:

TEAM	Fw	Ds	Cl	Gv	Tm	Wa	GAMES PLAYED	WON	LOST
FT.WORTH	--	20	18	4	10	26	124	78	46
DALLAS	13	--	15	9	11	32	129	80	49
CLEBURNE	17	16	--	10	12	22	126	77	49
GREENVILLE	5	4	5	--	5	11	60	30	30
TEMPLE	3	2	3	6	--	6	64	20	44
WACO	8	7	8	1	6	--	127	30	97

THE OFFICIAL TEXAS LEAGUE SCHEDULE OF 1906:

FORT WORTH vs GREENVILLE: at GV: APRIL 25,26,27 MAY 30,31 JUNE 1,2
                          at FW: MAY 13,14,15, 27,28,29

FORT WORTH vs TEMPLE: at TEMPLE: MAY 20,21,22,23 JUNE 18,19,20
                      at FORT WORTH:MAY 4,5,6 JUNE 3,4,5

Ft. Worth and Greenville were scheduled to meet 13 times before June 30, which was selected as the end of the first season when it became apparent that Greenville would drop out of the Texas League. Three games were called because of rain, May 15, June 1 and 2, leaving the teams with 10 playing dates. The 10 dates correspond to the newspaper accounts of 1906,indicating that Fort Worth won five times from the Hunters, not four as shown by the Ruggles' compilation.

Ft. Worth and Temple were also scheduled to meet 13 times in what would finally be the first season. The game of May 6 was rained out, and a make-up double header on June 3 resulted in one game ending in a ten inning one-one tie, thus yielding only 12 official games between the Panthers and Temple. Indications were that Ft. Worth won nine of the twelve, not ten as indicated by the records compiled by William Ruggles.

One less loss by Temple probably makes little difference, but in the case of the Greenville Hunters, the one additional loss means that in their only season in the Texas League, the Hunters were loser more often than winners. Ruggles' record had shown that they had broken even in games won and lost.

```
                  FIRST HALF 1906 TEXAS LEAGUE
    D=DALLAS C=CLEBURNE FW=FT.WORTH GV=GREENVILLE W=WACO T=TEMPLE



**************************************************************
FINAL STANDING OF TEXAS LEAGUE  FIRST HALF SEASON
Based on Contemporary Newspaper Accounts:
              WON  LOST  .Pct  GB

FORT WORTH    42    20   .678  ---
DALLAS        43    22   .662   1/2
CLEBURENE     38    24   .613   4
GREENVILLE    30    31   .492  11 1/2
TEMPLE        20    43   .317  22 1/2
WACO          15    48   .238  27 1/2

**************************************************************
FINAL 'OFFICIAL STANDINGS' OF THE TEXAS LEAGUE OFFICE

FORT WORTH    42    20   .678  ---
DALLAS        43    22   .662   1/2
CLEBURNE      38    24   .613   4
GREENVILLE    30    30   .500  11
TEMPLE        20    44   .313  23
WACO          15    48   .238  27 1/2
```

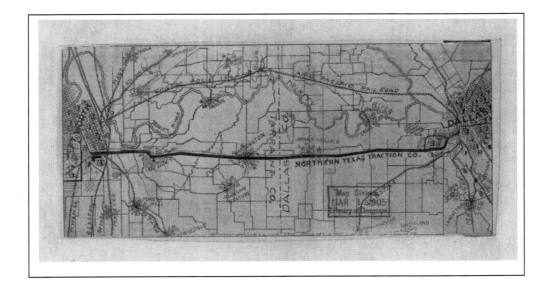

THE FIRST HALF "INTERURBAN SERIES" ENDED WITH FORT WORTH ON TOP

```
                1906 TEXAS LEAGUE DAY BY DAY SCORES - SECOND HALF
                   WINNER LOSER    STANDINGS:WON-LOST

SUNDAY    JULY 1    FT.WORTH  3   CLEBURNE  0   FT.WORTH 1-0
                    W-MERKEL      L-CRISS       DALLAS   1-0
                    DALLAS    4   WACO      0   CLEBURNE 0-1
                    W-PRUITT      L-HIATT       WACO     0-1

MONDAY    JULY 2    FT.WORTH  4   CLEBURNE  0   FT.WORTH 2-0
                    W-WALSH       L-ADAMS       DALLAS   2-0
                    DALLAS    6   WACO      3   CLEBURNE 0-2
                    W-WEBB        L-DOYLE       WACO     0-2

TUESDAY   JULY 3    FT.WORTH 11   CLEBURNE  5   FT.WORTH 3-0
                    W-DUPREE      L-SPEAKER     DALLAS   3-0
                    DALLAS   10   WACO      1   CLEBURNE 0-3
                    W-RODEBAUGH   L-JACKSON     WACO     0-3

WEDNESDAY JULY 4    FT.WORTH  8   WACO      3   FT.WORTH 4-1
                    W-JARVIS        L-BROWNING  DALLAS   4-1
                    WACO      6 FT.WORTH 4     CLEBURNE 1-4
                    W-HIATT         L-MERKEL    WACO     1-4
                    CLEBURNE  2   DALLAS    1
                    W-DICKSON     L-GARRET
                    DALLAS   10   CLEBURNE  5
                    W-PRUITT      L-WICKER

THURSDAY  JULY 5    FT.WORTH  6   WACO      1   FT.WORTH 5-1
                    W-WALSH       L-DOYLE       DALLAS   5-1
                    DALLAS    6   CLEBURNE  3   CLEBURNE 1-5
                    W-WEBB        L-CRISS       WACO     1-5

FRIDAY    JULY 6    WACO      5   FT.WORTH  4   DALLAS   6-1
                    W-JACKSON     L-DUPREE      FT.WORTH 5-2
                    DALLAS    3   CLEBURNE  0   WACO     2-5
                    W-CLARK       L-ADAMS       CLEBURNE 1-6

SATURDAY  JULY 7    DALLAS    2   FT.WORTH  0   DALLAS   7-1
                    W-RODEBAUGH   L-JARVIS      FT.WORTH 5-3
                    WACO      4   CLEBURNE  1   WACO     3-5
                    W-BROWNING    L-DICKSON     CLEBURNE 1-7

SUNDAY    JULY 8    FT.WORTH  4   DALLAS    1   DALLAS   7-2
                    W-WALSH       L-FERRIS      FT.WORTH 6-3
                    CLEBURNE  3   WACO      0   WACO     3-6
                    W-CRISS       L-HIATT       CLEBURNE 2-7

MONDAY    JULY 9    DALLAS    4   FT.WORTH  2   DALLAS   8-2
                    W-GARRET      L-MERKEL      FT.WORTH 6-4
                    WACO      4   CLEBURNE  2   WACO     4-6
                    W-DOYLE       L-SPEAKER     CLEBURNE 2-8

TUESDAY   JULY 10   FT.WORTH  4   WACO      0   DALLAS   8-3
                    W-DUPREE      L-JACKSON     FT.WORTH 7-4
                    CLEBURNE  5   DALLAS    0   WACO     4-7
                    W-ADAMS       L-WEBB        CLEBURNE 3-8
```

```
                    1906 TEXAS LEAGUE DAY BY DAY SCORES - SECOND HALF
                        WINNER LOSER  STANDINGS:WON-LOST


WEDNESDAY   JULY 11 FT.WORTH 7     WACO       3     DALLAS    8-3
                    W-JARVIS         L-HIATT         FT.WORTH  8-4
                    DALLAS    0     CLEBURNE 0       WACO      4-8
            5th Rain CLARK   vs  DICKSON            CLEBURNE  3-8


THURSDAY  JULY 12   FT.WORTH  2    WACO       1     FT.WORTH  9-4
                    W-MERKEL         L-BROWNING      DALLAS    8-4
                    CLEBURNE  5    DALLAS     1     CLEBURNE  4-8
                    W-DICKSON        L-RODEBAUGH     WACO      4-9


FRIDAY    JULY 13   FT.WORTH  4    WACO       2     FT.WORTH 10- 4
                    W-DUPREE         L-DOYLE         DALLAS    8- 5
                    CLEBURNE  8    DALLAS     3     CLEBURNE  5- 8
                    W-CRISS          L-FERRIS        WACO      4-10


SATURDAY JULY 14    WACO      2    FT.WORTH 1       FT.WORTH 10- 5
                    W-HIATT          L-JARVIS 1      DALLAS    8- 6
                    CLEBURNE 2     DALLAS     1     CLEBURNE  6- 8
                    W-ADAMS          L-GARRETT       WACO      5-10


SUNDAY    JULY 15   WACO      5    FT.WORTH 2       FT.WORTH 10- 6
                    W-JACKSON        L-DEATHRIDG     DALLAS    8- 7
                    CLEBURNE 2     DALLAS     1     CLEBURNE  7- 8
                    W-DICKSON        L-CLARK         WACO      6-10


MONDAY    JULY 16   FT.WORTH 3     WACO       2     FT.WORTH 11- 6
                    W-MERKLE         L-HIATT         DALLAS    8- 7
                    DALLAS vs CLEBURNE ppd           CLEBURNE  7- 8
                                     rain            WACO      6-11


TUESDAY   JULY 17   FT.WORTH 1     DALLAS     0 *   FT.WORTH 12- 6
                    W-DUPREE         L-WEBB          DALLAS    8- 8
                    WACO AT CLEBURNE RAIN            CLEBURNE  7- 8
                    *10 innings                      WACO      6-11


WEDNESDAY   JULY 18 DALLAS    2    FT.WORTH 1*      FT.WORTH 12- 7
                    W-RODEBAUGH L-JARIVS             DALLAS    9- 8
                    WACO 3         CLEBURNE 1**     CLEBURNE  7- 9
                    W-PHILLIPS  L-CRISS              WACO      7-11
                    *10 innings **13 innings


THURSDAY  JULY 19   DALLAS    2    FT.WORTH 1       FT.WORTH 12- 8
                    W-GARRETT        L-MERKEL        DALLAS   10- 8
                    WACO      5    CLEBURNE 4       CLEBURNE  8-10
                    W-HIATT          L-DICKSON       WACO      8-12
                    CLEBURNE 7     WACO       4
                    W-ADAMS          L-BROWNING


FRIDAY    JULY 20   DALLAS    9    FT.WORTH 0       FT.WORTH 12- 9
                    W-CLARK          L-DUPREE        DALLAS   11- 8
                    FT.WORTH FORFEITS                WACO      9-12
                    WACO      6    CLEBURNE 5       CLEBURNE  8-11
                    W-PHILLIPS  L-DICKSON
```

239

```
                1906 TEXAS LEAGUE DAY BY DAY SCORES - SECOND HALF
                    WINNER LOSER  STANDINGS:WON-LOST


SATURDAY JULY 21    CLEBURNE 2   FT.WORTH 1*   DALLAS    12 -8
                    W-CRISS      L-JARVIS      FT.WORTH  12-10
                    DALLAS   6   WACO     3    CLEBURNE   9-11
                    W-FERRIS     L-DOYLE       WACO       9-13
                    *10 innings


SUNDAY   JULY 22    CLEBURNE 2   FT.WORTH 1*   DALLAS    13-8
                    W-ADAMS      L-MERKLE      FT.WORTH  12-11
                    DALLAS   2   WACO     0    CLEBURNE  10-11
                    W-RODEBAUGH  L-BROWNING    WACO       9-14
                    * Game Protested

MONDAY      JULY 23 FT.WORTH 0   CLEBURNE 0 *  DALLAS    14-8
                    DUPREE vs DICKSON          FT.WORTH  12-11
                    DALLAS   4   WACO     1    CLEBURNE  10-11
                    W-GARRET     L-HIATT       WACO       9-15
                    *GAME CALLED 19TH TIED DARKNESS

TUESDAY  JULY 24    FT.WORTH 6   CLEBURNE 1    DALLAS    14- 9
                    W-JARVIS     L-MORAN       FT.WORTH  13-11
                    WACO    12   DALLAS   8    CLEBURNE  10-12
                    W-DOYLE      L-WEBB        WACO      10-15

WEDNESDAY JULY 25   FT.WORTH 2   CLEBURNE 0    DALLAS    14- 9
    5               W-MERKEL     L-ADAMS       FT.WORTH  14-11
                    DALLAS vs WACO at          CLEBURNE  10-13
                       Gatesville, rain out    WACO      10-15

THURSDAY JULY 26    FT.WORTH AT CLEBURNE       DALLAS    14-10
                         RAIN                  FT.WORTH  14-11
                    WACO     2   DALLAS   1*   CLEBURNE  10-13
                    W-BROWNING   L-GARRETT     WACO      11-15
                      *  at Gatesville, Texas


FRIDAY   JULY 27    CLEBURNE 4   FT.WORTH 1    DALLAS    14-11
                    W-DICKSON    L-JARVIS      FT.WORTH  14-12
                    WACO     5   DALLAS   2    CLEBURNE  11-13
                    W-HIATT      L-WEBB        WACO      12-15

SATURDAY JULY 28    CLEBURNE 4   FT.WORTH 2    DALLAS    15-11
                    W-CRISS      L-MERKEL      FT.WORTH  15-13
                    FT.WORTH 2   CLEBURNE 0*   CLEBURNE  12-14
                    W-BOLES      L-SPEAKER     WACO      12-16
                      * Called 7th for Train Schedule
                    DALLAS   2   WACO     0
                    W-FARRIS     L-DOYLE

SUNDAY   JULY 29    FT.WORTH 6   DALLAS   3    DALLAS    15-12
                    W-DUPREE     L-GARRETT     FT.WORTH  16-13
                    CLEBURNE 3   WACO     1    CLEBURNE  13-14
                    W-ADAMS      L-BROWNING    WACO      12-17
```

240

```
              1906 TEXAS LEAGUE DAY BY DAY SCORES - SECOND HALF
                        WINNER LOSER  STANDINGS:WON-LOST


MONDAY     JULY 30   DALLAS    3   FT.WORTH 2*   DALLAS    16-12
                     W-CLARK       L-JARVIS      FT.WORTH  16-14
                     CLEBURNE  7   WACO     5    CLEBURNE  14-14
                     W-DICKSON     L-HIATT       WACO      12-18


TUESDAY    JULY 31   DALLAS    2   FT.WORTH 0    DALLAS    17-12
                     W-FARRIS      L-MERKEL      FT.WORTH  16-15
                     CLEBURNE 12   WACO     3    CLEBURNE  15-14
                     W-CRISS       L-PHILLIPS    WACO      12-19
WEDNESDAY AUGUST 1
                     FT.WORTH  3   DALLAS   0    DALLAS    17-13
                     W-DUPREE      L-GARRETT     FT.WORTH  17-15
                     CLEBURNE  7   WACO 3        CLEBURNE  16-14
                     W-ADAMS       L-DOYLE       WACO      12-20


THURDAY    AUGUST 2  FT.WORTH  1   DALLAS   0    CLEBURNE  17-14
                     W-JARVIS      L-FARRIS      DALLAS    17-14
                     CLEBURNE  4   WACO     1    FT.WORTH  18-15
                     W-DICKSON     L-BROWNING    WACO      12-21


FRIDAY AUGUST 3      FT.WORTH  4   DALLAS   1    CLEBURNE  18-14
                     W-BOLES       L-CLARK       FT.WORTH  19-15
                     CLEBURNE  6   WACO     4    DALLAS    17-15
                     W-CRISS       L-JACKSON     WACO      12-22


SATURDAY AUGUST 4    FT.WORTH  4   DALLAS   2    FT.WORTH  20-15
                     W-DUPREE      L-GARRETT     CLEBURNE  18-15
                     WACO      4   CLEBURNE 3    DALLAS    17-16
                     W-DOYLE       L-SPEAKER     WACO      13-22


SUNDAY    AUGUST 5   FT.WORTH  4   WACO     0    FT.WORTH  21-15
                    *W-JARVIS      L-BRWONING    CLEBURNE  18-15
                     DALLAS vs CLEBUNRE,rain     DALLAS    17-16
                       * No HITTER                WACO      13-23


MONDAY     AUGUST 6  FT.WORTH  6   WACO     2    FT.WORTH  22-15
                     W-MERKEL      L-BROWNING    CLEBURNE  19-15
                     CLEBURNE  2   DALLAS   0    DALLAS    17-17
                     W-ADAMS       L-FARRIS      WACO      13-24


TUESDAY   AUGUST 7   WACO      5   FT.WORTH 4    CLEBURNE  21-15
                     W-DOYLE       L-DUPREE      FT.WORTH  22-16
                     CLEBURNE  4 * DALLAS   3    DALLAS    17-19
                     W-DICKSON     L-CLARK       WACO      14-24
                     CLEBURNE  2   DALLAS   0
                     W-DICKSON     L-GARRETT
                       *11 Innings
WEDNESDAY AUGUST 8   DALLAS    6   WACO     4*   FT.WORTH  23-16
                     W-FARRIS      L-BROWNING    CLEBURNE  21-16
                     FT.WORTH  3   CLEBURNE 2    DALLAS    18-19
                     W-JARVIS      L-ADAMS       WACO      14-25
                     * Played in Clarksville
```

THURSDAY AUGUST 9   WACO   6   DALLAS   5*   FT.WORTH 24-16
                          *Played in Clarksville   CLEBURNE 21-17
                      W-DOYLE   L-CLARK   DALLAS   18-20
                      FT.WORTH 16   CLEBURNE 4   WACO   15-25
                      W-MERKEL   L-SPEAKER

FRIDAY AUGUST 10   DALLAS   12   WACO   4   FT.WORTH 25-16
                      Played in Clarksville   CLEBURNE 21-18
                      Called 7th Train Sched   DALLAS   19-20
                      W-MALONEY   L-BROWNING   WACO   15-26
                      FT.WORTH 3   CLEBURNE 2*
                      W-DUPREE   L-CRISS
                      *10 innning

SATURDAY AUGUST 11   DALLAS VS WACO Ppd
                      train arrived late
                      FT.WORTH -CLEBURNE Ppd rain

SUNDAY   AUGUST 12 FT.WORTH 2   CLEBURNE 1   FT.WORTH 26-17
                      W-JARVIS   L-DICKSON   CLEBURNE 22-19
                      CLEBURNE 3   FT.WORTH 0   DALLAS   21-20
                      W-ADAMS   L-DUPREE   WACO   15-28
                      DALLAS   4   WACO   1
                      W-FARRIS   L-DOYLE
                      DALLAS   5   WACO   4
                      W-COOPER   L-MORRIS

MONDAY   AUGUST 13 FT.WORTH 5   CLEBURNE 2   FT.WORTH 27-17
                      W-MERKEL   L-CRISS   DALLAS   22-20
                      DALLAS   11   WACO   2   CLEBURNE 22-20
                      W-CLARK   L-JACKSON   WACO   15-29

TUESDAY   AUGUST 14 FT.WORTH 3   CLEBURNE 0   FT.WORTH 28-17
                      W-BOLES   L-DICKSON   DALLAS   23-20
                      DALLAS   7   WACO   1   CLEBURNE 22-21
                      W-GARRETT   L-SMITH   WACO   15-30

WEDNESDAY AUGUST 15
                      CLEBURNE 2 FT.WORTH 0   FT.WORTH 28-18
                      W-ADAMS   L-BOLES   DALLAS   24-20
                      DALLAS   2 WACO 0   CLEBURNE 23-21
                      W-FARRIS   L-BROWNING   WACO   15-31

THURSDAY AUGUST 16   CLEBURNE 9   FT.WORTH 6   FT.WORTH 28-19
                      W-CRISS   L-JARVIS   DALLAS   24-21
                      WACO   6   DALLAS   5   CLEBURNE 24-21
                      W-DOYLE   L-COOPER   WACO   16-31

FRIDAY AUGUST 17   CLEBURNE 6*   FT.WORTH 2   FT.WORTH 28-20
                      W-DICKSON   L-DUPREE   DALLAS   25-21
                      DALLAS   7   WACO   3   CLEBURNE 25-21
                      W-CLARK   L-MORRIS   WACO   16-32
                      * Shelton hits first 'over-the-fence'
                      home run of season at Gorman Park

```
                 1906 TEXAS LEAGUE DAY BY DAY SCORES - SECOND HALF
                      WINNER  LOSER   STANDINGS:WON-LOST


   SATURDAY AUGUST 18  FT.WORTH 9    WACO     0    FT.WORTH  29-20
                       W-MERKEL      L-BROWNING     DALLAS    26-21
                       DALLAS   4    CLEBURNE 3*    CLEBURNE  25-22
                       W-FARRIS      L-ADAMS        WACO      16-33
                       *11 innings


   SUNDAY   AUGUST 19  CLEBURNE 1    DALLAS   0*   FT.WORTH  29-21
                       W-CRISS       L-GARRETT     DALLAS    26-22
                       WACO     5    FT.WORTH 2    CLEBURNE  26-22
                       W-DOYLE       L-JARVIS      WACO      17-33
                       *12 innings


   MONDAY   AUGUST 20
                       FT.WORTH 5    WACO     1    FT.WORTH  30-21
                       W-DUPREE      L-BOWER       DALLAS    26-22
                       CLEBURNE vs DALLAS rain    CLEBURNE  26-22
                                                   WACO      17-34


   TUEDAY AUGUST 21    DALLAS-FT.WORTH Rain
                       CLEBURNE-WACO   Rain


   WEDNESDAY AUGUST 22
                       DALLAS    1   FT.WORTH 0   FT.WORTH  30-22
                       W-FARRIS      L-MERKEL      DALLAS    27-22
                       CLEBURNE 10   WACO     1   CLEBURNE  27-22
                       W-DICKSON     L-MORRIS      WACO      17-35




   THURSDAY AUGUST 23 FT.WORTH 4    DALLAS    2   FT.WORTH  32-22
                       W-JARVIS      L-GARRETT     CLEBURNE  29-22
                       FT.WORTH 3    DALLAS    1   DALLAS    27-24
                       W-DUPREE      L-CLARK       WACO      17-37
                       CLEBURNE 3    WACO      1
                       W-ADAMS*      L-BROWNING
                       CLEBURNE 6    WACO      0
                       W-ADAMS       L-BOWER
                       *Adams pitches no hitter, both ends
   FRIDAY AUGUST 24    DALLAS    11  FT.WORTH 1   FT.WORTH  32-23
                       W-FARRIS      L-MERKEL      CLEBURNE  30-22
                       CLEBURNE  5   WACO     0   DALLAS    28-24
                       W-CRISS       L-DOYLE       WACO      17-38


   SATURDAY AUGUST 25 FT.WORTH 5    WACO     1    FT.WORTH  33-23
                       W-BOLES       L-MORRIS      CLEBURNE  31-23
                       CLEBURNE 2    DALLAS   1    DALLAS    29-25
                       W-DICKSON     L-FARRIS      WACO      17-39
                       DALLAS   4    CLEBURNE 3
                       W-COOPER      L-DICKSON
```

```
                1906 TEXAS LEAGUE DAY BY DAY SCORES - SECOND HALF
                   WINNER  LOSER    STANDINGS:WON-LOST


SUNDAY AUGUST   26   FT.WORTH 2    WACO       0    FT.WORTH 35-23
                     W-DUPREE      L-DOYLE    1    CLEBURNE 32-24
                     FT.WORTH 4    WACO       1    DALLAS   30-26
                     W-MEREKEL     L-BROWNING      WACO     17-41
                     DALLAS   3    CLEBURNE 2
                     W-GRIFFITH    L-ADAMS
                     CLEBURNE 5    DALLAS     3
                     W-CRISS       L-FARRIS


MONDAY AUGUST   27   DALLAS   5    CLEBURNE 2    FT.WORTH 35-23
                     W-GARRET      L-CRISS       CLEBURNE 32-25
                     FT.WORTH-WACO off day       DALLAS   31-26
                                                 WACO     17-41


TUESDAY AUGUST  28   DALLAS     4  FT.WORTH 0    FT.WORTH 35-24
                     W-CLARK       L-JARVIS      CLEBURNE 33-25
                     CLEBURNE 9    WACO       3  DALLAS   32-26
                     W-DICKSON     L-BROWNING    WACO     17-42


WEDNESDAY AUGUST 29
                     DALLAS     2  FT.WORTH 0    FT.WORTH 35-25
                     W-FARRIS      L-DUPREE      CLEBURNE 34-25
                     CLEBURNE 5    WACO       3*  DALLAS  33-26
             *Game Played Under Protest         WACO     17-43
                     W-ANDERSON    L-MORRIS
THURSDAY AUGUST 30
                     FT.WORTH 8    DALLAS     3  FT.WORTH 36-25
                     W-MERKEL      L-CLARK       CLEBURNE 35-25
                     CLEBURNE 7    WACO       1  DALLAS   33-27
                     W-CRISS       L-BOWERS      WACO     17-44
                  *Waco Home Game at Corsicana


FRIDAY AUGUST   31   FT.WORTH 3    DALLAS     3  FT.WORTH 36-25
                     Boles   vs. Farris 11inng  CLEBURNE 36-25
                     CLEBURNE 5    WACO       4  DALLAS   33-27
                     W-ANDERSON    L-DOYLE       WACO     17-45
                  *Waco Home Game at Corsicana


SATURDAY SEPT 1      CLEBURNE 6    FT.WORTH 5    CLEBURNE 37-25
                     W-ADAMS       L-MERKEL      FT.WORTH 36-26
                     DALLAS     5  WACO       0  DALLAS   34-27
                     W-GARRETT     L-MORRIS      WACO     17-46


SUNDAY SEPTEMBER 2
                     CLEBURNE 2    FT.WORTH   0  CLEBURNE 39-25
                     W-DICKSON     L-MERKEL      DALLAS   36-27
                     CLEBURNE 2    FT.WORTH   0  FT.WORTH 36-28
                     W-DICKSON     L-DUPREE      WACO     17-48
                     DALLAS   10   WACO       1
                     W-CLARK       L-DOYLE
                     DALLAS     6  WACO       0
                     W-COPPER      L-BROWNING
```

244

THE TEXAS LEAGUE
1906
FIRST HALF STANDINGS

	Won	Lost	Pct.	GB
Fort Worth Panthers	42	20	.677	----
Dallas Giants	43	22	.662	½
Cleburne Railroaders	38	24	.612	4
Greenville Hunters	30	31	.491	11 ½
Temple Boll Weevils	20	43	.317	22 ½
Waco Navigators	15	48	.238	27 ½

SECOND HALF STANDINGS

	Won	Lost	Pct.	GB
Cleburne Railroaders	39	25	.609	---
Dallas Giants	36	27	.571	2 ½
Fort Worth Panthers	36	28	.563	3
Waco Navigators	17	48	.262	22 ½

COMPOSITE STANDINGS
THE TEXAS LEAGUE
1906

	Won	Lost	Pct.	GB
Fort Worth Panthers	78	48	.619	----
Dallas Giants	79	49	.617	----
Cleburne Railroaders	77	49	.611	1
Greenville Hunters	30	31	.492	xxx
Temple Boll Weevils	20	43	.317	xxx
Waco Navigators	32	96	.250	46

Note: Final Standings Are Based Upon Contemporary Newspaper Accounts

THE OFFICIAL TEXAS LEAGUE STANDINGS FOR 1906
William Ruggles Secretary of the Texas League

First Series
April 25- June 30

	Won	Lost	Pct.
Fort Worth Panthers	42	20	.677
Dallas Giants	43	22	.622
Cleburne Railroaders	38	24	.613
Greenville Hunters	30	30	.500
Temple Boll Weevils	20	44	.313
Waco Navigators	15	48	.238

Second Series
Jul 1- Sept 3

Cleburne Railroaders	39	25	.609
Fort Worth Panthers	36	26	.581
Dallas Giants	37	27	.578
Waco Navigators	15	49	.234

COMPOSITE SERIES
April 25-Sept 3, 1906

	FW	Ds	Cl	Gv	Tm	W	Played	Won	Lost	Pct
Fort Worth	---	20	18	4	10	26	124	78	46	.629
Dallas	13	---	15	9	11	32	129	80	49	.621
Cleburne	17	16	---	10	12	22	126	77	49	.613
Greenville	5	4	5	---	5	11	60	30	30	.500
Temple	3	2	3	6	---	6	64	20	44	.313
Waco	8	7	8	1	6	---	127	30	97	.236

* No Playoff: Championship Defaulted to the Cleburne Railroaders

THE CLEBURNE RAILROADERS
GAME BY GAME HITTING
HITTING RECORDS

FIRST HALF SEASON
1906
Page 1

Player columns (AB H for each):
1 ADAMS · 2 AKINS · 3 ARBOGAST · 4 CRISS · 5 POINDEXTER · 6 SHELTON · 7 SPEAKER · 8 WHITEMAN · 9 WRIGHT · 10 DICKSON · 11 COYLE · 12 MORAN · 13 N. CLAYTON · 14 EARTHMAN · 15 POWELL · 16 JONES · 17 RANSOM · 18 YAGER · 19 ANDERSON · 20 BATES · 21 FISHER · 22 PEESEE · 23 WOMACK · 24 PENNEL · 25 WHITE · 26 LEWIS

DATE	OPPONENT	W/L	SCORE	AB	H
04 25	DALLAS	L	4-0	36	7
04 26		L	4-1	30	2
04 27		L	7-4	41	11
04 28	FT.WORTH	L	4-2	33	5
04 29		L	4-3	41	6
04 30	1 WACO	W	6-4	31	4
05 1		W	7-1	35	11
05 2		W	8-3	36	12
05 3	DALLAS		RAIN	0	0
05 4		W	3-2	31	2
05 5		W	6-3	33	11
05 6			RAIN	0	0
05 7	GRNVILLE	L	17-4	37	11
05 8		L	1-0*	24	0
05 9		W	3-1	30	4
05 10	FT.WORTH	W	4-3	32	6
05 11		W	3-2	29	7
05 12		W	4-1	34	10
05 13	TEMPLE	W	7-5	35	13
05 14		W	11-6	41	13
05 15		W	16-3	41	13
05 16	GRNVILLE	L	4-2	34	9
05 17		L	10-0	29	5
05 18		W	8-4	34	8
05 19		W	9-0	36	11
05 20	WACO	L	3-2	31	3
05 21		L	4-1	31	7
05 22		W	3-1	31	3
05 23		W	8-1	38	11
05 24	TEMPLE	W	7-2	39	11
05 25		W	2-0	30	4
05 26		W	3-2	30	8
05 27	DALLAS	L	6-2	32	5
05		W	3-1	33	12
05 28		L	10-3	38	12
05 29		W	10-2	41	12

* Correction: May 2:
Newspaper Listed "EARTHMAN" in box score
Should be "WHITEMAN" AB: 5 H: 4

247

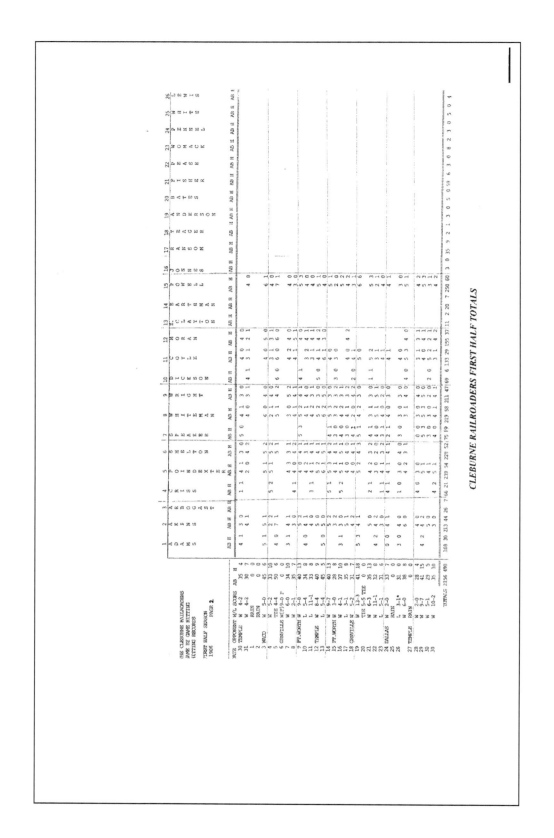

CLEBURNE RAILROADERS FIRST HALF TOTALS

THE CLEBURNE RAILROADERS
GAME BY GAME HITTING
RECORDS

SECOND HALF SEASON
1906

Page 3

DATE	OPPONENT	W/L	SCORE	AB	H	ADAMS AB	ADAMS H	AKEN AB	AKEN H	ARBOGAST AB	ARBOGAST H	COYLE AB	COYLE H	CRISS AB	CRISS H	DICKSON AB	DICKSON H	MORAN AB	MORAN H	POINDEXTER AB	POINDEXTER H	SHELTON AB	SHELTON H	SPEAKER AB	SPEAKER H	WHITEMAN AB	WHITEMAN H	WRIGHT AB	WRIGHT H	POWELL AB	POWELL H	WICKER AB	WICKER H	KELLOG AB	KELLOG H
07 1	FT.WORTH	L	3-0	32	6			4	0			4	0	3	1			4	0	4	1	3	1			3	1	3	0	4	2				
07 2		L	4-0	29	3	2	0	4	0							3	0	3	0	3	0	4	1	3	0	4	1	3	1						
07 3		L	11-5	36	8	3	0	4	3			4	0			1	0	4	1	3	1	4	1	4	0	5	1	4	1						
07 4	DALLAS	W	2-1	33	8			5	2			4	0			4	0			3	2	4	1	2	0	4	1	3	0	4	2				
		L	10-5	35	9	1	0	4	0			4	1							3	1	4	0	4	1	4	3	4	2	4	1	3	0		
07 5		L	6-3	35	10			5	0			4	2	4	0					4	2	4	2	3	0	3	1	4	1	4	2				
07 6		L	3-0	30	4	3	1	4	1			4	0					4	1	2	0	4	0	2	0	4	1	3	0						
07 7	WACO	L	4-1	32	4			4	0			4	1	1	1	2	0	4	0	4	0			3	1	4	0	3	1	3	0				
07 8		W	3-0	32	6			3	1			3	0	4	1			4	0	4	1			3	1	5	1	2	0	4	1				
07 9		L	4-2	34	6	5	0	3	1			4	1	2	1			2	0	4	1			4	0	4	0	4	1					2	1
07 10	DALLAS	W	5-0	32	7	3	1	3	1			3	0	4	2			4	1	4	0			4	0	3	2	4	0						
07 11		TIE	0-0	0	0																														
07 12		W	5-1	26	5			3	0			4	0	4	0	2	0	3	2	3	1			2	1	3	1	2	0						
07 13		W	8-3	36	12			5	2			5	3	3	1			4	2	4	1	5	2	3	0	3	0	4	1						
07 14		W	2-1	31	5	3	1	3	0	4	1	3	0					3	0	4	2	3	1	4	0			4	0						
07 15		W	2-1	35	10			4	0	4	2	4	1	4	4	4	0			3	1			4	2	4	0	4	0						
07 16		RAIN		0	0																														
07 17	WACO	RAIN		0	0																														
07 18		L	3-1	44	5			6	1	5	0	5	0	5	3			5	0	4	1			5	0	5	0	4	0						
07 19		L	5-4	36	10	1	0	4	1	4	3	4	0	1	0	4	3	0	0	4	1	5	1	2	0	4	1	3	0						
19		W	7-4	31	7	4	1	5	1	3	0	2	0							4	1	3	2	3	1	4	1	3	0						
07 20		L	6-5	32	10	0	0	3	2	4	1	3	0	4	2	2	0	1	0	4	2	1	0	2	1	4	1	4	1						
07 21	FT.WORTH	W	2-1	34	7			4	2	4	1	5	1	4	0			3	1	4	1			4	1	3	0	3	0						
07 22		W	2-1	28	6	2	0	4	0	3	0	4	2					2	0	4	3	4	0	3	0	2	1								
07 23		TIE	0-0 19n	70	9			8	1	8	0	8	0	8	4	7	1			8	0	2	0	6	0	8	2	7	1						
07 24		L	6-1	31	5			2	1	4	0	3	0					4	1	4	2	4	1	3	0	4	0	3	0						
07 25		L	2-1	30	6	1	0	4	0	4	1	4	0					2	0	4	1			4	1	4	1	3	2						
07 26		RAIN		0	0																														
07 27		W	4-1	31	10			4	0	0	0			3	1	3	1	4	1	4	1	4	3	4	2	2	1	3	0						
07 28		W	4-2	31	5	4	1	4	0			4	1	4	2			3	0			4	0	2	0	4	1	2	0						
28		L	2-0	25	5	3	1	2	1			3	0	3	0			3	2			3	1	2	0	3	0	3	0						
07 29	WACO	W	3-1	35	9	3	3	5	2			4	0					4	1	4	1	4	0	4	0	4	2	3	0						
07 30		W	7-5	36	16			4	2			3	1			4	1	5	3	3	0	5	3	4	2	4	2	4	2						
07 31		W	12-3	47	19			6	0			5	2	6	3			5	2	5	4	5	2	5	3	5	2	5	1						

THE CLEBURNE RAILROADERS
GAME BY GAME HITTING
RECORDS

SECOND HALF SEASON
1906   **Page 4**

DATE	OPPONENT	W/L	SCORE	AB	H
08 1	WACO	W	7-3	39	15
08 2		W	4-1	31	9
08 3		W	6-4	29	6
08 4		L	4-3	37	10
08 5	DALLAS		RAIN	0	0
08 6		W	2-0	29	8
08 7		W	4-3	39	9
08 7		W	2-0	31	9
08 8	FT.WORTH	L	3-2	32	6
08 9		L	16-4	36	8
08 10		L	3-2	34	7
08 11			RAIN	0	0
08 12		L	2-1	29	2
08 12		W	3-0	34	6
08 13		L	5-2	32	6
08 14		L	3-0	31	7
08 15		W	2-0	33	11
08 16		W	9-6	40	15
08 17		W	6-2	39	8
08 18	DALLAS	L	4-3	36	10
08 19		W	1-0	42	0
08 20 & 21			RAIN	0	
08 22	WACO	W	10-1	29	8
08 23		W	3-1	31	7
08 23		W	6-0	33	11
08 24		W	5-0	36	11
08 25	DALLAS	W	2-1	28	6
08		L	4-3	32	9
08 26		L	3-2	31	6
08		W	5-3	31	9
08 27		L	5-2	37	8
08 28	WACO	W	9-3	38	11
08 29		W	5-3	32	9
08 30		W	7-1	37	14
08 31		W	5-4	31	7
09 01	FT.WORTH	W	6-5	43	16
09 02		W	2-0	27	6
09 02		W	2-0	29	6
TOTALS				**2207**	**538**

Player totals (AB / H):

Player	AB	H
ADAMS	75	19
AKEN	260	60
ARBOGAST	134	33
COYLE	206	30
CRISS	143	57
DICKSON	70	11
MORAN	146	37
POINDEXTER	247	62
SHELTON	200	58
SPEAKER	224	52
WHITEMAN	255	72
WRIGHT	195	33
POWELL	23	8
WICKER	3	2
KELLOGG		
REEDER	18	5
ANDERSON	6	0

CLEBUNRE RAILROADERS SECOND HALF TOTALS

TEXAS LEAGUE 1906
EXTRA BASE HITS

Player	Doubles	Player	Triples	Player	Home Run
Whiteman	30	Whiteman	10	Salm	6
Boles	25	Salm	8	Hoffman	4
Maloney	22	Boles	7	McIver	4
Wilson	22	Phillips	7	Phillips	4
Cavender	21	Speaker	6	Boles	3
McAlister	20	Akin	6	Cavender	3
Meyer	20	Arbogast	6	Louden	3
Salm	20	Wallace	6	Moore	3
Maag	19	Louden	5	Shelton	3
Phillips	19	Poindexter	5	Whiteman	3
Shelton	19	Jackson	4	Arbogast	2
Louden	17	McIver	4	Erwin	2
Wallace	16	Meyer	4	Jackson	2
Speaker	16	Moran	4	Maloney	2
Fink	15	Powell	4	Stovall	2
Williams	15	Stevens	4	Wilson	2
Jackson	14	Walsh	4	Yohe	2
Carlin	13	Bero	3	Akin	1
Clayton, Harry	13	Erwin	3	Adams	1
Criss	13	Fink	3	Bero	1
Erwin	13	Maloney	3	Clayton	1
Poindexter	13	Murphy	3	Fischer	1
Stovall	13	Shelton	3	Garrett	1
Powell	12	Wilson	3	Gfroerer	1
Wright	12	Browning	2	Lucid	1
Akin	11	Cavender	2	Moran	1
Bero	11	Coyle	2	Poindexter	1
Moran	11	Gfroerer	2	Pruitt	1
Arbogast	10	McCulley	2	Ragsdale	1
Bigbie	10	Salm	2	Sullivan	1
Butler	10	Ury	2	Walsh	1
Hoffman	10	Adams	1	Speaker	1
Gfroerer	9	Doyle	1		
Moore	9	Jehl	1		
Reed	9	Reed	1		

Burleson	8	Bayard	1
McCulley	8	Benjamin	1
Raley	8	Burleson	1
Stevens	8	Butler	1
Hickey	7	Carlin	1
Murphy	6	Clayton	1
Curtis	5	Curtis	1
Dawkins	5	Dickson	1
Frederick	5	Fink	1
Kelsey	5	Garrett	1
McIver	5	Hackney	1
Merkel	5	Huddleston	1
Pease	5	Metz	1
Sheffield	5	Mooney	1
Wagner	5	Moore	1
Welch	5	Rodebaugh	1
Yohe	5	Sheffield	1
Doyle	4	Ransom	1
Ury	4		
Adams	3		
Dupree	2		
Farris	2		
Hiett	2		
Jehl	2		
Rodebaugh	2		
Browning	1		
Clark	1		
Cooper	1		
Coyle	1		
Dickson	1		
Fischer	1		
Hackney	1		
Webb	1		

Compiled from 1906 Newspaper Box Scores

OFFICIAL REACH											
FIRST HALF			Second Half			Combined Season			Published Statistics		
AB	H	BA	AB	H	BA	AB	H	BA	AB	H	BA
108	30	0.278	75	19	0.253	183	49	0.268	170	47	
213	44	0.207	260	60	0.231	473	104	0.220	465	101	0.217
26	7	0.269	134	33	0.246	160	40	0.250	321	72	0.224
133	29	0.218	206	30	0.146	339	59	0.174	323	59	0.183
66	21	0.318	143	57	0.399	209	78	0.373	192	76	0.396
69	6	0.087	70	11	0.157	139	17	0.122	139	22	0.158
155	37	0.239	146	37	0.253	301	74	0.246	296	78	0.264
239	54	0.226	247	62	0.251	486	116	0.239	476	115	0.242
228	52	0.228	200	58	0.290	428	110	0.257	422	111	0.263
75	19	0.253	224	52	0.232	299	71	0.237	287	77	0.268
219	58	0.265	255	72	0.282	474	130	0.274	466	131	0.281
211	47	0.223	195	33	0.169	406	80	0.197	395	77	0.195
11	2	0.182				11	2	0.182			
20	7	0.350				20	7	0.350			
250	60	0.240	23	8	0.348	273	68	0.249	263	69	0.262
3	0	0.000				3	0	0.000			
35	9	0.257				35	9	0.257	35	8	
2	1	0.500				2	1	0.500			
3	0	0.000	6	0	0.000	9	0	0.000			
59	6	0.102				59	6	0.102	58	7	
5	0	0.000				5	0	0.000			
3	0	0.000				3	0	0.000			
8	2	0.250				8	2	0.250			
3	0	0.000				3	0	0.000			
5	0	0.000				5	0	0.000	50	11	
4	1	0.250				4	1	0.250			
			3	0	0.000	3	0	0.000			
			2	1	0.500	2	1	0.500			
			18	5	0.278	18	5	0.278			
2153	**492**	**0.229**	**2207**	**538**	**0.244**	**4360**	**1030**	**0.236**	**4358**	**1061**	

TEXAS LEAGUE PITCHING RECORDS

GREENVILLE HUNTERS

Player	FIRST Won	Lost	Did Not Play SECOND Won	Lost	TOTAL Won	Lost	Pct.
Curtis, Don	1	0			1	0	1.000
Dougherty	1	0			1	0	1.000
Doyle, William	12	2			12	2	.857
Huddleston, Tom	2	7			2	7	.222
Jackson, W.R.	2	7			2	7	.222
Moore, Farmer	9	5			9	5	.643
Phillips	1	1			1	1	.500
Spencer, Charles	2	4			2	4	.333
Stovall, Sam	0	1			0	1	.000
Whittenberg, Ben	0	1			0	1	.000
By Forfeit	0	3			0	3	.000
	30	31	0	0	30	31	.492

WACO NAVIGATORS

	FIRST Won	Lost	SECOND Won	Lost	TOTAL Won	Lost	
Bower,			0	3	0	3	.000
Browning, Dutch	3	4	2	17	5	21	.192
Burns,	1	4			1	4	.200
Cook,	0	1			0	1	.000
Daniels,	0	3			0	3	.000
Doyle, William			7	10	7	10	.412
Dunbar, Tom	4	7			4	7	.364
Dunham,	0	3			0	3	.000
Ellison	0	1			0	1	.000
Hiett, Henry	4	11	4	6	8	17	.320
Hornsby, Everett	0	1			0	1	.000
Jackson, W R			2	4	2	4	.333
Lower, John	1	4			1	4	.200
Morris, C H			0	6	0	6	.000
Oehme,	1	4			1	4	.200
Ort	0	1			0	1	.000
Phillips,			2	1	2	1	.667
Simpson, Guy	0	1			0	1	.000
Smith			0	1	0	1	.000
Zook, Earl	1	3			1	3	.250
	15	48	17	48	32	96	.250

TEXAS LEAGUE PITCHING RECORDS

TEMPLE BOLL WEEVILS

Did Not Play

Player	FIRST Won	Lost	SECOND Won	Lost	TOTAL Won	Lost	Pct.
Blue, Barney	0	1			0	1	0.000
Goehring,	0	1			0	1	0.000
Jones, Doc	0	6			0	6	0.000
Merkel, Charles	4	9			4	9	0.308
Moore, Fred	0	1			0	1	0.000
Nowotny	1	0			1	0	1.000
Simpson, Guy	2	0			2	0	1.000
Vance, Neal	6	11			6	11	0.353
White, Bobby	0	8			0	8	0.000
Whittenberg, Ben	2	0			2	0	1.000
Wicker	2	4			2	4	0.333
Womack	1	2			1	2	0.333
By Forfeit	2	0			2	0	1.000
	20	43			20	43	0.317

CLEBURNE RAILROADERS

Player	FIRST Won	Lost	SECOND Won	Lost	TOTAL Won	Lost	Pct.
Adams, Rick	12	6	12	6	24	12	.667
Dickson, Walter	12	5	14	7	26	12	.684
Criss, Dode	8	4	11	6	19	10	.655
Speaker, Tris	2	3	0	4	2	7	.222
Womack	2	2			2	2	.500
Anderson, Wingo	0	1	2	0	2	1	.667
Moran, Charley	0	0	0	1	0	1	.000
Jones, Doc	0	1			0	1	.000
Wicker	0	0	0	1	0	1	.000
Lewis, Cal	1	0			1	0	1.000
Gibson,	0	1			0	1	.000
Yeager, Travis	0	1			0	1	.000
By Forfeit	1	0			1	0	1.000
	38	24	39	25	77	49	.611

TEXAS LEAGUE PITCHING RECORDS

DALLAS GIANTS

Player	FIRST		SECOND		TOTAL		
	Won	Lost	Won	Lost	Won	Lost	Pct.
Rodebaugh, Eddie	13	3	4	1	17	4	0.810
Pruiett, Charles	11	5	2	0	13	5	0.722
Farris, Frank	5	4	10	6	15	10	0.600
Garrett, Jess	7	3	6	9	13	12	0.520
Clark, Richard DICK			7	6	7	6	0.538
Cooper, Ike			3	1	3	1	0.750
Lower, John	4	3			4	3	0.571
Stovall, Sam	2	2			2	2	0.500
Maloney, James			1	0	1	0	1.000
Ables, Harry	1	0			1	0	1.000
Ward,	0	1			0	1	0.000
Webb, Cleon	0	1	2	4	2	5	0.286
Griffith,			1	0	1	0	1.000
	43	22	36	27	79	49	0.617

FORT WORTH PANTHERS

Player	FIRST		SECOND		TOTAL		
	Won	Lost	Won	Lost	Won	Lost	Pct.
Boles, Walter			4	1	4	1	0.800
Clark, Richard DICK	5	5			5	5	0.500
Deathridge,			0	1	0	1	0.000
Doyle, William	1	0			1	0	1.000
Dupree, Alex	13	1	11	7	24	8	0.750
Huddleston, Tom	3	2			3	2	0.600
Jarvis, Red	8	5	8	9	16	14	0.533
Merkle, Charles			10	10	10	10	0.500
Walsh, Leo	12	5	3	0	15	5	0.750
Wicker,	0	2			0	2	0.000
	42	20	36	28	78	48	0.619

TEXAS LEAGUE PITCHING RECORDS 1906

Pitcher	Team	First Half		Second Half		Total		
		W	L	W	L	W	L	PCT.
Rodebaugh, Eddie	Dallas	13	3	4	1	17	4	0.810
Walsh, Leo	Fort Worth	12	5	3	0	15	5	0.750
Dupree, Alex	Fort Worth	13	1	11	7	24	8	0.750
Pruiett, Charles	Dallas	11	5	2	0	13	5	0.722
Dickson, Walter	**Cleburne**	**12**	**5**	**14**	**7**	**26**	**12**	**0.684**
Adams, Rick	**Cleburne**	**12**	**6**	**12**	**6**	**24**	**12**	**0.667**
Criss, Dode	**Cleburne**	**8**	**4**	**11**	**6**	**19**	**10**	**0.655**
Moore, Frank Farmer	Greenville	9	5			9	5	0.643
Doyle, William	Grv/Waco	13	2	7	10	20	12	0.625
Ferris, Frank	Dallas	5	4	10	6	15	10	0.600
Jarvis, Red	Fort Worth	8	5	8	9	16	14	0.533
Clark, Richard Dick	Fort Worth	5	5	7	6	12	11	0.522
Garret, Jess	Dallas	7	3	6	9	13	12	0.520
Merkel, Chares	Fort Worth	4	9	10	10	14	19	0.424
Lower, John	Waco-Dallas	5	7			5	7	0.417
Dunbar, Tom	Waco	4	7			4	7	0.364
Huddleston, Tom	Grv/Ft.Worth	5	9			5	9	0.357
Vance, Neal	Temple	6	11			6	11	0.353
Hiatt, Henry	Waco	4	11	4	6	8	17	0.320
Jackson W.R.	Grv/Waco	2	7	2	4	4	11	0.267
Speaker, Tris	**Cleburne**	**2**	**3**	**0**	**4**	**2**	**7**	**0.222**
Browning, Dutch	Waco	3	4	2	17	5	21	0.192

The following statistics are the official figures as released by the Texas League for national publication.

OFFICIAL BATTING AVERAGES FOR THE TEXAS
LEAGUE 1906

CLEBURNE RAILROADERS:

Player	Club	Games Played	At Bat	Runs Scored	Hits	Batting Average
Adams	Cl	54	170	19	47	0.276
Akin	Cl	113	465	49	101	0.217
Arbogast	Cl	86	321	28	72	0.224
Coyle	Cl	85	323	34	59	0.183
Criss	Cl	52	192	20	76	0.396
Dickson	Cl	41	139	9	22	0.158
Fisher	Cl	16	58	4	7	0.121
Moran	Cl	84	296	36	78	0.264
Poindexter	Cl	123	476	52	115	0.242
Powell	Cl	65	263	40	69	0.262
Ransom	Cl	12	35	10	8	0.229
Shelton	Cl	108	422	58	111	0.263
Speaker	Cl	84	287	35	77	0.268
Whiteman	**Cl**	**120**	**466**	**75**	**131**	**0.281**
Wright	Cl	117	395	45	77	0.195
White	Cl T	16	50	4	11	0.220
Cleburne Totals		**1176**	**4358**	**518**	**1061**	**0.243**

DALLAS GIANTS	Club	Games Played	At Bat	Runs Scored	Hits	Batting Average
Burleson	Ds	44	153	13	32	0.209
Farris	Ds	30	94	3	13	0.138
Fink	Ds	123	429	55	101	0.235
Garrett	Ds	33	99	10	13	0.131
Hackney	Ds	25	89	8	19	0.213

258

Player	Club	Games Played	At Bat	Runs Scored	Hits	Batting Average
Maloney	Ds	116	447	43	110	0.246
Metz	Ds	17	52	7	12	0.231
Meyers	Ds	87	320	49	93	0.291
Pruiett	Ds	22	70	13	17	0.243
Ragsdale	Ds	101	380	43	95	0.250
Rodebaugh	Ds	26	83	7	17	0.205
Sullivan	Ds	74	252	39	50	0.198
Ury	Ds	91	327	34	69	0.211
Williams	Ds	87	324	39	76	0.235
Bigbie	Ds	127	450	44	84	0.187
Dallas Totals		**1003**	**3569**	**407**	**801**	**0.224**

OFFICIAL BATTING AVERAGES FOR THE TEXAS LEAGUE 1906

FORT WORTH PANTHERS

Player	Club	Games Played	At Bat	Runs Scored	Hits	Batting Average
Berry	FW	23	68	5	10	0.147
Boles	FW	125	487	77	116	0.238
Carlin	FW	123	478	50	129	0.270
Cavender	FW	124	453	80	103	0.227
Clayton	FW	122	405	41	83	0.205
Dupree	FW	52	157	9	27	0.172
Erwin	FW	93	326	35	80	0.245
Gfroerer	FW	115	416	63	99	0.238
Jarvis	FW	32	91	9	11	0.121
Salm	FW	120	443	64	115	0.260
Walsh	FW	23	70	8	13	0.186
Wilson	FW	127	476	56	126	0.265
Clark	FW Ds FW Ds	37	112	4	16	0.143
Kitchens	W	24	71	7	9	0.127
Fort Worth Totals		**1140**	**4053**	**508**	**937**	**0.231**

GREENVILLE HUNTERS

Player	Club	Games Played	At Bat	Runs Scored	Hits	Batting Average

		Games Played	At Bat	Runs Scored	Hits	Batting Average
Curtis	GV	27	102	15	26	0.255
Moore	GV	19	57	10	10	0.175
Raley	GV	50	202	23	50	0.248
Snedden	GV	56	182	22	34	0.187
Reed	GV T	48	172	23	44	0.256
Doyle	GV W	50	147	14	31	0.211
Jackson	GV W	96	370	32	85	0.230
McIver	GV W	112	420	74	107	0.255
Phillips	GV W	86	347	40	79	0.228
Louden	GV Ds	113	418	57	94	0.225
Maag	GV Ds	113	455	68	113	0.248
Stephens	GV Ds	98	343	33	83	0.242
Huddleston	GV FW	15	49	7	15	0.306
Greenville Totals		**883**	**3264**	**418**	**771**	**0.236**

OFFICIAL BATTING AVERAGES FOR THE TEXAS LEAGUE 1906

TEMPLE BOLL WEEVILS

Player	Club	Games Played	At Bat	Runs Scored	Hits	Batting Average
Frederick	T	35	135	9	25	0.185
Kelsey	T	21	71	10	13	0.183
McCully	T	61	256	39	59	0.230
Moore	T	44	166	21	45	0.271
Pease	T	63	241	35	59	0.245
Sheffield	T	39	134	9	36	0.269
Sullinger	T	31	111	16	20	0.180
Vance	T	24	70	9	14	0.200
Yohe	T	58	222	22	49	0.221
Merkel	T W	38	128	12	24	0.188
Wallace	T W	79	341	49	95	0.279
Butler	T Ds	44	172	15	44	0.256
Temple Totals		**537**	**2047**	**246**	**483**	**0.236**

WACO NAVIGATORS

Player	Club	Games Played	At Bat	Runs Scored	Hits	Batting Average

Bayard	W	29	106	11	22	0.208
Bero	W	117	449	29	83	0.185
Berry	W	16	61	7	11	0.180
Browning	W	46	218	9	23	0.106
Dawkins	W	38	126	18	31	0.246
Dunbar	W	16	44	2	9	0.205
Fisher	W	20	64	2	14	0.219
Hiatt	W	28	83	3	10	0.120
Hillery	W	17	68	3	11	0.162
Hoffman	W	67	238	18	54	0.227
Jehl	W	25	80	7	20	0.250
Lower	W	12	35	1	4	0.114
Morris	W	10	20	0	4	0.200
Murphy	W	63	224	22	42	0.188
Palm	W	47	218	9	29	0.133
Reitz	W	22	69	6	11	0.159
Wagner	W	42	147	17	30	0.204
Welsh	W	92	350	23	76	0.217
Westlake	W	16	48	1	8	0.167
Waco Totals		**723**	**2648**	**188**	**492**	**0.186**
1906 Texas League Totals		**10201**	**37230**	**4342**	**8598**	**0.231**

THE MINOR LEAGUEs: 1906
LISTED BY CLASSIFICATION: *AAA A B C D*

Pacifica Coast League	AAA
American Association	A
Arkansas-Texas League	D
Central League	B
Connecticut League	D
Cotton States League	D
Eastern League	A
Georgia State League	D
Illinois-Iowa-Indiana (Three-I League)	B
Interstate Association	C
Kansas State League	D
Kentucky-Illinois-Tennessee (The Kitty League)	D
New England League	B
New York State League	B
Northern Copper Country League	C
Pennsylvania-Ohio-Maryland League	D
South Atlantic League (Sally League)	C
South Central League	D
South Texas League	C

The 1906 Texas League Rules for Umpires
Issued by President Doak Roberts
The Rules were adopted from the Pacific Coast League

To the Official Umpres:

Gentleman:

You are hereby notified by the officers of the league are determined to stop unnecessary kicking and to stamp out rowdyism in every form. You have been previously told, we desire to reiterate, that you would have absolute charge of the field during process of the games, and it is the intention of the officers of the league to give you full and absolute support. You are hereby given to understand that you are, by the rules, given full authority to order any player, captain, or manager to do or omit to do any act which you may deem necessary to maintain your dignity and retain the respect of players and spectators.

No player (except the captain) is to be allowed to question any decision of the umpire. The captain of each team is the only member of the team who is to present or urge any point or to take part in and discussion with the umpire. You are hereby directed to notify each captain that the rules well be enforced exactly as they are printed, and that for each violation the prescribed penalty will follow. Make all decisions promptly as you see them. Never attempt to "even up" after having made a mistake. Any player throwing down his bat on a called strikes, or in any manner tending to hold you up to contempt or ridicule, is to be fined, and if such conduct is persisted in, he should be put out of the game.

If the batsman offers to argue with you, or leaves the batter's box to do so, it is your duty to instruct the pitcher to proceed with the game, and if he "puts'em over", call strikes, whether the batsman is in the batting position or not. Batters have frequently delayed games unnecessarily in this manner. No possible good ever comes of it, the only effect being to annoy and delay our patrons, whose pleasure and convenience it is our duty to consider at all times. Many of the players have acquired the habit of trying to "bluff" you into calling the fourth ball; that is to day, when three balls have been called immediately upon the delivery of the next ball pitched by the pitcher, the batter, without waiting for your decision, will throw his bat aside and proceed to first base. If it happens that the call "strike", as frequently is the case, he will proceed to "kick" and his friends and partisans of his club in audience will roast you.

For every such offense fine the batter not less than $5. In every instance where you levy a fine, report the same to the treasurer of the league. Report by mail the name of the player, the date and amount of the fine. Every fine levied must be reported and collected by you from the manger of the player's team before calling the next game, and the player so fined not allowed to play until the payment is made to you of the fine.

Positively do not remit a fine. Once it is levied it is your duty to report the same. Your failure to do so will result in the infliction of a penalty upon you.

Players should not be allowed to curse or abuse an umpire, and any player using vulgar or profane language should be fined and in a flagrant case should be removed from the game and may be suspended.

The officers in the this league will not retain in their employ an umpire who will tolerate any kind of rowdy baseball, and any player indulging in offensive or quarrelsome conduct during the game must be removed.

We desire our umpires to understand that they will be backed up and supported by the league, and if they fail to enforce the rules on account of manifest weakness, we do not want them. All teams must look alike to you and be given an even break. Always treat the visiting team fairly. You can not remain an umpire in the this league if you develop into a "home" umpire. It is our desire to secure umpires with "nerve" and we shall support them at all times.

You are hereby instructed to do everything possible to have the game played speedily and to keep the players on the move at all times, particularly in changing innings, and to have the batsman take their places promptly and be ready to take their turn at bat. A great deal of time has been lost in the past and games have been delayed unnecessarily. You thereby "nipping in the bud" trouble before it develops. Baseball can never be successful when players are allowed to do as they please and the officers in the league are fully alive to this fact.

In conclusion we urge you to compel respect from all: by so doing, your task will be an easy one.

Do I own the ball, or does it own me.....

Special Thanks to those individuals who were kind enough to respond to my many questions about the men of Naught Six:

Henry Slayton, Cleburne, Texas
Janie V. Conner, Abilene, Texas
Senola Howard, Fort Worth, Texas
Coleman Liggins, Cleburne, Texas
Jodie Adams, Euless, Texas
Mary Perry, daughter of Dode Criss, Euless, Texas
Mrs. Rufus B. Shell, Corsicana, Texas
Mrs. Bennie Adam, Paris, Texas
Clyde Head, Cleburne, Texas
J. Owen Wilson, Jr, Austin, Texas
Mrs. Joe P. (Martha) Macken, daughter of Owen Wilson, Austin, Texas
Jack Maupin, Richardson, Texas
George Schepps, Dallas, Texas
Margaret McCowen, Fort Worth, Texas
Nancy Lous McClellan, Daughter of George Jackson, Arlington, Texas
Ron Maxfield, Corsicana, Texas
Louis Swartz, Corsicana, Texas
Betsy Hudon, UTA Librarian
Tris Speaker Cobb, Hubbard, Texas
Frank Dickson, Sr. Albuquerque, New Mexico
JoDell McCLean, Cleburne, Texas
Michael Kelsey, Temple, Texas
Leo Hackney, Greenville, Texas

Out of curiosity I began to collect the story of the Cleburne team of 1906, chasing down anyone that might help me in this quest. Along the way I met many interesting and congenial folks who were more than willing to share stories about their fathers or uncles who were a part of this fascinating story. The list above is no doubt only a partial listing of those generous souls. Originally I had no idea that I would be publishing the results of my quest, and so unfortunately many others names that should have been included were lost or forgotten. Much of what has been written in these pages were shared verbal adventures, which otherwise would have been lost in the darkness of times past. My thanks to all who were kind enough to respond to my many questions.

Wiley

If you love baseball, you never have to grow up.....
Wiley Whitten actually age 3, but the feeling remains the same even as the days go by...

This post card picture does not indicate where Hardin is located. Likely Hardin, Kentucky, but could be Hardin, Missouri, or perhaps Hardin County, Tenneessee. A fading pencil insription indicates that one of the players is the husband of the writer, but there is no postmark. Ten players and their manager, 1906.

George Whiteman's Final Games with the 1918 Boston Red Sox: Whiteman is fourth from the left, front row. George Ruth is fifth from left, top row..The Babe

COUNTRY BALL

In 1906 the hierarchy of baseball started with the major leagues, then the professional minor Leagues, which consisted of AAA to D ball, next was the semi-professionals, who were sponsored by local companies who bought the teams uniforms, with the teams playing nearby communities. Dode Criss and Tris Speaker were signed by Roberts off of that type of amateur teams. Finally there was "country ball" where communities of perhaps 100-300 people would challenge close by communities for bragging rights. The men played in their work clothes. Mostly farm and ranch boys with just enough equipment, probably shared, played on any flat, reasonably smooth ground. Games were attended by men, although a few young girls might be watching. It was not a place that a woman would go. The games were played hard and with determination. A few might feel good enough to stroll into town in hopes of landing on a semi-pro team. But most stayed at home, keeping the farm going. These two pictures likely taken hundreds of miles apart, yet both have a similarity as if they had been directed by the same photographer. Unfortunately, neither picture is identified as to exact time or place. Just a baseball moment caught in time.

270

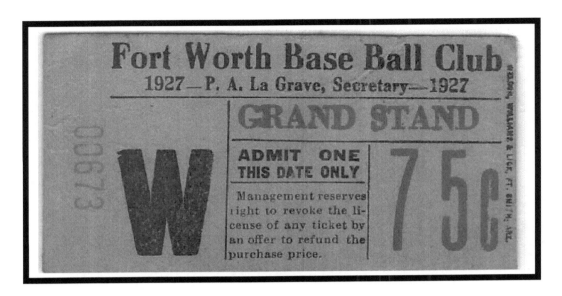

Paul LaGrave

Growing up in Fort Worth there seemed to be nothing unusual about going to LaGrave Field to watch baseball, that is until a relative came to town, and when the name LaGrave was mentioned, there was a bit of awkward laughter: a ball park called *The Grave*. Until that point I had not thought about the peculiar name.

In the modern world, the right to attach your name to a stadium carries a heavy price tag, which can create an awkward and embarrassing situation. In Denver the name of their arena in honor of Pepsi Cola's large dollar created an affectionate backlash to commercialism, with the fans calling the arena *The Can*. And talk about awkward situation, just ask the fans in Houston about Enron Stadium.

When Fort Worth moved from Haines Field to their new park on the west side of North Main, it was named *Morris Park* in honor of their manager. But what happens when the manager quits or is fired? Well, in the case of Fort Worth, you change the name to that of the team, hence *Panther Park*. When the 1911 park became obsolete, a new park was constructed in 1925 due east, carrying with it the name Panther Park.

Fort Worth did not have an officially named park until 1902, when Frank M. Haines, whose primary contribution to baseball in Fort Worth was allowing the team to occupy land on his firm's premises. Before that, the city ball fields were informally named in reference to the proximity of notable architectural structures, i.e., Spring Palace Grounds, and T&P Grounds.

In 1929 the beloved secretary of the team, Paul A. LaGrave, died. Panther Park name was soon replaced by a tribute to Mr. La Grave, and so came the name LaGrave Field. While the name has remained, as well as the exact site, there have now been three different parks that have carried the same name since 1929. The original park built in 1929 burned 20 years later, and thanks to the generosity of the Brooklyn Dodgers, the new version of the park was constructed, and kept occupied until the end of the 1964 season.

When Carl Bell brought the Cats back to life, he opted for the historical, and called his new park LaGrave Field.

To the future Baseball fans:

Mia DuBose
Meagan Benson
Perry DuBose
Kayleigh Benson
Cole Smith
Logan DuBose
Ryan Whitten
Luke Smith
Miranda Whitten
Phoebe DuBose
Madalyn DuBose

Not to forget our wonderful children,

Darren, Tara, Kari,   Jason, Jake and Adam

**Cleburne Railroaders' Number One Fan
His faith in his team was redeedmed:
They were**
The Champions of Naught-Six

Railroader Photographer Archie Shaw (left), his daughter Margeret McCowen holding a copy of her father's famous composite photograph of the 1906 Cleburne Railroaders

The 1906 GROESBECK, TEXAS Team:Won 40 Lost 31

Cleburne, Texas
Home of the Champions of Naught Six

Roy Akin enjoyed a long minor league career. Roy is #19 in this championship photo of the 1914 Waco Navigators of the Texas League.

The Knothole Gang

INDEX

1, Aiken; 2, Poindexter; 3, Dickson; 4, Criss; 5, Arbogast; 6, Shelton, Capt.; 7, Moran; 8, Roberts, Mgr.; 9, Wright; 10, Coyle; 11, Adams; 12, Speaker; 13, Whiteman; 14, Mascot.
CLEBURNE (TEX.) TEAM—CHAMPIONS TEXAS LEAGUE.

THE CHAMPIONS OF NAUGHT SIX:
THE CLEBURNE RAILROADERS

-30-

Made in the USA
Lexington, KY
05 December 2011